THE INVASION OF INDIAN COUNTRY IN THE TWENTIETH CENTURY

American Capitalism and Tribal Natural Resources

THE INVASION OF INDIAN COUNTRY IN THE TWENTIETH CENTURY

American Capitalism and Tribal Natural Resources

By DONALD L. FIXICO

 University Press of Colorado

Published by the University Press of Colorado
P.O. Box 849
Niwot, Colorado 80544

The University Press of Colorado is a cooperative publishing enterprise supported, in part, by Adams State College, Colorado State University, Fort Lewis College, Mesa State College, Metropolitan State College of Denver, University of Colorado, University of Northern Colorado, University of Southern Colorado, and Western State College of Colorado.

The paper used in this publication meets the minimum requirements of the American National Standard for Information Sciences — Permanence of Paper for Printed Library Materials. ANSI Z39.48-1984

Library of Congress Cataloging-in-Publication Data

Fixico, Donald Lee, 1951–
    The invasion of Indian country in the twentieth century : American
capitalism and tribal natural resources / Donald L. Fixico.
        p. cm.
    Includes bibliographical references and index.
    ISBN 0-87081-498-2 (cloth : alk. paper). — ISBN 0-87081-517-2
(pbk. : alk. paper)
    1. Indians of North America—Government relations. 2. Natural
resources—United States. 3. Indians of North America—Land tenure.
4. Indian reservations—United States. I. Title.
E93.F515   1998
333.2—dc21   98-28488
                                                                                     CIP

07 06 05 04 03 02   10 9 8 7 6 5 4 3

to
Mr. Bennie Mott and Mr. Melvin Thompson
for understanding the importance of a college
education and for helping me as a young man
working for a college education.

CONTENTS

ILLUSTRATIONS

PREFACE

L ike many people, I have often been stuck in traffic jams in large cities and observed countless automobiles wasting gasoline. Then, while driving through industrial centers with tall smokestacks spewing the remains of burning coal or oil, I have been forced to breathe thick, hazy air with a grayish tint. I have read about polluted rivers where dead fish float on the surface and animals avoid drinking the water. Perplexing questions about humanity and the environment have frustrated me: "What is happening and why?" "Where will it end?" "How can this wastefulness in America be stopped?" Then I think about the land—the homeland of my Native American forebears whose tribes had special relationships with the earth—and how my ancestors and other Indian people have suffered at the hands of American capitalists in this age of greed, the twentieth century. My feelings run deep and have compelled me to write about the suffering of the land and the Indian people—and the government policies that have threatened to change them forever.

This book is divided into two parts. Part 1 focuses on a theorized internal model of Indian society, emphasizing six essential elements that are being bombarded by federal policies that alter tribal ways of life. Part II addresses both the capitalistic pressure on tribal natural resources and the strategies that Native Americans have adopted to defend such resources. The book does not focus on one region or one tribe. Rather, it brings an overall, insider's perspective to Indian life in Indian Country as Native societies were subjected to increasing pressure from federal policies and American capitalists seeking to control and grow wealthy from Indians' natural resources.

The underlying thesis is that American capitalism, deriving from a tradition of Eurocentrism, has continued through the twentieth century to exploit tribal nations for their natural resources, thus forcing Indian leadership to adopt modern corporate strategies to ensure the survival of their nations and people. The following pages present case histories of certain tribes that have been exploited during this era. My logic in selecting these cases was to depict various policy periods affecting certain Indian natural resources, involving different tribes in different parts of Indian Country. The case studies of Part 1 also stress little-known events of Indian exploitation, all sparked by the white society's eagerness to harvest tribal natural resources. My objective is to bring more attention to the struggles of these Indian groups.

Furthermore, the book hypothesizes that six fundamental elements—person, family, clan or society, community, nation, and spirituality—are imperative to constituting Indian society in general. This theory proposes an internal model of analysis and demonstrates the ways in which external forces of American capitalism and federalism have threatened this model. Certainly, there are other well-known cases that could be used and other incidents that some people are convinced deserve attention. And to be sure, a number of different cases set important precedents in federal Indian law relating to tribal natural resources. But the case histories explored in the first half of the book have been selected to provide a geographic balance among the various tribes victimized by harmful federal policies. The second half analyzes the Native responses and new methods that Indian leaders have adopted to deal with the accelerating demands for their natural resources and the pressures of capitalism.

The situation in each case exemplifies a certain characteristic about traditional Indian life that is vulnerable to the pressures of mainstream consumption. Chapter 1 concerns the Indian "individual" and the natural resource of land, or "mother earth," as it is known to Native Americans. The focus here is a traditional Muscogee Creek elder named Jackson Barnett, who was out of his natural element when dealing with the ambitious mainstream culture. As a group, the Muscogee Creeks were once one of the largest tribes in the Old South, possessing enormous land areas. They underwent allotment—that is, they were allotted small parcels of land on an individual basis—in the early 1900s after surviving the Trail of Tears in the 1830s and reestablishing a relationship with the land in the Indian Territory during the nineteenth century.

Chapter 2 demonstrates how one Indian "family" (an extended family with numerous relatives) was shattered when whites consumed with greed decided these Indians should be murdered for the royalty moneys they had received for their oil-rich land. The tragic fate of these Osage—once called the richest people in the world due to the large royalties paid to them in the 1920s—epitomized the worst expression of American greed and Indian exploitation. Chapter 3 focuses on the Indian "community" and water issues, telling the story of the peaceful Pueblo communities who united with others when forced to fight to regain their lands, lands made even more valuable by the limited water supply in their region. Probably the oldest continuing Indian communities in North America, the Pueblo depended on water to support their agricultural lifestyle.

After the individual, family, and community, the final kinship element among Native Americans is the "tribe." In this regard, Chapter 4 presents the case of the Klamath, a tribe that met legal extinction when the U.S. government declared it terminated by law—that is, when all federal trust responsibilities toward the tribe were withdrawn. The Klamath held the largest timberlands in America, and after termination, their properties sold on the open market for huge profits. Thousands of acres of rich timberland on their reservation in the Pacific Northwest fell into the hands of white opportunists.

Chapter 5 deals with the animal world of the Great Lakes, involving the fight waged by the Chippewa of Wisconsin for their legal rights to fish and hunt. In the court battle that ensued, very real concerns about the totem animals of various Chippewa clans were ignored. The next chapter describes one tribe's relationship with the "spirituality" of a holy place—specifically, the Lakota (Sioux) and their Black Hills in South Dakota, which were mined in the early years for gold and recently for other minerals. It depicts the struggle between two diametrically opposed sets of values—those of the Indians, who hold their religious beliefs supreme, and those of the white capitalists, who are motivated by the quest for wealth, including the gold that has lured so many Americans throughout U.S. history. The Lakota relationship with the Black Hills is special, and Indian traditionalists respect the sacredness of a given area—the homeland and its environment.

Chapter 7 directly addresses the environment and its natural resources of oil, gas, uranium, coal, and water. Energy companies see these resources as a means of enrichment; Indian traditionalists, by contrast, view them as an integral part of the homeland to which they themselves belong. For Native Americans, natural rights are preeminent, but the mainstream society has found it difficult to understand this and to accept and respect the Indians' treaty rights. Members of the largest tribe that is dependent upon fishing, the Chippewa, reside in Minnesota, Wisconsin, and Michigan, and their legal right to fish has been contested in all three states. (Chapter 7 is a revised version of a piece I originally wrote for *The Plains Indians of the Twentieth Century*, edited by Peter Iverson and published in 1985.) Chapter 8 discusses a coalition of tribes who are fighting for their rights and resources with modern expertise, as the Council of Energy Resource Tribes (CERT) seeks to do, while facing new problems spawned by the energy crises, U.S. bureaucracy, and Indian criticism. Chapter 9 shows the way in which Indian leaders have turned to the federal judicial system and white people's law to defend their natural resources and develop their own line of defense in tribal courts within their tribal governments. Chapter 10 stresses traditional Indian leadership and describes the rise of sophisticated tribal leaders who fight to save the last vestiges of the natural resources on their homelands. Wanton greed continues today, and Indians who lack education and sufficient business experience continue to be taken advantage of by America's capitalistic society.

The last chapter illustrates a collective, traditional Indian philosophical approach toward the environment and stresses the alarming fact that accelerating demands have reduced the world's natural resources to dangerously low levels. It is my hope that important lessons can be learned from the philosophy, traditions, and history of the Native Americans before it is too late.

Numerous people and research institutions have been very helpful and supportive as I worked on this volume over a period of several years.

In particular, I am most appreciative of the work done by Marcus Pascale and Karen Keifer (former research assistants), who filed away countless pieces of information and made numerous treks to the library, even during the coldest months in Wisconsin. At the University of Wisconsin–Milwaukee, John Boatman, lecturer in ethnic studies and coordinator of American Indian Studies, has always been supportive of my work, and so has former associate dean Richard Meadows and former dean William Halloran of the College of Letters and Science. In fact, Dean Meadows spared time from his busy schedule to read and offer suggestions for early drafts of this project. Since those days, the Department of History at Western Michigan University–Kalamazoo has continued to support my work, and I am particularly grateful to Dr. Ronald Davis, chairperson of the History Department, and to former dean Douglas Ferraro of the College of Arts and Science, former provost Nancy Barrett, and President Diether Haenicke. I am also thankful for the daily services of Alberta Cumming,

Lori Klingele, Rena Lynema, and graduate student assistant Scott Gyenes. I appreciate the computer skills and the help offered by Mark Liberacki at Western Michigan University. Dr. Hans Stolle of the Geography Department was gracious in making the map for this book. I am grateful for the comments on the book from my good friend, Prof. Peter Iverson of Arizona State University. A sabbatical allowed me to complete the final stages of the book, and I must apologize to my graduate students—Mary Younker, Rob Galler, Dixie Haggard, Barbara Sears, and Maribel Izquierdo-Rodríguez—for being away so much of the time. In addition, I am grateful to Dr. Terry Straus of the University of Chicago (previously at NAES College in Chicago) for allowing me access to the school's library and archives of tribal newspapers.

This research project has involved various trips to Oklahoma to conduct research in the libraries and archives of my home state. While researching materials on the Osage and Muscogee Creek at the Special Collections in the McFarlin Library, University of Tulsa, I was helped by Lori Curtis, assistant curator, and the rest of the staff there. At the Western History Collections of the University of Oklahoma in Norman, Curator Donald DeWitt, Ray Miles, Ann Blevins, and others offered their assistance. At the Carl Albert Center, Curator Todd J. Kosmerick, Carolyn Hanneman, and Michael Lovegrove helped me. Gathering photographs is always subjective, and I am grateful for the help I received from John R. Lovett, photographic archivist, and the rest of the staff at the Western History Collections. My research also took me to the Oklahoma Historical Society, and I appreciate the assistance Robert Nespor and Bill Welge provided in helping me find materials on Creek allotment and Osage oil, as well as in locating photographs.

I am also grateful for the assistance from the archivists and staff members at the Dwight D. Eisenhower and Harry S. Truman Presidential Libraries. I appreciate the help offered by archivists and staff at the Federal Archives and Records Center at Suitland, Maryland. In particular, John Aubrey, of the Newberry Library in Chicago, has been most helpful in making suggestions about where to look and what to look for; in addition, Dr. Jay Miller, formerly of the D'Arcy McNickle Center for the History of the American Indian at the Newberry Library, and Dr. Frederick Hoxie, vice president of the Newberry Library, have shared their center's tribal newspapers and their advice. I also thank Kathleen Baxter and other staff members at the National Anthropological Archives of the National Museum of Natural History, Smithsonian Institution. My research has taken me to the Special Collections of the Zimmerman Library at the University of New

xiv   *Preface*

Mexico–Albuquerque, where Rose Diaz was again very helpful, as were Joanne Colley and other staff members. In my research for photographs, Stella De Sa Rego, the photoarchivist, and her assistant were most accommodating. I also appreciate the help of Kent Carter, Barbara Rusk, Margaret Hacker, and other staff members at the Federal Archives and Records at Fort Worth, Texas. It is at Fort Worth that I saw the thumbprint signature of Jackson Barnett that brought him so much wealth and so much pain. I thank Jim Pierce, chief administrative officer of the Council of Energy Resource Tribes, for the valuable information he provided.

Dr. Leonard Bruguier of the University of South Dakota graciously read and commented on the chapter on the Black Hills. At the Montana Historical Society Library, Charles Rankin, Brian Shovers, Connie Geiger, Ellie Arguimbau, Jodie Foley, and Bob Clark kindly assisted me while I was researching Lee Metcalf's papers in Helena. I am also indebted to Kenneth Duckett and Hilary Cummings of the Special Collections of the University of Oregon Library at Eugene and to Melissa Dermer, who proofread an early draft of the manuscript and caught numerous mistakes. All of the people involved were most kind in suggesting improvements and directing me to collections of papers. I am also grateful to Luther Wilson of the University Press of Colorado for his friendship and support of this book.

Most important of all, I am indebted to my wife, Professor Sharon O'Brien, and to our young son, Keytha, for allowing me the time to complete this book. They are always there for me, and yet I feel that I am always keeping them waiting. Finally, I should stress that the following words are my own, and I alone bear responsibility and for any mistakes they may contain.

INTRODUCTION TO
INDIAN AND WHITE VALUES

W hen the first Europeans arrived in the Western Hemisphere during the sixteenth century, they sought the land and its natural resources for their own benefit, intent on enriching their homelands. First the Spanish, then the French, followed by the Dutch, the British, and even the Russians laid claims along the Pacific coastline for new empires. During the 1500s and 1600s, the conquerors of the new age of European imperialism in the Western Hemisphere scarcely recognized the Native inhabitants who utilized the natural resources for their own livelihood. Within a short time, they assaulted the Native populations and took whatever they wanted. They were unabashed in their greed, displaying an obdurate attitude that was shared by their successors in later centuries. Following the Industrial Revolution in the United States during the late 1800s, an increasingly urban America sought fuels to run its modern factories and railroads and later its automobiles and airplanes. With little government involvement (by today's standards at least), the "laissez-faire" attitude of capitalism became the guiding force of the economy as competition intensified for natural resources such as oil, coal, uranium, and water.

This study, consisting of various case histories of Indian-white competition for natural resources in Indian Country during the last 100 years, focuses on a struggle between two different cultural worlds, contrasting the values of American capitalism and the traditional values of the Indian nations. Incongruent in philosophies, goals, values, and cultures, American Indians and Anglo-Americans clashed and remained intertwined in a growing crisis of competition, just as their forebears once were. The only things that they experienced in common were the land and its natural resources. As the white American capitalists took much from the Native inhabitants, the two orders of life clashed with deadly consequences. For the Indians, homelands were lost; for the Euramericans, new settlements, towns, and empires were built. And in the process, the land and its environment were severely depleted.

The first five chapters focus on certain basic elements of Indian society, presenting case histories of selected tribes with various natural resources, all of which have been profoundly affected by federal policies in the twentieth century. Chapter 1 focuses on the "person" and land relations, as told in the sad story of Jackson Barnett, a Creek full-blood. Chapter 2 is centered on the "family" or "extended family" unit and the exploitation of oil in land belonging to the Osage. The third fundamental element, "community," is explored in Chapter 3, which stresses the legal fight for water rights. Chapter 4 depicts the "tribal nation," the last concrete quality of the Native infrastructure. Here, the focus is on the Klamath, who survived but lost much of their timber to white capitalists. Chapter 5 is about the importance of "clan" (or "society" for Western tribes), explaining the significance of human relationships and respect for the plant and animal worlds—the natural environment. Chapter 6 considers the abstract element of "spirituality" among Indians, as exemplified in the efforts of the Sioux to reclaim their beloved Black Hills. These six basic elements are pertinent to the life of all Native America. They are internal and innate, giving Indian society cohesion—unless they are weakened by outside forces.

Woven throughout the last 100 years of Anglo exploitation of Indian people and their lands are recurrent themes of cultural dominance, ethnocentrism, and racism. The Anglo-American culture of the twentieth century is driven by capitalistic ambitions to acquire wealth. By contrast, American Indians are members of tribal nations whose philosophies stress a kinship and interrelatedness with all creation. And the conflicting dynamics of the two very different systems have yielded a history of anguishing human and environmental exploitation.

The roots of American capitalism are steeped in the early European settlement of the Western Hemisphere and actually originate in the struggle for land in Europe, where this resource existed in limited supply and quality. The privileged owned the land and all its natural resources, and rights of ownership became an important part of societies with class systems that passed land from one generation to the next via inheritance. Generally, landowners were members of the wealthy noble classes who paid taxes on their lands, an obligation that was envied by those people who had no property of their own and felt fortunate to work the land for the wealthy. The possession of land represented status and power, compelling nations to go to war for territories against weaker rulers of smaller nations. Wood from the forests of the land meant ships could be built, and cleared areas permitted farmers to produce grains and raise livestock. Coal and oil supplied heat, and the discovery of silver and gold brought instant wealth.

Life for the first Europeans in America was a continuing struggle for survival. Families emerged as the basis of settlements, towns, and eventually cities, but individualism became a strong characteristic of the American experience and American capitalism. This trait soon became imbedded in the American character, as well; it was then coupled with an ethic of survival at all cost, even killing if necessary, as conflict and competition also became a part of the American experience. Soon, the Euramericans became the dominant population. The new American mainstream demonstrated a general unwillingness to share permanently, especially with people of a different culture— whether they were new European immigrants, Indians, Hispanics, or African Americans. The seeming abundance of natural resources and land in America seemed to validate John Locke's philosophy of private property, as expressed in his *Two Treaties of Civil Government* and his attack on the divine right of kings to rule.

Lockean ideas gained popularity in America, especially during the eighteenth and nineteenth centuries. Adam Smith introduced the concept of "laissez-faire" as an ideal of free enterprise in his book *The Wealth of Nations*—a concept that, when put in action, enabled the individual American to seek property with little interference from state and federal governments. This profit system inspired ambition, productivity, and innovation, but unfortunately, it also fostered greed and deception.

The late nineteenth century marked the rise of modern America and changes as described by Richard Hofstader in his *Age of Reform*, but it excluded minorities, especially American Indians due to their traditional values. In the Indian nations, the reservations and the people also entered an era of change—an era of decline and poverty. A similar state of poverty exists in Indian Country today, as measured against the white American standards.

While the battle for natural resources continues throughout Indian Country, fundamental qualities of Indian life have also changed and are now vulnerable to total loss. These fundamental qualities, addressed in Part 1, consist of the "self" or "person"; the "extended family" unit; the "clan" or "society"; the "community"; the "tribe" or "nation"; and the "spirituality" of relatedness. Although Indians are, of course, individuals, they fundamentally view themselves as members of a group. The basic unit of group emphasis is the family, and the kinship relationship of all families constitutes a community or village/town; more than one community forms a tribal nation. (Although many tribes have traditional clans or societies, some do not.) The kinship of the people is of utmost importance. In earlier times, when life was harsh and filled with danger, living and working in a group improved chances for survival, and group values consequently superseded individualism. Democratic equality within the group made everyone feel more secure, although societal development created a different status between the genders and within male and female groups. The need to belong to a group introduced social controls, determined behavior, shaped values, and restricted individual activity, such as accumulation of wealth, unless it benefited the people as a whole. Biologically, the people were related, but this relatedness extended beyond the concrete reality of life on earth. The people felt a relatedness with all things in a spiritual context. This philosophical relatedness provided emotional comfort, a perspective on the role of humans, and a worldview that everything is interconnected within a balanced order sanctioned by the Creator.

The opening chapter in Part 2 addresses the demands created by the mainstream lifestyle on the natural resources of Indian Country. The ways in which Indian nations and their tribal leaders have responded to these demands and organized nationally is discussed in Chapter 8. Chapter 9 demonstrates how tribes and their leaders have used the courts and the law to protect their tribal resources. Chapters 10 and 11 illustrate effective tribal leadership at work, in the context of a general environmental philosophy that offers a lesson for the world.

Throughout the twentieth century, Indians have found their traditional order of life challenged legally by non-Indians and the U.S. government. In fact, the continual emphasis on the non-Indian values of the mainstream, dominant culture overshadows the elemental qualities of traditional Indian life, as portrayed in this book. It is important to recognize that these fundamental qualities have survived in the tribal communities against great odds, even as issues related to the exploitation of tribal resources have been lost in the intricacies of federal policies, federal-Indian law, and competition for big dollars in a capitalistic marketplace.

For the white society, the Industrial Revolution unleashed the forces of free enterprise and optimistic demands that would be met at the expense of American Indians and their lands. Profits were to be made by taking risks and by bending the law if necessary, which was particularly easy if there was little law to bend. Even today, society is largely ruled by "the profit motive harnessed to the powerful impulses of self-interest," as Paul Blumberg noted in *The Predatory Society: Deception in the American Marketplace.* Clearly, the twentieth century is the age of American economics.

In the courts of the white people's law, Indian rights regarding natural resources such as water and even the right to hunt and fish have been vigorously contested. Tribal leaders and the Council of Energy Resource Tribes (CERT), founded in 1975, have had to fight hard to protect their natural resources and uphold their traditional philosophies. American capitalism has moved the Indian-white struggle for land and natural resources into the courts—the arena of federal-Indian law.

Placing all of this in perspective, the twentieth century has brought significant destructive changes to Indian Country. Tribal leaders, Indian people, and their legal rights, traditional values, and natural resources are in jeopardy. In a final stand, the leaders and their people will have to protect their lands from the ravishing excavations of energy companies. Every day of every year, the tribes are required to defend their natural resources. The realization that American capitalism's encroachment upon Indians has involved fraud, exploitation, and murder would no doubt shock Adam Smith, Karl Marx, and John Maynard Keynes, considered the three great economists of all time.

As America has developed within the last 100 years, wealth has become a determining factor of one's place in society. The possession of wealth also brings power, especially in politics and in community, motivating many white Americans to concentrate their energies on acquisition and destruction of obstacles that stand in their way—unfortunately including American Indians. Greed has become the driving force in seizing land and using its natural resources without regard to the consequences, without concern for the future. Sadly, this has set a precedent for other Americans of different backgrounds and for the rest of the world The tragic outcome of this ethic can be seen in the brutal exploitation that Indians have experienced, as individuals and as a community, throughout the twentieth century—the age of greed.

NATURAL RESOURCES ON INDIAN LANDS

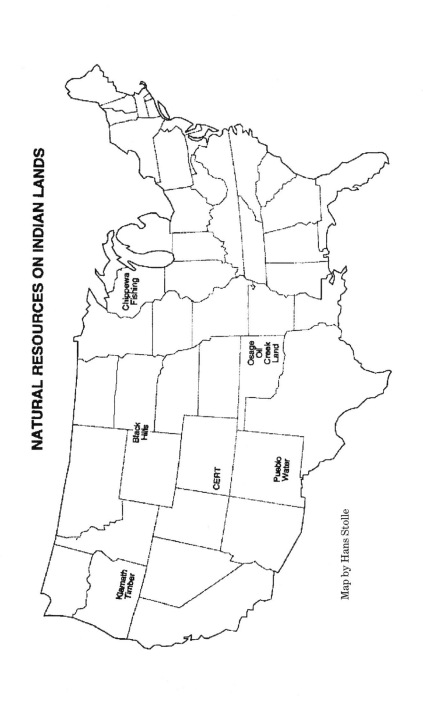

Chippewa
Fishing

Osage
Oil
Creek
Land

Black
Hills

CERT

Klamath
Timber

Pueblo
Water

Map by Hans Stolle

THE INVASION OF
INDIAN COUNTRY IN THE
TWENTIETH CENTURY

American Capitalism and Tribal Natural Resources

PART ONE

ELEMENTS OF INDIAN SOCIETY AND POLICIES

1

JACKSON BARNETT AND THE ALLOTMENT
OF MUSCOGEE CREEK LANDS

Jackson Barnett, a full-blood Muscogee Creek,[1] epitomized the exploitation of many Indian people during the allotment of tribal lands between 1887 and the mid–1920s. Caught in the capitalist web of the white world, the Creek and other allotted Indians found their lives chaotic and threatened upon being assigned individual lands by the government. From all sides, greedy whites and selfish mixed-bloods pressured and cheated the full-bloods, lusting after their royalties and their oil and gas lands. Allotment of tribal lands under the Dawes Act of 1887 and subsequent amendments divided tribal members and created factions for and against the allotment of those lands. Without the support of their kinspeople and lacking business experience, individual Indians such as Jackson Barnett fell victim to free enterprise profit making.

The federal policy of Indian allotment was designed to individualize Native Americans and destroy their communal orientation. Furthermore, the most basic element of Indian society—the person or self—came under ruthless attack. The idea of "self" being interconnected with community and environment is well documented in the case of Jackson Barnett. However, he and other Indian people found they had to reorient their thinking as they lived adjacent to or within white society, which stressed individuality. Learning to cope became a means of survival, as sadly proved by Native people such as Jackson Barnett during the allotment years.

Barnett's sad story began during the late 1800s when his people, the Muscogee Creek, experienced political strife as they tried to find

1. Jackson Barnett, Creek, richest Indian. Courtesy, Western
History Collections, University of Oklahoma Library.

a balance between retaining the old ways and becoming like the whites. The adult life of Jackson Barnett illustrated the confusion experienced by a single Indian person trapped between the dynamic changes of a traditional Native culture entangled with the white society. In this dilemma, Indian people had to make critical decisions involving their lands while alien pressures compounded their problems. The traditional "person" did not comprehend the land leases and property sales involved in the federal government's allotment policy, thus pulling them from the old world they knew.

Creation stories from long ago say that Jackson Barnett and his tribespeople descended from "Ekv' nv," or mother earth, as many tribes know it, with each generation deepening the relationship between the people and the earth. According to Muscogee Creek oral history, the people received the substance of life from "Ekv' nv," created by the Master of Breath, "Hesaketvmese," who breathed the spirit of life into people. Muscogee origin accounts tell of their ancestors emerging from the earth and encountering the forces of fire from the four cardinal directions.[2] The Creek were in awe of the fires, and the power of nature over their lives appeared obvious to them; they respected the ways and laws of nature. Nature compelled the people to observe the earth's gifts of life to the plants, which nourished and sheltered the animals, thus enabling all to live. All things were related and belonged to nature's order or system, leading the Muscogee Creek to develop kinship relations with the earth's plants and animals as expressed in clans and animism.

Astonishingly, the Muscogee Creek survived President Andrew Jackson's policy of removing Indians to territory west of the Mississippi during the 1830s. Thirty years later, they endured the American Civil War that brought destruction to their homes in Indian Territory. As a tribe, their relationship with "Ekv' nv" persisted in spite of the Dawes Act and its amendment, which mandated that their land be carved up and distributed to tribal members. In the name of "civilization," the Creek would be transformed into individual farmers, which jeopardized tribal identity, caused factionalism, and netted large losses of their new homelands. Traditionalists in the late 1800s who underwent allotment, like Jackson Barnett, felt a loss of spirit and lacked an understanding of the whole situation. Even the wise elders with generations of traditional knowledge did not have an answer, and they blamed the white people for what was happening to them.

Factionalism among the Muscogee Creek has always existed, but fortunately, the tribe endured through even the most crucial times. External issues had also threatened tribal unity, especially as more Creek began to live nontraditionally. But in time, the pressures of issues related to the white world became more powerful than the internal cohesion of Creek society, creating persistent havoc. Even after their removal from their original homeland in the Southeast to lands in the West, the Muscogee Creek waged at least three civil wars within their tribe, basically pitting those members favoring more progressive ways against those wanting to retain traditional culture. In 1872, the Sands Rebellion divided the Creek when the majority of the tribe elected Colonel Samuel Checote, a mixed-blood and a former Confederate, as chief over Sands, also known as Oktarharsars Harjo, a full-blooded Union or Loyal Creek with an estimated 300 support-ers. Checote prevailed.[3] A decade later, the conservative full-bloods attempted another restoration under Isparhecher, who led 350 Loyal Creek (who stayed neutral in the Creek's internal civil war). In what was known as the Green Peach War of 1883, Isparhecher failed to re-store the traditional government and society.[4]

Intertribal political problems forced the Muscogee Creek to re-vise their tribal government. Internally, the primary concern involved maintaining law and order; externally, the tribe faced continual pres-sure from the United States to allot their lands. Moreover, both local whites and a state government coveted the lands, hoping to expand white settlement.

Eager non-Indians on former Creek lands and in other areas of the territory lobbied congressmen from nearby states to introduce federal legislation for white settlement and Oklahoma statehood. The Creek had much to lose. White opportunists did not want the Creek and other Indians to control Oklahoma Territory and the new state. Having little political influence in Washington, the Creek and the other Five Civilized Tribes could not muster sufficient outside support for their own state, and they witnessed control of the situation slipping from their grasp.

Lawless turmoil followed as bands of whites, blacks, and other Indians camped throughout the Muscogee Creek Nation and the rest of Indian Territory. Increasing crimes challenged the Creek Lighthorse to maintain peace and order. Robbers, murderers, and livestock rus-tlers plagued the Muscogees and other tribal nations. The Cookson Hills in nearby Cherokee Territory became the hideout for local out-laws such as Ned Christie and the famed female outlaw Belle Starr.[5] Although the tribes attempted to maintain tribal laws, their efforts conflicted with the territorial law being enforced from Fort Smith, Arkansas.

· Outlaws and general disorder undermined Creek authority, which played into the hands of white opportunists who wanted the best land of the territory for themselves. Simultaneously, federal agents trav-eled among the Creek to urge acceptance of the allotments. To the disadvantage of the Creek, the U.S. Congress entertained legislation in the interests of non-Indians wanting statehood for Oklahoma Terri-tory.

As the end of the troubled 1800s approached, the Creek employed another method of fighting allotment to save the old ways. Soon, the Muscogee Creek entered the courtroom and petitioned Congress to express their support for traditionalism and their opposition to allot-ment. The Muscogee Creek National Council sent a message to President William McKinley during October 1889 to remind him of the eighteen ratified treaties that the United States had signed with their tribe.[6]

During these unstable years, the U.S. Congress passed the Dawes Land Allotment Act (in 1887), but it initially excluded the Muscogee Creek and other members of the Five Civilized Tribes, many of whom had become successful farmers. The allotment policy individualized Indians for mainstream assimilation, with the purpose of dissolving reservations, and the Oklahoma statehood movement appeared to engulf the Creek and the other Five Civilized Tribes.

Wanting to control their own destiny, the Muscogee Creek wrote their own constitution during the early 1890s, consisting of ten articles that defined their new form of government; one company of Lighthorse would enforce the tribal laws in each Creek town.[7] Working to overcome division within the tribe, the Muscogee Creek realized the need to solidify their nation against the United States.

The new constitution enabled the Muscogee Creek to begin regulating their natural resources. Section 376 stipulated that no less than three tribal citizens in a group could mine coal in the nation. Section 392 stated that members had to obtain a license from the treasurer of the nation and file a bond with good security for contracting with any railroad company to furnish ties from timberlands or other materials.[8] Outside pressures for Creek resources convinced the tribe to remain united, but the greater battle proved to be waged among tribal members themselves.

Continual factionalism, pitting full-blood traditionalists against mixed-blood progressives, frustrated the Muscogee Creek, and the momentum of allotment undermined the tribe, causing many families to fragment. Fathers and sons disagreed, brothers fought each other, and the individual person had to choose between the old ways and the new.

In an effort to protect their people, members of the tribal council passed a resolution in opposition to the allotment of their lands. Section 120 of the resolution, dated November 5, 1894, stated: "We still believe that the Government of the United States will prove true to her many pledges and keep perfect faith with our people and will aid instead of obstruct our present form of government to the end that we may enjoy peace and happiness in our sacred home, for which we have paid full compensation."[9]

At the close of the nineteenth century, the sovereignty of the Muscogee Creek was threatened on the political front as well. Politically ambitious white officials of Oklahoma Territory campaigned for statehood. Realizing they might be consumed by the movement, the

Creek and other members of the Five Civilized Tribes pushed for a state of their own, which would be called Sequoyah and encompass the eastern half of Indian Territory. The reservations fought the movement for Oklahoma's statehood until Kansas Senator Charles Curtis, a part Kaw-Osage who would become vice president of the United States, introduced the Curtis Act of 1898, a law that negated all the Indian reservations in Indian Territory, except for that of the Osage , who held mineral rights in common as a tribe. As a part of the statehood plan, the territorial legislature introduced a radical bill to relocate all of the Indian population from the eastern half of the territory to the western portion.[10] This proposal threatened to combine the western and eastern tribes, but resistance from the Indian nations prevented this from happening.

The Dawes Act had excluded the Five Civilized Tribes, and the Muscogee Creek at least avoided allotment for the next fifteen years. Increasing non-Indian support for allotment could not be averted. As other tribes experienced allotment, the Creek realized what the ultimate outcome would be. Unable to overcome the white desire for their lands and the government's aggressive policy of allotment, the National Council of the Muscogee Creek, in 1893 and 1899, authorized tribal representatives to negotiate with the Dawes Commission and the leaders of the Five Civilized Tribes and report back to the council.[11] The Muscogee strove to hold their nation together, but opposition to allotment and the trespassing of whites wanting their lands added to the troubles of the tribe. In preparation, Isparhecher, the principal chief, appointed Samuel Haynes, James R. Gregory, Napoleon B. Moore, and Wallace McNac as members of a national committee to help the Dawes Commission in identifying and enrolling the Muscogee Creek for allotment.[12] Finally, special legislation in an amendment approved on March 1, 1901, mandated that the tribe ratify the allotment agreement by March 25.[13] Section 7 of the Indian Appropriation Act, passed in 1902, stipulated that "any deceased Indian to whom a trust or other patent containing restrictions upon alienation [that] has been or shall be issued for lands allotted him [his estate] may sell and convey lands inherited from such descendant."[14] This law proved detrimental to the Creek as they lost more lands and properties such as homes and livestock.

At five o'clock on January 3, 1903, 255 Muscogee Creek received the first allotments,[15] and it was not long before others did as well. Frustrated with all the actions launched against them, many Creek refused their allotments, thereby creating "surplus" lands that could possibly pass to white settlers and land speculators. William Foulke, a journalist for *Outlook* magazine, reported on the fraud consuming the Creek, describing the debauchery committed by whites and the land sharks who were cheating the Muscogees out of their allotted lands due to the carelessness of the federal government.[16] The task of supervising Indian land distribution was monumental, and any mistakes occurred unfairly at the expense of the Indians.

The allotment program officials continued assigning allotments to the Creek and established the tribal roll, later known as the Dawes Roll. The Muscogee government initially made the roll with the help of an Indian agent, and the secretary of the interior and the commissioner of Indian affairs reviewed the roll for final approval.

As early as 1901, Chitto Harjo, a full-blood Creek, urged resistance against allotment and the ways of the white people. This last patriotic fight for traditionalism became known as the Crazy Snake Rebellion. Also known by the name of Wilson Jones, Harjo was a town mekko (Creek king) and a member of the House of Kings in the Muscogee Creek National Council. Born in 1846, he grew up among the Upper or Loyal Creek who sided with the Union during the American Civil War, fighting to protect themselves against Confederate soldiers. In protest to the allotment, Harjo led ninety-four "Snake" followers, who took their name from one of the Creek clans. Attempting to establish a new Creek government based on ancient tribal laws of "Ekv' nv," the Snakes gathered at Old Hickory stompground, five miles east of Henryetta, Oklahoma. (Harjo himself lived twelve miles east of Henryetta at the foot of Tiger Mountain.) As the Snakes gathered, U.S. troops and federal marshals were ordered in, and the two sides fought near Seminole and Wewoka. The action of the Snakes incited Choctaw traditionalists to oppose allotments, and federal officials had to use force to defeat them as well.[17]

Immersed in turmoil, the House of Warriors of the Muscogee Creek government passed a series of twenty-five laws on December 7, 1903, to maintain the strength of the government.[18] Harjo had been a member of the government, and his action divided both the tribal government and the communities.

Finally breaking the strength of the Snakes, federal officials arrested Harjo and some of his followers, and court charges were filed against them. A federal court convicted them, although Harjo and the Snakes continued to voice their opposition, claiming that allotment officials cheated their tribespeople during the assignments of land. Their protests fell on deaf ears as non-Indians and proallotment Indians campaigned for Oklahoma Territory to become a state in the union.

The Muscogee Creek continued to suffer at the hands of white opportunists and the devastating allotment program. Confused and bitter, they felt a horrible injustice had been done to them. In a letter dated 1904, the National Council appealed to President Theodore Roosevelt for help: "As a people we have kept our faith with the U.S. government. ... Knowing your intense honesty, your hatred of shams ... we turn to you, Mr. President, feeling that you will understand us better than Congress. ... You know the West—you know our hopes and our ambitions; and we appeal again to your sense of justice and fair dealing."[19] The council failed.

In 1906, Indian Territory joined with Oklahoma Territory as non-Indian officials happily anticipated statehood. The growing interest in Oklahoma and the statehood movement convinced Chitto Harjo and several of his Snakes to make one last effort and plan a delegation to Washington. The delegates insisted that the Treaty of 1832 be upheld and believed that they had won a victory. Government officials opposed the Snakes's intentions, but Harjo insisted that justice would prevail.[20]

In Washington, little concern was given to the Muscogee and other Indian groups, although a special Senate investigating committee surveyed the old Indian Territory to evaluate Indian progress. On November 23, 1906, the Senate committee held a hearing in Tulsa for the purpose of hearing from the Creek. An estimated 500 people jammed the Elk's Lodge Hall or stood nearby. In a plea on behalf of his people and future generations, Chitto Harjo spoke against the allotment program. Clutching his hat in his hands, with a sober look on his face, his eyes sincere, he stood before the committee to speak: "Now I hear the Government is cutting up my land giving it away to other people. ... It can't be so for it is not the treaty. These people who are they? They have no right to this land. It never was given to them. It was given to me and my people and we paid for it with our land back in Alabama. The black and white people have no right to it. Then how can it be that the Government is doing this? ... It wouldn't be justice. I am informed and believe it to be true that some citizens of the United States have title to land that was given to my fathers and my people by the government. If it was given to me, what right has the United States to take it from me without first asking my consent?"[21]

During the next several weeks, Harjo waited to testify against the allotment policy before a Senate committee. He realized the sovereign significance of the treaties between his tribe and the United States. He iterated the rights of his people under the treaties and described the relationship between his people and the United States as positive until the civil war.

In summary, the fight to save the old ways and opposition to white settlers wanting allotment of Indian lands produced skirmishes at Hickory Ground and Wewoka. Exaggerating these events, the Oklahoma City Daily Oklahoman, the Muskogee Daily Phoenix, the Eufaula Indian Journal, and other regional newspapers described the hostilities as an "Indian war." Rumors circulated that black freedmen had joined the Snakes in an all-out war against white settlers, provoking them to arm themselves and travel in mobs in search of the Snakes and freedmen.[22] In the end, federal marshals and Loyal Creek defeated Harjo and his Snakes, arresting almost all of them. Swept under by a new era of change, Crazy Snake died in April, 1911, at the house of a Choctaw friend, Daniel Bob.[23]

Filled with confusion and anger against the white people, Chitto Harjo, through his loyalty to tribal ways, inspired other traditionalists of the Five Civilized Tribes. Mostly full-blood Cherokee formed a secret society known as the "Pin Indians," so named because they wore insignias proclaiming their opposition to allotment. Their membership reached approximately 5,000 full-bloods under Cherokee leader Red Bird Smith, and they called themselves the Keetoowah Society. A Muscogee Creek hostile to allotment, Eufaula Harjo, helped Smith to unite other Creek, Cherokee, and supporters from the Chickasaw and Choctaw to join them. With members from all four tribes, they then called themselves the Four Mothers Society. Seeking ways to escape the allotment experience, they sent a delegation to Washington to convince the federal government to let them keep their community usage of land and traditional customs. The government denied this request.. Furthermore, although members of the Four Mothers Society had struck an agreement to buy land from Mexico, the United States refused to give them permission to sell their allotments.[24] Unable to succeed in these efforts, the traditionalists had to remain in their communities, feeling the paternalistic pressure of the federal government controlling their lives.

On May 21, 1908, the Senate passed legislation to remove restrictions from part of the lands of the allottees of the Five Civilized Tribes. The federal government listed Creek tribal members alphabetically, according to degree of Creek blood. In addition, the Dawes roll included Creek freedmen who had moved with the Creek to Indian Territory, and they were regarded as part of the Creek tribe.[25]

The next major problem occurred when the allotments of several Muscogee Creek were found to have large pools of oil, which soon brought the Indians windfalls of royalty payments. Instantly wealthy, these individuals began buying anything that they wanted. The easy acquisition of white goods was very disruptive, threatening the traditional cultural values these Indians had known from birth.

Wosey John Deer, a Muscogee Creek woman (roll number 9546), had oil on her land, to her misfortune. With her windfall and under the custody of her dishonest guardian, W. J. Cole of Sapulpa, Oklahoma, she invested in cattle of high breed. On one occasion, she ordered the butchering of one of her bulls worth $500 simply to eat him. Once word of Wosey's newfound wealth spread, she was harassed "at every turn by designing persons wishing to use any possible means" to take advantage of her. One of those persons was her alleged guardian, Cole, who forced her to divorce her husband, Albert Deer. She could not read or write, and friends found her beaten up on one occasion.[26]

In another situation, the death of Willie Berryhill left a sizable estate of more than $40,000 that his heirs fought over.[27] Another wealthy Muscogee Creek used his newfound wealth to purchase a wooden horse as an ornament for his yard and then purchased two phonographs to play just two records.[28] Henry Ford's Tin Lizzies soon caught the attention of wealthy Muscogee Creek, and some wanted the best automobiles made. Lucinda Pittman, a wealthy Creek who lived in Muskogee, wanted a Cadillac but did not like the available color (the cars were customarily black). Lucinda selected an item of a very unusual color at a store in Muskogee and demanded that the salesman at the Cadillac dealership paint the car that shade. In addition, she wanted it upholstered in matching material. This odd request confounded the Cadillac salesman, but he finally acquiesced to the demands of the rich Creek woman.[29]

In the following weeks, stunned people watched her oddly colored Cadillac leaving a trail of dust on the roads around Muskogee; and she frequently traveled to Tulsa and Oklahoma City. Among rich Indians in Oklahoma, she made the Cadillac a popular car, and the company profited from Lucinda Pittman's unusual choice of color. Soon, pink, crimson, and sea-green automobiles became the trend throughout Oklahoma and, indeed, the United States.[30]

Eastman Richards, a tall full-blood, was another wealthy Muscogee Creek. His allotment of barren land proved useless for farming or raising stock, but oil underground brought him unmeasured wealth. On September 7, 1923, Eastman generously donated $50,000 to the American Baptist Home Mission Society for Bacone College.[31] Frustrated in his dealings with non-Muscogee Creek, he surrounded himself with family and friends and financed the development of his own town. Against the advice of his guardian, he chose a site in McIntosh County in Oklahoma and had the town that would bear his name— Richardsville constructed for an estimated $1 million.[32] In later years, the town disintegrated from lack of activity.

One of the several Muscogee Creek exploited for their royalty money was Katie Fixico of Okmulgee.[33] A full-blood Muscogee Creek, Katie had an estate worth $1 million from oil royalty payments. She married John Daniels, who signed a petition declaring that she was competent to handle her own business affairs, but eleven days later, he asked that she be declared legally "incompetent." During the period of uncertainty that ensued, the Exchange Trust Company of Tulsa was made guardian of Katie's estate, but fraud had already been committed, and Katie Fixico Daniels was bilked out of $80,000 by her former guardian, V. V. Morgan, and an unscrupulous attorney.[34]

The most famous case of allotment fraud among the Muscogee Creek involved Jackson Barnett. In 1842, at Buzzard Hill along the Canadian River, Jackson Barnett was born to Siah and Thlesophile Barnett. Jackson, who had a half brother named Tecumseh, had a difficult young life but learned to survive. He received an allotment of 160 acres; the Dawes Roll listed him as number 4524, age forty-eight, from Tuckabatchee town of the Muscogee Creek Nation.[35] He grew up in obscurity as a conservative full-blood and had joined the Snake faction for a while, which opposed allotment of tribal land. As the years passed, Jackson continued to live on his land outside of Henryetta. His life was quiet, rather peaceful, with the usual trips into town. Jackson Barnett obtained his riches when an oil company discovered oil in 1912 beneath his otherwise worthless allotted land, said to be so rocky and barren that it would not even support a jackrabbit.[36]

In 1912, a field clerk helped Jackson lease his allotment to an oil company. Another company that also wanted his land succeeded in establishing his "incompetency," and the Okmulgee County court appointed him a "guardian" named Carl J. O'Hornett and secured another lease for the Barnett allotment. The two oil companies compromised on a settlement, and the drilling for oil on Jackson's land commenced in the Cushing field. The two companies paid royalties to the Creek agency to be invested in liberty bonds or paid to O'Hornett for Jackson's living expenses. In spite of his accumulating wealth, growing by each day, the traditionalist Jackson Barnett continued to live a humble existence near Henryetta.[37]

In 1919, Jackson Barnett consented to donate $25,000 to build a Baptist church in Henryetta. People soon learned about his wealth, and one preacher in Muskogee thought that Jackson could easily give $200,000 and stated that "if we do not get this money the lawyers and the [Interior] department will get it as they have always done."[38] During December, the Baptists sent a committee to discuss the proposed donation with Cato Sells, the commissioner of the Bureau of Indian Affairs (BIA). Then, on February 11, 1920, Gabe E. Parker, the superintendent of Indian affairs at Muskogee, said that the department approved of a plan to devote half of Jackson's $1,500,000 to charities, which included a hospital for Indians at Henryetta.[39] At one point, three persuasive individuals and a minister convinced Jackson to donate the money. Commissioner Sells was convinced that Barnett sincerely wanted to do this. Unable to write his name, Jackson signed the paperwork with his thumbprint.[40]

The news of the old full-blood and others like him became locally famous, as word spread that oil was making them rich. Learning about the wealthy elderly Creek Indian, an attractive brunette named Anna Laura Lowe decided to met the rich Barnett. In a investigation a few years later, an attorney from New York reported to Cato Sells that the dark-haired woman actually schemed to kidnap Jackson Barnett and had talked to several people about helping her. She met Barnett for the first time on January 30, 1920. On the following day, she arrived at his house in a taxi and drove him and a black caretaker to Okemah, where Jackson thought she was taking him to a store. Annie Lowe "gave Jackson whiskey on the way to Okemah, that Jackson refused to drink and that thereupon she turned the bottle up to his lips and practically forced the liquor down him."[41] Lowe wanted to obtain a marriage license but was refused at Okemah. She then had the taxi drive them to Holdenville, the county seat of the next county, but the clerk there also refused her. Later that day, she told Jackson's guardian, Carl O'Hornett, that she loved Barnett and intended to marry him. O'Hornett did not believe her and opposed the plan of marriage.

During the evening of February 22, Lowe returned at nine o'clock with a man and his wife. They persuaded Jackson to get into their car and told the black caretaker that Jackson would be back the next morning. The threesome and Barnett drove all night to Coffeyville, Kansas, where Anna Lowe obtained a marriage license in the city of Independence. Next, she found a justice of the peace named Bicket to marry them at the Metropolitan rooming house in Coffeyville. Bicket later reported that Jackson Barnett had likely been given whiskey and appeared "doped" during the brief marriage ceremony.[42] Lowe took Jackson to Missouri for a second marriage to ensure that she really was the new (and wealthy) Mrs. Jackson Barnett. Protecting her greedy interest before the second wedding, Lowe and her attorney, Harold McGugin, one-time Republican candidate for governor of Kansas, convinced Barnett to thumbmark a letter that rescinded his earlier generous donations.

The investigating attorney had discovered that Annie Laura Lowe was a scoundrel and a prostitute. She had been married twice before, and during 1914, 1915, and part of 1916, she worked the hotels in Tulsa to find rich men. During the rest of 1916 and 1917, she did the same in Kansas City, and in 1918 and 1919, she traveled to the oil fields in

Oklahoma and Texas looking for men who had struck it rich. At least a half-dozen bellboys at various hotels swore that they were hired by Lowe as go-betweens to arrange her dates, and hotel clerks, a manager, and an assistant manager supported claims that Lowe was a manipulating prostitute; one house detective said that he threw her out of a hotel.[43]

On one occasion, Lowe bilked a man in Kansas City out of $5,000 in cash by drugging him. Going rapidly through this money due to her taste for expensive clothes and high living, she also attempted to blackmail an oilman in 1916 and 1917. She had her clutches on two wealthy part-Cherokee Indians as well.

The commissioner of Indian affairs and Carl O'Hornett tried to annul the marriage, but Jackson Barnett seemed content with it and convinced them to temporarily drop their suit.[44] In May, Mrs. Barnett, Jackson, and Mrs. Barnett's sixteen-year old daughter arrived at the agency to request a larger monthly allowance, but their request was initially denied. They also wanted to build a house in Muskogee, but County Judge Hugh L. Murphy of Okmulgee County denied their wish. While the judge and the agency discussed the request, the Barnetts traveled to Muskogee to look for a place to buy. Wirt Randolph, of Wynnewood, Oklahoma, who was also Mrs. Barnett's brother, accompanied the couple and represented their business interests in looking at the Buell place, located four and one-half miles northwest of Muskogee. Mr. Buell wanted to sell the house and the furniture inside since it was especially "designed and installed by Mr. Teupe of Kansas City."[45] During November and December, the Barnetts attracted publicity from the newspapers reporting on Jackson's wealth as the press watched their every action. During the night, the Barnetts moved their household goods to Muskogee, having purchased a house and filled it with furniture. O'Hornett and Judge Murphy agreed to increase the Barnetts' living allowance to $2,500 per month.[46]

The publicity surrounding Jackson Barnett made him a target for many opportunists, and some were persistent. On December 18, 1920, the opportunistic Casey succeeded in getting Barnett into Reverend Cameron's office in Henryetta to reinstate his donations to the Baptist organization. All the confusion compelled Victor Locke, superintendent of the Five Civilized Tribes, to send a memorandum prepared by his law clerk and a second memorandum to the Interior Department, stating that Barnett had been adjudged "incompetent" by one of the courts in Oklahoma and that he had a guardian, Carl O'Hornett. The relationship between the probate courts of Oklahoma and the Interior Department were in conflict. Mrs. Barnett's attorney, McGugin, met with the special assistant to the attorney general to prepare a petition to BIA Commissioner Charles H. Burke, saying that Barnett's guardian had failed him. McGugin arranged for the Barnetts to go to Washington to speak to Commissioner Burke about their needs and the unhelpful guardian, O'Hornett.[47]

During 1921, one report related that Mrs. Barnett and an attorney named McGugin had Jackson drinking in an automobile. A bystander remarked that, as McGugin and Mrs. Barnett were giving Jackson some air, McGugin remarked, "Yes, we are airing him out in the car; and we are going to air him out of some money."[48]

With her attorney's help, Mrs. Barnett arranged to receive Liberty Bonds in the amount of $550,000, then she created a trust for Jackson. Next, she turned over to McGugin, as his portion of the distribution, bonds worth $125,000 or perhaps more.[49] During these months, Mrs. Barnett also looked for a private girls' school for her daughter, Maxine Lowe Barnett, and applied to Mrs. Barstow's School in Kansas City with the understanding that Jackson would pay for all the expenses.[50]

All during this time, the marriage seemed dubious; a legal petition had been filed against it, provoking Mrs. Barnett to take Jackson to Washington, D.C., to see Commissioner of Indian Affairs Burke in order to arrange the division of Barnett's estate in the amount of $1,100,000, half going to his wife and the other half to a school for orphans in Oklahoma. Jackson signed the paperwork with his thumbprint.

In July 1922, a solicitor for the Interior Department rendered a legal opinion that the department, not the probate court, had authority over Jackson Barnett and his estate; thus, the donations would be carried out. The conflict between the probate court and the Interior Department resulted in a court case in the U.S. District Court of New York, heard by Judge John Knox. The judge ruled that fraud had occurred regarding the generous donations, and ordered that they would not be carried out; furthermore, because Jackson had, "at the insistence of his wife," been "declared to be incompetent by a court of California [and Oklahoma], and guardians of the person and estate were then appointed ... that property of Barnett [should remain in] the custody of the Secretary of the Interior."[51]

Judge Knox appointed Elmer Bailey as Jackson's new guardian and questioned Jackson before making his decision about the case. A sample of the judge's questions and Jackson's answers follows:

Q. And what about the money while you are alive?
A. I am going to keep it and eat off it.
Q. What was that?

A. I am going to keep it and eat off it all the time while I live.
Q. Do you know where that money is now?
A. No.
Q. Did you ever make a gift to this school [Bacone], giving them the money after you died?
A. I do not know.
Q. Do you remember having signed any papers?
A. I do not know.[52]

To get a better understanding of the situation before making his decision, Judge Knox called Jackson to the stand; Jackson did not understand the nature of the oath, so the bailiff did not swear him in to testify. Based on the answers to his questions, Judge Knox stated

> that he [Jackson] is a harmless, kindly, mentally undeveloped man, who was extremely bored at the court proceedings and had no comprehension of their significance. He was able to impart information as to where he lived, as to the number of and type of his automobiles, and that he was possessed of several cow ponies. ... He was aware, too, of his ownership of a farm of about seventy acres and that he had another piece of property on which there was an oil well. Also that money came to him from the oil well, but he did not know the amount of his income. When asked if he had any idea of a million dollars, he answered, 'No.' [53]

News about the Jackson Barnett case reached Congress, and some members informed President Calvin Coolidge. The Department of Justice intervened on Barnett's behalf due to the government's responsibility to a "ward" of the state, leading to forthcoming court cases in the District of Columbia, suits against Mrs. Barnett in California, and suits against her attorneys in Oklahoma and Kansas. In Oklahoma, a state supreme court decided that O'Hornett and Bailey were illegally appointed guardians for Jackson Barnett, and those appointments were nullified. In the end, Jackson was named in the proceedings of more than twenty-one cases; in most of these cases, the old full-blood was questioned and subjected him to mental testing.[54]

To escape publicity, Mrs. Barnett moved herself and her wealthy husband to southern California in 1923, where they purchased a house that one newspaper reported cost $100,000. For the next five years, the Barnetts lived in splendor, although Jackson's estate continued in a state of legal limbo. A court in Oklahoma subpoenaed Jackson in 1926 and charged him with contempt for ignoring a summons for the proper supervision and protection of his estate. A new date of September 27, 1926, was set for a grand jury hearing in Muskogee, Oklahoma.[55] The court ordered a marshal from the state to deliver Jackson Barnett for the trial, which involved two issues: "one an accounting of property said to be in excess of $1,000,000," the other seeking "an annulment of the Indian's marriage, charging fraud and undue influence."

Mrs. Barnett attempted to drag Jackson away from Deputy Marshal Bailey and the policemen, while degrading them by yelling, "Oklahoma bandits," "highwaymen," and "robbers." She also refused to listen to the writ of summons from the court.[56] An outraged Mrs. Barnett hired attorneys to protest to Federal Judge R. L. Williams that her husband was kidnapped and that the summons improperly named only Jackson Barnett. Declared an "incompetent" by the county court of Okmulgee, Jackson was under the jurisdiction of the court. Mrs. Barnett's lawyers claimed she should also have been summoned. "They dragged him right off the porch ... without giving him time to so much as pack his bag," exclaimed Mrs. Barnett.[57] She threatened that the doctor said Jackson, seventy-six years old at the time, was ill, and she warned against the long drive to Oklahoma. "My husband was [sic] a sick man," she said. "If they attempt to drive to Oklahoma, I think the trip will kill him."[58] However, Bailey drove Jackson to San Bernadino and put him on a train to Muskogee. Angry at the court action, Mrs. Barnett stormed to Oklahoma to take her husband back to California.

Arriving on a warm August day, Mrs. Barnett registered at the Severs Hotel in downtown Muskogee. Demanding to see her husband immediately, she had the marshal arrange a meeting with Jackson. The marshal took precautions and decided to hold the meeting in his office. Learning about Mrs. Barnett's arrival, news reporters gathered at the Severs Hotel, hoping for an interview. One reporter knocked at her door and had it slammed in his face. "You won't see me," she shouted, while locking the door. "You can get your information regarding Jackson Barnett from the Oklahoma Outlaw!"[59]

While in custody of the court, Jackson wanted to remain in Muskogee at the farmhouse that he had purchased a few years earlier. Deputy Bailey said that Jackson had told him that he was homesick and that his wife would not let him visit Oklahoma for three years. "I was glad to see the officers that came to arrest me," said Jackson.[60] The next morning, he asked to see his farmhouse, a bungalow of small stone design located on several acres at 48th and Okmulgee Streets, on the west side of Muskogee. It is "the only house he really loves in the world," said the deputy.[61] The marshal's office arranged to drive Jackson to his farm and had a green roadster waiting for him and Deputy Bailey. Meanwhile, Mrs. Barnett was hunting for Jackson. Leaving the federal building, she saw him and flew down the steps toward the car. "Jackson! Jackson! I want to see you!" she cried. Jackson grinned without saying a word as the car backed up and drove away. He then motioned for the green roadster to go faster. In a rage, Mrs. Barnett, who was wearing a dashing dress with a tiny white hat pulled down over her coal-black hair, reportedly made quite a scene.[62]

Back in Oklahoma, Jackson was at peace. His mind and soul were reunited with "Ekv' nv," where he could touch the earth and smell the cut hay in the wind. Separated from his brethren Muscogee Creek, he at least was with the homeland again for a while. "I jus' soon not have money. I like hors', pigs, hogs. I stay here and run my farm. Woman, she can go 'way. I live with Caesar [farm caretaker Cecil Elliot]. We run farm all right. That's only t'ing I know. She got lot of money now. Henry Roan had lot of money. So have I. Don't t'ink some t'ing happen. Don't take no chance," said Jackson.[63] Full of plans, Jackson wanted to cut down the brush around his farm and buy new furniture for the house.

Mrs. Barnett had plans of her own. "I won't turn my husband back to those blood-hounds," she threatened. "I'm going to take care of him. I'm fond of him. I guess, I picked him out for a husband. And I didn't kidnap him as they say. All they want is his money. People were always writing to him in California asking for donations. He doesn't know enough to avoid all of them."[64] Mrs. Barnett vowed to fight the court-decreed separation of their marriage to the end. But the government said that divorce proceedings would not be necessary since the marriage was performed without the consent of Jackson Barnett's guardian. At the end of August, a determined Mrs. Barnett moved in with Jackson at the farmhouse and ordered it completely refurnished by a furniture store in downtown Muskogee. However, Mrs. Barnett declined to say whether she had come back to Muskogee to live permanently.[65]

During 1926, the grand jury hearing began, and similar cases were developing elsewhere. As the proceedings started, a new witness, J. J. Johnson, the hotel operator at Okemah, testified that he was the driver of the automobile used to take Jackson and Anna Laura Lowe to be married in the famous kidnapping case.[66] As the Barnett case proceeded, other Muscogee Creek also shared local knowledge involving the estates of Effie Fife, Katie Fixico, Eastman Richards, Jeanetta Marshall, Wosey Deer, and Maude Lee Mudd in court. Muscogee Creek chief C. W. Hill sent a message to the nation, stating that these individuals and all Creek needed legal protection.[67] For these wealthy Muscogee Creek, money only brought disaster and disruption to their lives, leading to exploitation, abuse, and court litigation. The white society's money bought only temporary happiness but caused permanent harm.

In 1928, a federal grand jury in Muskogee investigated criminal charges against Charles Burke and Albert Fall, but the Department of Justice dismissed the case. Later, in 1928–1929, a committee of the U.S. Senate called for a full investigation of the handling of Jackson Barnett's affairs.[68] No government officials were found guilty of wrongdoing, and Barnett proved himself to be fundamentally well aware of the situation, even though all of the investigation was conducted in the alien, white system of justice.

To support their extravagant lifestyle in the white world, the Barnetts requested extra money from Jackson's trust fund at Christmas, asking for $6,000 in 1928.[69] Jackson Barnett spent his remaining years in southern California. In Los Angeles, many remembered him pretending to direct streams of traffic on Wilshire Boulevard from the corner sidewalk outside his expensive home.[70]

The windfall money from his oil made Barnett wealthy beyond belief and brought drastic changes to his life. His wealth propelled him into a bewildering world, where he felt alienated from the American mainstream even as his new lifestyle ostracized him from his own people—the Muscogee Creek. Jackson Barnett surely felt alone and outcasted, a feeling that goes against the Indians' social emphasis on belonging to a people and to "Ekv' nv." To maintain a perspective for security's sake, his personal interests remained the same in spite of his wealth. He had few and simple pleasures, and his love in life included a few horses.[71] He did not want to change to suit the white world, but his wealth altered him due to the new status and unwanted publicity it brought. Most of all, his notorious wife, Anna Laura Lowe, changed his life during their thirteen years of marriage and worked steadily to spend Jackson Barnett's money until Secretary of the Interior Harold Ickes quickly telegraphed Superintendent A. M. Landman to suspend payments to the Barnetts on April 3, 1934.[72]

Removed from his homeland of Oklahoma, Jackson lived the rest of his days in California. Deemed "incompetent" by a court, his late years of wealth and controversy ended when he passed away peacefully in his sleep at the age of ninety-four. His spirit, confused and torn between the old Creek ways and the rich lifestyle of the white world, could finally rest. He died in 1934, dubbed "the world's richest Indian." Preparations for his burial began at Forest Lawn Cemetery in California, but the United States government halted the proceedings. Government agent John W. Dady in California, acting under telegraphed instructions from Commissioner of Indian Affairs John Collier in Washington, appeared at the mortuary and ordered the funeral to be postponed until the decision about whether to bury Jackson Barnett there or at Henryetta in Oklahoma was made.[73] Collier favored burying Barnett in Oklahoma and telegraphed Dady that he would let him know of the decision the following day, June 1, 1934.[74]

The death of Jackson Barnett produced a new controversy, for he left no will. His estate was estimated at $4 million in cash, securities, and real estate in Los Angeles and Riverside Counties in California and in Creek County in Oklahoma.

Immediately after Jackson's death, attorney Omar R. Young filed a petition in a court in Long Beach, California, on behalf of Barnett's twenty-one-year-old nephew, Hubert Howard Barnett. The nephew's petition claimed that Jackson had five nieces and three nephews living who would be his rightful heirs.[75]

At Muskogee, Oklahoma, other relatives filed another petition. Will Conner, 40, from Hanna, and Nettie Conner Bear, 43, of Eufaula, filed in behalf of seven other heirs—Wynie Conner Hendrix, 57, of Ardmore; John Conner, 36, of Eufaula; Rebecca J. Baker, 63, of Schooton; Nathan Williams, 59, of Okemah; Susie Conner, 45, of Sasakwa; Emma Conner Burgess, 40, of Sasakwa, and May or Hanna Conner, 35, of Sasakwa.[76]

In the end, 200 "heirs" had emerged in Oklahoma, California, Kentucky, New Mexico, Tennessee, Indiana, and Ohio. Another "wife," with two children, also made a claim to the Barnett estate. At this stage, people named Barnett from all parts of the country were receiving calls from lawyers suggesting that they claim relationship to Jackson Barnett; eventually, an estimated 1,000 people claimed to be relatives.[77]

Fifteen years of litigation followed Jackson's death before his estate was settled. Mrs. Barnett had employed attorneys, including Harold McGugin, to argue for her interests. During the presentation of the evidence, it was disclosed that large sums had been transferred to Mrs. Barnett and her lawyers by Barnett's thumbprint signature.[78] The U.S. District Court ruled that the transfers were illegal and that Mrs. Barnett and her lawyers knew of Jackson's mental "incompetence" to handle large sums of money. A court order called for her to be ejected from the Barnett home in Los Angeles, in spite of a petition filed by her friends and supporters seeking to stop the procedure.[79]

In the final outcome, the court annulled the Barnett marriage in 1934, based on the conclusion that Jackson did not understand the meaning of marriage vows; the marriage was ruled invalid. After the fifteen years it took to resolve the heirship of Jackson Barnett's estate, his rightful heirs received appropriate shares as determined by the court. Judge Robert L. Williams in the federal district court at Muskogee, Oklahoma, rendered his decision on December 16, 1939.

Based on the Dawes allotment rolls, the court recognized thirty-four claimants, mostly full-bloods, as descendants of Siah Barnett, listed as Jackson's father.[80]

White greed for Indian allotted land proved unrelenting, affecting tribes and individuals such as Jackson Barnett. This was unfortunate enough by itself, but to take advantage of an elderly person who understood little about the mainstream society was even worse. This sad tale presents the exploitation of one Muscogee Creek full-blood but also reveals that white greed knew no limits, leading one person of a culture to exploit another of a different culture, even as other opportunists waited to have their chance, too. Traditionalist like Jackson Barnett lived in a nightmare of confusion, feeling trapped in a life no longer like the one they had known as children. The once proud spirit of each exploited allotted Indian was crushed by the momentum of the white capitalist system, which then abandoned the traditionalist Indian in a modern world.

The general prophecy of the Muscogee Creek is that the world will come to an end when the people no longer celebrate the harvest of the green corn in their "busk" ceremony, and tribal prophets warn that the sky will rain blood; when the trees are cut, their sap will be blood, announcing that when the last of the Indians disappear from the land, the land will fall beneath the waters of the ocean.[81] Jackson Barnett had simple pleasures—his horses and his love for the land—and his death, like the tribal prophecy, promised chaos.

The sad story of the exploitation of Jackson Barnett was only one of many cases of unscrupulous whites taking advantage of the Muscogee Creek and allottees of other tribes. It was even more unfortunate if the allottees had oil on their lands, as many Osage did in the early decades of the twentieth century.

NOTES

1. Muscogee Creek is also spelled Muskogee Creek, and quite often the Muscogee are referred to as Creek. Their original pronunciation was "Muscogulge," as discussed in J. Leitch Wright Jr., *Creek and Seminoles: Destruction and Regeneration of the Muscogulge People* (Lincoln: University of Nebraska Press, 1986), p. XIV.
2. The origin account of the Muscogee Creek states that the people emerged from the earth and faced four fires—a blue fire from the south, a black fire from the west, a white fire from the east, and a red and yellow fire from the north, which they chose to use. See John R. Swanton, "Social Organization and Social Usages of the Indians of the Creek Confederacy," in *Forty-Second Annual Report of the Bureau of American Ethnology,*

1924–1925 (Washington, DC: U.S. Government Printing Office, 1928), pp. 33–78.

3. Angie Debo, *The Road to Disappearance: A History of the Creek Indians* (Norman: University of Oklahoma Press, 1966), pp. 191–213 (this was first published in 1941); see also "Speech of Hon. Samuel Checote, After the Signing of the Agreement of Peace at Muskogee, August 10, 1883," Box 2, Alice Robertson Papers, Special Collections, McFarlin Library, University of Tulsa, Oklahoma.

4. Debo, *Road to Disappearance*, pp. 249–284.

5. Theda Perdue, *Nations Remembered: An Oral History of the Five Civilized Tribes, 1865–1907* (Westport, Conn.: Greenwood Press, 1980), pp. 26 and 74.

6. "Memorial of the Muscogee Nation by Its National Council to the President and Congress of the United States, October, 1889," Western History Collections, University of Oklahoma, Norman.

7. The Lighthorse company consisted of a captain and four privates, elected every two years by vote of the district, to carry out the orders of the judge. The constitution further established that the nation would be divided into six districts, replacing the emphasis on traditional tribal towns, with each one having a judge and a prosecuting attorney; see *Constitution and Laws of the Muskogee Nation*, compiled and codified by A. P. McKellop, (Muskogee, Indian Territory: F.C. Hubbard, 1893), pp. 15–16, Western History Collections, University of Oklahoma, Norman.

8. Ibid., pp. 127–133.

9. Section 210 of Muscogee Creek Tribal Council Resolution, November 5, 1894, Creek File, Western History Collections, University of Oklahoma, Norman.

10. Thos. A. Osborne, President of the West Side Circle Railway Company of Topeka, Kansas, to J. B. Harrison, Indian agent, Indian Rights Association Papers, Incoming Correspondence, 1888, microfilm, Reel 13, Marquette University Library, Milwaukee, Wisconsin.

11. *Acts and Resolutions of the National Council of the Muskogee Nation of 1893 and 1899, Inclusive* (Muskogee, Indian Terrritory: Phoenix Printing, 1900), pp. 75–76, Western History Collections, University of Oklahoma, Norman.

12. "Isparhecher to Muscogee Creek," April 1, 1899, Box 33, Alice Robertson Papers, Special Collections, McFarlin Library, University of Tulsa, Oklahoma.

13. "Act of 1901." Allotted Muscogee Creek Land, Creek File, Western History Collections, University of Oklahoma, Norman.

14. *U.S. Statutes 22*, 245, 275.

15. "Deeds to Creek Lands Recorded," *Muskogee Daily Phoenix*, January 3, 1903, Box 42, Alice Robertson Papers, Special Collections, McFarlin Library, University of Tulsa, Oklahoma..

16. William Dudley Foulke, "Despoiling a Nation," *Outlook* 91 (January 2, 1909): p. 44.

17. Debo, *The Road to Disappearance*, pp. 376–377.

18. *Rules of the House of Warriors*, Adopted December 7, 1903. (Okmulgee,

Indian Territory: Chieftain Printing House, n.d.), Western History Collections, University of Oklahoma, Norman.

19. Muscogee Creek Tribal Council to President Theodore Roosevelt, 1904, Creek File, Western History Collections, University of Oklahoma, Norman.

20. Daniel F. Littlefield Jr. and Lonnie E. Underhill, "The Crazy Snake Uprising of 1909: A Red, Black, or White Affair?" *Arizona and the West* 20, no. 4 (Winter 1978): 309.

21. Testimony of Chitto Harjo, November 23, 1906, Elks Lodge, Tulsa, Oklahoma Territory, in Western History Collections, University of Oklahoma, Norman.

22. Littlefield and Underhill, "Crazy Snake Uprising," pp. 313–316.

23. Stanley A. Clark to Joe Dukes, May 14, 1939, Box entitled "Creek Historical Manuscript and Documents," Special Collections, McFarlin Library, University of Tulsa, Oklahoma.

24. Debo, *The Road to Disappearance*, pp. 308–309.

25. *Alphabetical List of Creek Indians by Blood and Creek Freedmen* (Showing All Adult Creek Indians by Blood and All Adult Creek Freedmen, The Respective Allottees Who Are Affected by the Enactment of the Removal of Restriction Bill) included in a Conference Report, passed Senate May 21, 1908, Sixtieth Congress, 1st sess., *Final Form of H.R. 15641*, [Regarding] *An Act for the Removal of Restrictions From Part of the Lands of Allottees of the Five Civilized Tribes, and for Other Purposes*, Western History Collections, University of Oklahoma, Norman.

26. Acting Superintendent of Commissioner of Indian Affairs, August 29, 1925, Booklet 1925 Miscellaneous Departmental, Box 2, Entry number E314, Record Group 75, and U.S. Probate Attorney Peter Deirman to Creek National Attorney A. J. Ward, December 27, 1922, Records of the Bureau of Indian Affairs, Five Civilized Tribes Agency, Records of the Office of the Superintendent, Correspondence With the Commissioner of Indian Affairs, 1919–1923, Booklet, Miscellaneous Departmental, January to August, 1923, Box 1, Entry number E314, Record Group 75, Federal Archives and Records Center, Fort Worth, Texas.

27. U.S. Probate Attorney Peter Deirman to Creek National Attorney A. J. Ward, December 27, 1922.

28. C. B. Glasscock, *Then Came Oil: The Story of the Last Frontier* (Indianapolis and New York: Bobbs-Merrill, 1938), p. 229.

29. Ibid.

30. Ibid.

31. Acting Superintendent to Commissioner of Indian Affairs, October 10, 1923, Booklet 1923 miscellaneous, September to December Inc., Box 1, Entry number E314, RG 75, Records of the Bureau of Indian Affairs, Records of the Five Civilized Tribes, Records of the Office of the Five Civilized Tribes Correspondence With the Commissioner of Indian Affairs, 1919–1923, Federal Archives and Records Center, Fort Worth, Texas.

32. Glasscock, *Then Came Oil*, p. 229.

33. "Find Fraud in Indian Estate," *Tulsa Daily World*, July 30, 1926, Folder "Clippings," Box 1, Entry number E314, RG 75, Records of the Bureau of Indian Affairs, Records of the Five Civilized Tribes, Records of the Office

of the Five Civilized Tribes Correspondence With the Commissioner of Indian Affairs, 1919–1923, Federal Archives and Records Center, Fort Worth, Texas.

34. *Alphabetical List of Creek Indians by Blood and Creek Freedmen.* The difficult early life of Jackson Barnett and his troubled adult years are described in Benay Blend, "Jackson Barnett and the Oklahoma Indian Probate Court," Master's thesis, University of Texas, Arlington, 1978.

35. Glasscock, *Then Came Oil*, p. 156.

36. Angie Debo, *And Still the Waters Run: The Betrayal of the Five Civilized Tribes* (Princeton, N.J.: Princeton University Press, 1973), p. 338 (originally published by Princeton University Press in 1968).

37. Ibid., p. 339.

38. Ibid.

39. In the United States District Court, Southern District of New York, E31–91, *Jackson Barnett, A Mental Incompetent, by Elmer S. Bailey, Hist "prochein ami," plaintiff v. The Equitable Trust Company of New York and the American Baptist Home Mission Society, defendants,* pp. 4–5, I:202, Reel 6, microfilm, John Collier Papers, copy at Newberry Library, Chicago, original at Yale University.

40. John J. Brady, Attorney and Counselor at Law, to Cato Sells, Commissioner of Indian Affairs, Confidential Inspection Report, April 28, 1920, I:202, Reel 6, microfilm, John Collier Papers, Newberry Library, Chicago.

41. Ibid.

42. Ibid., pp. 4–5.

43. Ibid., p. 6.

44. Debo, *Still Waters Run*, p. 339.

45. J. Garfield Buell to Superintendent Victor M. Locke Jr., December 1, 1921, Booklet Miscellaneous "B": 1921, Box 1, Entry E315, RG 75, Records of the Bureau of Indian Affairs, Records of the Five Civilized Tribes, Federal Archives and Records Center, Fort Worth, Texas.

46. Debo, *Still Waters Run*, p. 340.

47. U.S. District Court, E31–91, p. 8, I:203, Reel 6, microfilm, John Collier Papers, Newberry Library, Chicago.

48. Ibid., pp. 2–4.

49. Ibid., pp. 22–23.

50. Superintendent Victor M. Locke Jr. to Miss Maude Woy, September 12, 1921, Booklet Miscellaneous "B": 1921, Box 1, Entry E315, RG 75, Records of the Bureau of Indian Affairs, Records of the Five Civilized Tribes Agency, Federal Archives and Records Center, Fort Worth, Texas.

51. U.S. District Court, E31–91, Reel 6, Part I, 203, microfilm, John Collier Papers, p.17, Newberry Library, Chicago.

52. Ibid., p. 16.

53. Ibid.

54. Debo, *Still the Waters Run*, p. 346–347.

55. "Seize Barnett for Contempt!" *Muskogee Daily Phoenix*, August 21, 1926, Folder "Clippings," Box 1, Records of the Bureau of Indian Affairs, Records of the Five Civilized Tribes Agency, RG 75, Entry number 317, Federal Archives and Records Center, Fort Worth, Texas.

56. Ibid.
57. Ibid.
58. "Barnett's Wife May Seek Writ to Get Husband," *Muskogee Daily Phoenix*, August 26, 1926.
59. Ibid.
60. S. Arne, "No More Women! for Jack Barnett," *Muskogee Times-Democrat*, August 24, 1926.
61. "Mrs. Barnett Moves to Home of Husband," *Muskogee Daily Phoenix*, August 31, 1926.
62. Arne, "No More Women! for Jack Barnett."
63. Ibid.
64. Ibid.
65. "Mrs. Barnett Moves to Home of Husband."
66. "Cab Driver to Tell of Elopement," *Muskogee Daily Phoenix*, July 7, 1926.
67. "Creek Chief Calls Upon His People," *Muskogee Daily Phoenix*, July 7, 1926.
68. Debo, *Still Waters Run*, pp. 347–348.
69. Acting District Superintendent to Commissioner of Indian Affairs Charles Burke, November 14, 1928, Booklet, Miscellaneous Departmental Letters, 1928–1929, Box 2, Entry number E314, Record Group 75, Federal Archives and Records Center, Fort Worth, Texas.
70. Glasscock, *Then Came Oil*, p. 156.
71. Ibid.
72. Telegram from Secretary of Interior Harold Ickes to Superintendent A. Landman, April 3, 1934, Booklet Miscellaneous Departmental 1934, Box 3, Entry E314, Record Group 75, Records of the Bureau of Indian Affairs, Records of the Five Civilized Tribes Agency, Federal Archives and Records Center, Fort Worth, Texas.
73. "Burial Rites for Barnett Halted by U.S.," *Daily Oklahoman*, June 1, 1934, Folder "Creek Indians," Oklahoma Historical Society, Oklahoma City.
74. Telegram, Commissioner of Indian Affairs John Collier to Superintendent John W. Brady, May 31, 1934, Booklet Miscellaneous Departmental 1934, Box 3, Entry E314, RG 75, Records of the Bureau of Indian Affairs, Records of the Five Civilized Tribes Agency, Federal Archives and Records Center, Fort Worth, Texas.
75. "Burial Rites for Barnett."
76. Ibid.
77. Debo, *Still Waters Run*, p. 349.
78. "A Poor Indian," *Winners of the West* 15, no. 8 (August 1938), Folder, "Creek Biographies," Oklahoma Historical Society, Oklahoma City.
79. Memorandum From the Secretary of the Interior, November 8, 1938, regarding Jackson Barnett Estate, Reel 28, microfilm, John Collier Papers, Newberry Library, Chicago.
80. Debo, *Still Waters Run*, p. 349.
81. Swanton, "Social Organization and Social Usages," pp. 77–78.

2

THE OSAGE MURDERS AND OIL

The murders of the Osage for the royalty money they had re ceived from oil has been called the "reign of terror," and they represented the most blatant expression of the greed for Indian lands. In one notorious case, more than a dozen murders occurred within one family. Following a three-year investigation, the federal government linked the killings to one master criminal—William K. Hale, self-proclaimed "King of the Osage." During the mid-1800s, white settlers pushed the Osage from their native lands, leading to their removal to Indian Territory. According to the allotment policy, after the tribe was given a reservation, the Osage were assigned tracts of land and headrights to mineral development on an individual basis. The history of the "reign of terror" began in the early 1900s when oil was discovered on Osage land.

Among the Osage, as among other Indian groups, the family unit was and continues to be crucial to the existence and identity of the people as a whole. In fact, the family unit was often perceived as being more important than the individual family members. Strength was found in numbers, and hunting or fighting for survival was more effective when the family worked together in a cooperative effort. Father, mother, children, grandparents, aunts, and uncles actually constituted the "extended family"—an elemental quality of native society. The bond between the members was a deep devotion because being connected by blood was the strongest link possible. The elders, adults, and youths represented continuity, and the family always carried this quality forward—unless it was disrupted by some destructive force, as happened to the Osage Kyle family during the "reign of terror."

The Osage murders involved one particular family whose members found themselves experiencing sudden changes from their traditional lifestyle due to the windfall wealth from oil royalties. Caught in the dangerous void between traditional tribal ways and the materialism of America's Roaring Twenties, this family and other oil-rich Osage became targets of hideous murder plots. The worst of American capitalism—murderous avarice—resulted in the killing of more than a dozen Osage all related to one family. They were killed for their headrights to oil royalties. Although many people would welcome the wealth from oil revenues on their lands, it brought only heinous destruction to these people and provoked the worst actions that any group of people could do to another.

The story began when the United States pressured the Osage at various intervals into signing three treaties involving the cession of approximately 100 million acres of land. The Indians received $166,300 in livestock, horses, farming equipment, money, and annuities.[1] The first treaty in 1808 surrendered over 50 million acres in present-day Missouri and Arkansas, and the treaty in 1818 ceded a small section of 1.8 million acres in what is today western Arkansas and eastern Oklahoma. Finally, in 1825, the Osage signed a treaty with the United States to cede all their lands, more than 45 million acres in Missouri, Oklahoma, and Arkansas. By this treaty, they agreed to move to a reservation in southern Kansas. The rush of additional settlers to Kansas and Nebraska and the popular movement for territories forced the federal government to take away the Osage reservation in 1870. In return, the United States compensated the Osage, who purchased a new reservation located in the northeast area of Indian Territory.[2]

In 1871, the Osage moved to their new reservation, which consisted of 1,470,559 acres purchased from the Cherokee. The new reservation was bordered by the ninety-sixth meridian on the east, the Arkansas River and the former Muscogee Creek Nation on the south and west, and the Kansas border on the north. The new land satisfied the Osage, and fortunately, it remained unwanted by white settlers, who could not sink their plows into the thickly wooded areas of hard oaks and stands of hickory. In many parts, scrub oaks known as blackjack trees crowded the land, interspersed with streams and open meadows dividing rocky hills and the blackjacks. Stretching to the west, thick prairie grass took over, and in other areas, tall bluestem grass up to fourteen inches high covered the reservation. Throughout the entire new Osage Reservation, deer, turkey, quail, beaver, otter, raccoon, coyote, timber wolf, and buffalo, farther to the west, fed off the land and the woods.[3] The land was suited only for difficult homestead-ing, and no one guessed that large pools of oil rested below the surface of the new reservation. Following their removal to this land, the Osage began to reconstruct their nation and government during late nine-teenth century when more white settlers expressed interest in the dark, rich soil of eastern Indian Territory.

In 1875, James Bigheart became the appointed Osage chief. With some support from the tribe, he drafted the early tribal legislation to establish law and order, although the United States did not recognize the Osage' accomplishments. In 1881, the tribe elected Bigheart the first chief, a post he held until the turn of the twentieth century. These busy years involved oil and mineral exploration, and Bigheart signed the first oil and gas lease, enabling the Osage to begin accumulating oil wealth. From 1900 until June 28, 1906, when the Allotment Act was signed, no formal Osage government existed, although the old constitution of the 1880s remained on the records. Under Section 9 of the new act, the tribe elected a principal chief, an assistant principal chief, and eight members of the Osage Tribal Council every two years.[4]

Early towns on the reservation, such as Grayhorse and Fairfax, which had approximately 2,000 residents, brought the Santa Fe Rail-road to the area. In future years, the thriving town of Barnsdall, for-merly called Bigheart, attracted the Missouri Pacific Railroad. The following years were devoted to farming, mostly among the mixed-bloods and intermarried individuals and the Little Osage, a full-blood band who had purchased farms from white settlers living near the Kansas border.[5] The federal government directed the Osage and other Indians in agriculture; thus, farming dominated life on the Osage Res-ervation (despite the fact that most of the land was inhospitable to the plow) until the unexpected discovery of oil spawned instant towns such as Avant, Okesa, Bolanger, Herd, Osage, Personia, Foraker, Gainola, Frankfort, Burbank, Pure, Nelogany, Pershing, Grayhorse, Remington, Hulah, and Wildhorse. Actually, many of these sites oper-ated as lively oil field camps for several years. After World War I, the decade of the twenties and increasing wildcatting for oil produced notorious towns like Denoya (first called Whizbang), Talco, Tallant, Apperson, Cooper, Carter Nine, Lynam, Atlantic Field, Naval Re-serve, Webb City, Hardy, Bowring, Big Bertha, Phillips No. 2, and Little Chief.[6]

The oil boom began in 1895 when a New Englander named Henry Foster moved from Rhode Island to Independence, Kansas. Becom-ing familiar with the Indian settlements in the area, he applied to the secretary of the interior for a lease of the Osage Reservation. While waiting for the lease to be approved, Foster died, and his brother

2. Oil gusher in Oklahoma. Courtesy, Western History Collections, University of Oklahoma Library.

Edwin assumed the obligations and pursued the rumor that oil existed beneath the Osage Reservation. On March 16, 1896, Edwin B. Foster and the Osage National Council (formed in 1881), represented by James Bigheart, principal chief, Saucy Chief, president of the council, and several other Osage, signed their names to the lease or marked the documents with their Xs.[7]

Foster's lease included "oil and gas mining" over the entire Osage Reservation for a period of ten years, but the tribe sublet mostly the eastern half. As a part of this blanket lease, Foster agreed to pay a royalty of ten percent of all crude pumped from the reservation and $50 a year per gas well, as long as the well was used. The market value of oil at the place of production determined the royalty to be paid to the national treasurer of the Osage Nation.[8]

In less than a month, Saucy Chief led a protest and filed a complaint with the secretary of the interior. He contended that the full Osage Council had not met when the lease had been presented and that the contract lacked the approval of the majority of the Osage Tribe. The Osage agent supervised an investigation into the matter and reported that two white men had taken about fifty Osage across the Arkansas River to Cleveland in Oklahoma Territory, where the white men plied the Osage with whiskey and induced them to sign a protest against the Foster lease.[9]

When the first oil well on the Osage land was drilled in 1897, there was no immediate confirmation of the future large oil holdings on this land. Two years later, Foster's Osage Oil Company drilled on the eastern side of the Osage Reservation near Bartlesville, a town in the Cherokee Nation. A limit of fifty barrels pumped daily discouraged Foster, convincing him that the well's production was not commercially profitable when measured against the cost of drilling and forcing him to cap the well. Falling deeper into debt for his operational costs, Foster sold more stock in his company and continued to wildcat. The second well brought good results, and though several experimental wells that followed produced dry or nearly dry holes, the seventh well struck the best results in the entire Kansas-Indian Territory oil field.[10]

Wildcatting elsewhere, Foster virtually ignored the possibility of oil on the Osage Reservation. Pursuing black gold instead, in 1900 he arranged for a sublease on the reservation in large land blocks after the entire reservation was surveyed in tracts measuring half a mile in width and three miles in length extending east to west. Each rectangular tract received a number, and subletters leased in the eastern part of the Osage on a bonus and royalty basis. The conditions required payment to Foster at interests of one-eighth (later one-sixth) of the royalty and a bonus of $1 to $5 per acre.[11]

In the following year, Foster consolidated his interests to form the Indian Territory Illuminating Oil Company (ITIO), which he incorporated at Trenton, New Jersey, with a capital base of $3 million. ITIO owned and controlled all the rights and properties of the Osage and Phoenix Oil Companies, and it supervised the subleasing of the Osage Reservation.

A growing number of oil strikes convinced the Alameda Oil Company to finance the first well of a sublessee on Lot 40, and this encouraged Foster's ITIO to drill additional wells. Shortly thereafter, Foster's company announced plans to drill wells at the rate of one every twenty days. Standard Oil Company promised to buy the crude at its refinery at Neodesha, Kansas, for $.88 per barrel, and ITIO also announced that leases covering approximately 6,000 acres had been sold to New York and St. Louis companies.[12]

In 1902, the rail shipments of crude oil to the Neodesha refinery amounted to 37,000 barrels from 13 wells, 6 of which had been drilled that year. In January 1903, Foster's ITIO reported that it and its sublessee had drilled 30 wells. Seventeen wells struck oil, 2 produced gas, and 11 became dry holes. A year later, 361 wells rose among the blackjacks and bluestem grass on the Osage; 243 pumped oil, 21 produced gas, and 97 were dry. By 1906 throughout the eastern Osage Reservation, 783 wells became a part of the countryside—544 producing oil, 41 yielding gas, and 198 proving dry. In that year alone, the wells on the reservation yielded more than 5-million barrels of oil annually, and ITIO had disbursed $2,686,627 from the blanket lease to the Osage.[13] The eastern half netted approximately 70,000 leased acres of pumping wells, 165,000 acres of non–oil producing acres, and 430,000 acres of unleased land.[14]

The turn of the century brought a tremendous push for Indian Territory by whites eager to control the new state for its farming and grazing potential. David Payne and his raiders from Kansas had ignited a "boomer" movement, advocating white settlement in Indian Territory, the last vestige for a total Indian homeland. Rumors of oil and increasing gushers turned the heads of white opportunists toward the Osage as many white men married Osage women. These avaricious whites and an increasing number of mixed-bloods pressured the federal government to extend the allotment program of land to the Osage, for they and the Five Civilized Tribes had been left out of the original Dawes Land Allotment Act in 1887.[15] The last push to civilize the Indians had begun. Three years later, only thirteen reservations remained in Indian Territory, and the bureaucrats aimed their efforts at statehood. To escape allotment, the Osage Tribe sent a delegation to Washington with a memorial to the House of Representatives dated January 25, 1888, requesting that House bill 1277 be amended to exclude the Osage Tribe from allotment.[16]

Although the Dawes legislation originally excluded the Osage, outsiders and mixed-bloods began influencing the Osage to make individual land claims of the reservation. By 1892, most of the Osage favored establishing individual claims of land, compelling the federal government to send the Cherokee Commission (officially called the Jerome Commission) to Pawhuska, the capital of the Osage Nation, to supervise allotment of the Osage and to sell the surplus land. A large number of tribal members, mostly mixed-bloods, favored allotment, but the full-bloods firmly resisted, especially in regard to the existing members on the tribal rolls, claiming that many did not belong and should not benefit from the allotment.[17]

The full-blood faction received support from the Cherokee, whose many traditional members opposed allotment. Furthermore, the Osage held ambitions to become the sixth Civilized Tribe, wanting to join the Cherokee, Muscogee Creek, Choctaw, Chickasaw, and Seminole in hopes of converting Indian Territory into an "Indian state." Some 279 Osage signed a proposition indicating this desire to the Cherokee Commission and opposed ceding land on any terms.[18] On the Osage Reservation, the tribe experienced factionalism, pitting tribal members against each other. This division had existed since the 1860s, with mixed-bloods standing against full-bloods as the two sides clashed over the issue of assimilation into the white society or retaining traditions. In the 1920s, the tribal roll classified the people in two groups: those who had half Osage blood or more and those who had less than half Osage blood. The classifications had to be approved by the assistant secretary of the interior.[19]

As the number of intruders in the Osage Reservation grew, another effort was made to allot the reservation when the Osage Commission was formed on May 18, 1894, consisting of James S. Hook as chairperson, John A. Gorman, and John L. Tullis. Under instructions approved by the secretary of the interior, a full council of Osage agreed to any negotiations with the approval of a majority of male adults. The Osage Commission was advised not to use any pressure in order to obtain Osage approval of the allotment, but this effort failed because the full-blood contingent disapproved of the tribal roll, saying it consisted of too many mixed-bloods; they issued an "ultimatum" to purge certain undeserving names from the tribal annuity roll. In the following year, the federal government decided that this issue needed to be resolved before further action could proceed.[20]

The Osage tribe argued about the legal status of its membership, yet it had had the foresight to establish laws affecting the business, membership, and wills of its tribal members. Under Article V of the constitution dated 1881–1882, a tribal judge held the authority to supervise the heirship of property being divided equally among a man's widow and children (when they became eighteen years old for males and fifteen for females). If the wife remarried and died, then the estate remained with the first set of children.[21]

Numerous Osage mixed-bloods had already assimilated into white society, and they had a business interest in improving their lands or their pocketbooks. The full-bloods seemed regressive and appeared content to live in camps and villages in the south-central and south-

western part of the Osage Reservation, where they practiced tribal
customs and lived communally. Life seemed to be changing about them
as other tribes were undergoing allotment and white settlers were
pushing into Indian Territory, and the traditional Osage struggled.
From the time of their move from Kansas until about 1906, smallpox,
pneumonia, and tuberculosis reduced the tribal population from nearly
4,000 to fewer than 2,000 members.[22]

To control the influx of non-Osage, the tribal constitution read
that "any white man or citizen of the United States ... to marry an
Osage woman, shall first be required to make known his intentions to
the National Council by applying for a license ... and take an oath to
support the Constitution and abide by the laws of the Osage Nation."[23]
Children of mixed parentage, becoming mixed-bloods, "shall have equal
right, in proportion to their number, with the full-blood Indians in all
the benefits to be derived from this [Treaty of 1868] and all former
treaties with the Osage."[24]

The mixed-bloods' interest in allotment prevailed, over the interests of the stubborn full-blood faction. On November 28, 1904, the
Business Committee, also called the National Council, consisting of a
principal chief and eight councilmen, passed a resolution to appoint a
delegation of nine persons, an interpreter, and the local agent to represent the tribe in Washington and advocate allotment. To prove their
intention, the Osage passed a bill at the final general tribal election in
February 1906, which the delegation presented in Washington. The
bill represented a compromise of all the tribal factions and was introduced in the House of Representatives. After several amendments,
Congress approved the bill on June 28 as the Osage Allotment Act of
1906. An important provision allowed the secretary of the interior to
grant competency, at his discretion, to those Osage who could read
and write sufficiently to conduct business. Tribal members could sell
or lease their lands, except for their homestead allotments of 160 acres
each, which would stay in trust status for twenty-five years. To help
establish the membership, the principal chief had three months after
the passage of the act to file with the secretary of the interior a list of
individuals fraudulently claiming to be tribal members. The real membership list could not include the name of any person or his descendants placed on the roll prior to December 31, 1881, when the Osage
adopted their constitution. During the following weeks, approximately
160 enrollment applications flooded into the National Council.[25]

The Osage Allotting Commission, composed of Charles E.
McChesney, Cassius R. Peck, and Black Dog, began to allot the Osage
Reservation into 160-acre parcels to the 2,229 tribal members. Imme-
diately thereafter, tribal members complained to them about fraudu-

lent members and the procedure for allotment.26 Finally, the tribe devised a lottery plan, and Interior Secretary Ethan A. Hitchcock approved it. The tribe held a public drawing on July 8–9 at the opera house in Pawhuska. Allotment Commissioner McChesney reported to the commissioner of Indian affairs that "a full-blood boy was blindfolded and revolved a keg called the 'name wheel,' drawing there from at each revolution a card containing the name of some member of the tribe. A mixed-blood boy was blindfolded, and from a revolving key called the 'number wheel' he drew at each revolution a card containing a number to correspond to the name drawn."27 The lottery attracted many mixed-bloods, but the full-bloods expressed little interest and stayed away. The census for 1910 revealed that the Osage belonged to eleven tribal bands.28

In the end, the commission distributed a total of 1,465,380.56 acres, with each Osage receiving 657.41 acres to do with as he or she pleased—at least as far as the surface rights were concerned. Tribal members held all subsurface or mineral rights in common, but each Osage had a "headright," meaning that he or she would receive an equal share of all mineral income; the tribe declared it illegal to sell such headrights.29 The allotment commission completed the distribution by 1908, and on March 31, 1909, it was discontinued.

The Osage tribal roll for disbursing royalties contained names of those members on the list as of January 1, 1906, and all children born to them by July 1907. In addition, nonenrolled Osage children of white fathers were included, with no distinction made based on sex, age, or degree of Osage blood.

Needless to say, Pawhuska became a bustling site. It became known as the seat of the Osage Agency, and the full-bloods lined up there to receive their quarterly moneys on the first and second days of the payment periods. The agency paid the mixed-bloods two or three days later; all of these transactions kept eight men busy for four or five days. Meanwhile, waiting like hungry dogs, merchants and white opportunists looked forward to doing business with the Indians, and creditors made sure to collect their full payments before the Indians spent all of their money. Many bootleggers who sold whiskey illegally to the Osage later claimed they made their entire living off the Indians. A general estimate on moneys paid to the Osage (including payments for grazing permits, pipeline damages, and other revenues in addition to oil and gas) from July 1, 1904, to May 13, 1905, was said to be $108,567 in the form of gas and oil royalties.30

In the following years, royalty money flowed with the oil. In 1917, a headright was worth $2,719; in 1920, the amount spiraled upward to $8,090. An average Osage family of five had an astounding income of

$40,450 annually. In 1925, the same family received more than $65,000 per year.[31] (In comparison, on an average, other tribes averaged less than $200 in annual income in 1928.[32]) Such unimaginable wealth enticed whites to get at Osage oil money. One full-blood, named Don Dickenson, had a typical experience: He met a white woman, and after a whirlwind courtship lasting just one week, he married her. Three days later, she left him and took $100,000 in alimony with her![33]

Upon the deaths of tribal elders, headrights passed on to descendants who legally inherited claims to the Osage mineral rights in common. In one case, the respected elder Lizzie Q. Kyle had inherited eight headrights. People speculated that upon her death, all of the eight headrights passed to her last living daughter, Mollie Burkhart. All of the unfortunate deaths aroused suspicion and prompted a federal investigation, but an Osage family had been eliminated, disrupting the community and stressing the destruction caused by the intrusion of another culture.

In 1905, Congress received pressure from oil companies to not renew Foster's blanket lease, which would not expire until March 1906. Several Osage leaders also traveled to Washington to voice concerns over the renewal of the lease. In addition, other oil companies and individuals interested in getting into the lucrative oil business claimed that Foster monopolized the Osage oil interests, thus violating the federal antitrust laws. After investigating the complaints, on March 3, 1905, near the end of the session, Congress compromised by renewing the Foster lease and all the subleases made by ITIO on a total area of 680,000 acres on the eastern side of the Osage Reservation. All original provisions of the Foster lease were made applicable for another ten years, with the exception that the gas well royalty was increased from $50 to $100 for each well. The fate of the western half of the Osage Reservation remained undetermined until 1912.[34]

The rush for oil land in the Osage area pressured the tribal government and the tribal members, and havoc abounded. In one situation, the Barnsdall Oil Company cut the fence of T. J. Leahy, a mixed-blood allottee who complained that workers from the oil company trespassed across his farm and hauled lumber to build an oil derrick. Filled with anger, Leahy removed the lumber and repaired his fence. The oil drillers asked Barnsdall Superintendent Hugh Pitzer for written permission to cut the fence and to haul lumber again for their well, and Leahy obtained arrest warrants for the oil workers. This conflict of interests went to court, and the ruling favored the rights of the mixed-blood over the leasing rights of the oil company.[35]

Several months prior to the Barnsdall incident, Leahy met with other mixed-bloods who wanted to protect their interests. In January

1911, they formed the Osage Protective Association (OPA) to block the government's renewal of the Foster lease and to gain support for distribution of the mineral estate to tribal members. The OPA worked in Washington to lobby for favorable legislation (albeit to no avail), especially in the interest of the rest of the tribe.[36] Finally, in March 1921, Congress passed a law removing all restrictions on allotments of Osage with less than one-half Indian blood. Known as Public Law 360, the measure included oil, gas, coal, and other minerals, providing that "all valid existing oil and gas leases on the 7th day of April, 1931, are hereby renewed upon the same terms and extended, subject to all other conditions and provisions thereof, until the 8th day of April, 1946, and as long thereafter as oil or gas is found in paying quantities."[37]

Trying to gain control over their own affairs, the Osage formed a committee and requested the National Council to lease the western land on terms that would be more profitable to the tribal members. Royalties of one-third and one-sixth of eastern Osage lands were suggested. Because some Osage farmed and had ranches, the tribe argued that no company should be permitted to drill for oil without written consent" from the allottee of the land involved. The Osage National Council continued to discuss the leasing procedure and decided that a lease should be allocated by sealed bids to be conducted at specific times, with the lease going to the highest bidder.[38] The drilling activities on the reservation increased, and by November 1, 1921, the Osage Reservation had a total oil production of 20,625,127 barrels; gas production had reached 33,918,985 cubic feet. Various companies drilled a total of 1,244 oil and gas wells during the fiscal year ending June 30, 1921, with the total royalties and rentals paid during June 1921 amounting to $544,835.[39]

In May 1912, the Osage National Council instructed the principal chief to sign four leases that covered most of the western half of the reservation, but the secretary of the interior disapproved of this action. On July 13, the Interior Department decided to try various suggestions for developing the western half of the Osage Reservation. The Department of the Interior recommended that Osage land be leased in parcels of 300 to 5,120 acres, but no individual could have more than 25,000 acres. According to the Interior Department's view regarding the best way to bring revenue to the Osage and other Indians, policy required the United States agent at Pawhuska periodically advertise tracts available for leasing on sealed bids. Anyone wanting to lease a tract had to request in writing that the land be offered for bidding, and each bid required a certified check for ten percent of the bonus and the first year's rental. The leases for the western half of the reservation lasted for ten years from the date of approval by the Department of the Interior, with the stipulation that no lease would extend beyond December 8, 1931. The Interior Department set the royalty amount on gas at one-sixth of the market value at the well, and the petroleum royalty was set at one-sixth of the gross production at the actual market value.[40] While the Osage became rich, the oil companies became wealthier.

The pressure for more individuals and oil companies to work the Osage land brought about the public lease auctions. At these auctions, oil companies could bid for the oil lease rights on each 160-acre tract of land. With huge amounts of money to be made, the amounts paid for these leases increased enormously. In 1912, the first public lease auction was held, and over the following fifteen years, an amazing total of twenty-eight auctions occurred. The pace of wildcatting and lease purchasing, as well as the amount of wealth to be had, caught the attention of officials at the Department of the Interior. On November 29, 1922, Interior Secretary Albert Fall informed Commissioner of Indian Affairs Charles Burke that drilling would be halted as much as possible due to the "oil situation in this country," referring to the rumors of fraud leading to the Osage murders, the Elk Hills controversy in California, and the Teapot Dome scandal in Wyoming.[41] The authority and actions of the Interior Department affecting so many oil leases provoked attention from the public and other sectors of the federal government.

Meanwhile, in Oklahoma, an oil boom was happening. "Colonel" Ellsworth E. Walters was from nearby the Pawnee town of Skeedee (described as "just a wide place in the road)," and he earned fame as the auctioneer. Paid $50 to $100 for his work at an auction, the colonel became a friend of the Osage and received a diamond-studded badge worth approximately $3,000 and a large diamond ring for handling mineral leases that made them rich. For example, in one auction on June 29, 1922, the Gypsy Oil Company paid $1,600,000 for a single 160-acre lease. Total sales of that day's auction skyrocketed to almost $11 million. On March 18, 1924, a company from Bartlesville, Oklahoma, paid a record $1,990,000 for a lease. The total sales of that auction finished at $14,156,800! This enormous amount of money was divided among the 2,229 Osage headrights. Customarily, Colonel Walters held the auctions in the shade of a huge tree at the Osage Agency in Pawhuska, and it achieved fame as the "million-dollar elm." Sometimes, the colonel held the auctions at the Constantine Theater, and later the Kihekah Theater in Pawhuska was used.[42]

Trains from Tulsa and Muskogee, Oklahoma, transported oilmen, wildcatters, and their geologists to the auctions, and several came from even farther away. Under the elm, wooden bleachers were constructed for oil barons such as Bill Skelly, E. W. Marland, Frank Phillips, G. F. Getty, and his son J. Paul Getty. They stayed at Pawhuska's thriving hotels, crowded with oil tycoons and people of all types wanting to get into the oil business and others like Anna Laura Lowe wanting to enjoy the wealth. Carl Coker Rister called Pawhuska the "Osage Monte Carlo," and the *Petroleum News* referred to it as the federal government's "Biggest Gambling Center."[43]

The never-ending flow of money unfortunately attracted the worst types of individuals, and with them came whiskey, drugs, and trouble. The Roaring Twenties for the nation became the Troubled Twenties for the Osage as the worst kind of greed led to the epidemic of murders that would be called the "Osage Reign of Terror." Outside of Pawhuska, the outlaw Al Spencer and his gang of train and bank robbers used the Cross Timbers of blackjacks as hideouts. In fact, so much crime of all types occurred that one might think the murders of a few Indians might be overlooked. Alarmed and angry at that prospect, the Osage Tribal Council pointed out to the U.S. Bureau of Investigation[44] that at least two dozen Osage had been killed, and this was being ignored! For their own protection, many Osage families began stringing electric lights completely around their homes, to fend of possible assailants at night. Fearing for their lives, they bought guns and bullets to protect themselves, and some decided to leave the state.

Operating quietly to catch the murderers, the bureau sent agents into Osage country to pose as cowhands and cattle buyers. Soon, they discovered that all evidence led to one William K. Hale, who proudly named himself "King of the Osage." Originally from Texas, he was working as a cowhand driving cattle through Indian Territory to Kansas cowtowns when he chose to stay on the reservation. His wife joined him, and in 1900, they lived in a tent during their early days on the Osage range, grazing and fattening cattle for market. Realizing better opportunities lay in Grayhorse, an Osage town, Hale soon moved there and encouraged his nephew, Ernest Burkhart, to join him. Since he befriended many Osage, his business prospered, and twenty years later, he owned or leased many thousands of acres of Osage range and had accumulated vast holdings of cattle, horses, city real estate, and banking interests. The Osage trusted him; he had even been a pallbearer at Anna Brown's funeral. She had held a headright to Osage oil. Pretty Anna Brown, a thirty-five-year-old full-blood , was found dead on May 28, 1921, at the bottom of a canyon located in a wooded ravine near Grayhorse, with a nearly empty bottle of corn whiskey nearby and a bullet lodged in her head. At the time, she was divorced from Ode Brown, a white man and ex-cowboy who lived in Ponca City.[45]

An investigation by the U.S. Bureau of Investigation and the ensuing court evidence revealed that the day before her death, two cars had stopped in front of Anna's house. From one car, a "tall, spare built man, without a coat" said, "Anna, get in." An unidentified red-headed woman sitting in the same car urged Anna to go with them. Testi-

3. William K. Hale, self-proclaimed "King of the Osages." Courtesy, Western History Collections, University of Oklahoma Library.

mony at the court disclosed that people in the two cars, now including Anna Brown, partied at one roadhouse and then another. Authorities estimated that she was killed early the following morning.[46]

In court, the murderer, Kelsie Morrison, confessed to killing Anna Brown and told about the connection with William Hale. "I killed Anna

Brown sometime in May 1921, about 2:30 in the morning, near Fairfax. ... I was pretty drunk. Byron Burkhart and I carried Anna down to the canyon ... my ex-wife Catherine Coe, accompanied us. ... Then we got her drunk and took her home. We left Anna in the canyon drunk. We got Anna drunk in order to kill her." Morrison described how Byron Burkhart got the whiskey at Ralston, which they gave to Anna about eleven o'clock at night. "Byron helped me carry Anna to the ravine, she was lying there drunk. We held her up in a sitting position." Morrison admitted that he directed Burkhart how to hold Anna while he shot her in the head. Immediately afterward, they left, heading for Hale's house.[47]

Morrison stated that he and Hale talked about an hour. "Hale said he'd wait a few days and if Anna's body wasn't found he'd hire some cowhand who would find it," Morrison testified. The agreement was that if Morrison killed Anna Brown, Hale would cancel a $600 debt that Morrison owed him. About three weeks later, Hale gave Morrison a car and paid him $1,060, and in 1923, Hale paid Morrison $2,000 for some business property that Morrison owned in Fairfax.[48]

Anna had no children. She left an estate of approximately $100,000, half of which would go to her mother, Lizzie Q. Kyle, who was very old and lived with Anna's sister, Mollie Burkhart, and Mollie's husband, Ernest. Her other heirs included her sisters—Mollie, Mrs. Rita Smith (wife of W. E. Smith)—and a half sister named Mrs. Grace Bigheart. Exactly sixty days after Anna's death, Lizzie Q. died at home, and her will stated that her estate of approximately $200,000 in addition to the $50,000 left by Anna Brown would go to Mollie Burkhart and her children.[49] Actually, the real benefactors were Ernest Burkhart and William Hale, who had convinced his nephew to marry Mollie.

Another unexplained murder happened in 1921. Joe Grayhorse, an Osage, died very suddenly after making a land deal with William Hale. Then, in the following weeks, Charles Whitehorn, related by blood to the Kyle family, was found dead near Pawhuska, his hometown. Friends last saw him alive there at about 9 P.M. on May 14.[50] About May 22, his body was found on a hill, a short distance north of town, with two bullet holes between his eyes. He obviously had not put up a fight to save his life as no cuts or scratches were evident to indicate resistance. Whitehorn had married Hattie Smitherman, a white woman, and suspicion had it that she killed him for his inheritance. She was arrested twice but was released both times for lack of evidence.[51]

Less than a year later, on March 26, 1922, one Anna Sanford (allottee number 407), a full-blood restricted Osage, died under mysterious circumstances. (Restricted Indians were those under federal trust protection.) Anna Sanford was married to a white man named Tom McCoy, and shortly after her death, McCoy married a woman who, coincidentally, was William Hale's niece.[52]

More suspicion began to point toward Hale and his nephew, Ernest Burkhart, a veteran of World War I. Suspicions mounted when George Bigheart, a rich Osage, lay dying of poisoned whiskey and Hale and Burkhart took him to a hospital in Oklahoma City. Bigheart asked for his attorney, William Vaughn, who traveled from Pawhuska and talked with him at the hospital. No one ever learned what the conversation was about. As expected, Bigheart died the next day, and soon afterward, Vaughn caught the MK&T train that night to return to Pawhuska. The following morning, Vaughn was found dead on the railroad right-of-way.[53] If speculation is correct, the lawyer stood in Hale's way to wealth: He could figure on an estate valued at $2.5 million, with an annual headright income of $250,000. Already rich, Hale wanted more, but at least ten Osage had to die first. And anyone standing in his way would be eliminated.[54]

Henry Roan (Roan Horse, allottee number 721), a cousin of Anna Brown's, became the next victim. On February 6, 1923, Roan was found dead in his automobile. For some unexplained reason, his car had been abandoned in an isolated range pasture on the reservation. It was never determined how long he had been dead, but it was certain that he had been murdered, for a 45-caliber bullet had been shot through his head. Interestingly, Hale held a policy worth $25,000 on Roan from Capitol Life Insurance Company, a very large sum of money in those years.[55]

Federal agents from the U.S. Bureau of Investigation observed that Mollie Burkhart, Ernest's Osage wife, had inherited the fortunes of her mother and her two murdered sisters, estimated at more than $100,000 a year.[56] Rumors named William Hale and his nephew, Ernest Burkhart. The Roan killing proved the rumors to be correct. Henry Roan was murdered on government-restricted land, and William K. Hale and John Ramsey were charged with the crime. In a related crime, the state of Oklahoma charged Ernest Burkhart as the conspirator who had arranged the nitroglycerin explosion that killed W. E. and Rita Smith and their housekeeper in Fairfax at 3:00 A.M. on March 10, 1923.[57]

When the trial began in Pawhuska in January 1926, Ernest Burkhart took the stand. By this date, his wife, Mollie Brown Burkhart, had received an inheritance from some of the murdered Indians, equal to more than $100,000 annually. She appeared, wrapped in a blanket, riding in a limousine without a chauffeur before the Pawhuska courthouse each day of the trial. Noting that she showed no emotion and little interest in the trial, reporters speculated that she did not understand the details or importance of the proceedings.[58]

So the infamous trials of the Smiths' murderers began. Early in the proceedings when prosecutors asked Burkhart about his business or line of work, he answered contemptuously, "I don't work. I married an Osage."[59] The trial resulted from a three-year investigation conducted by the U.S. Bureau of Investigation. One federal agent acted as a Texas cattle buyer, another posed as an insurance salesman, and a third agent passed himself off as a medicine man on the reservation.[60]

Over the two weeks of the trial, the mounting evidence and testimony convinced Ernest Burkhart that he could not win his case even with all of his wife's money and the powerful influence of his uncle. He changed his plea to guilty and threw himself upon the mercy of the court, asking for a term of life imprisonment. In turning state's evidence, Burkhart named his uncle, William K. Hale, as the person responsible for the murder conspiracy. He testified that Ace Kirby was the assassin who had actually blown up the Smith home and family. And he named one Henry Grammer as a go-between. By coincidence, both Kirby and Grammer had been killed between the time of the crime and the time when they might have been called to the witnesses stand.[61]

On the morning of June 21, 1926, the courtroom was crowded. Shortly after ten o'clock, Judge Jesse J. Worten ordered Burkhart to stand for his decision. The debonair Burkhart smiled. The judge asked him if he knew any reason why the sentence should not be passed; he replied in the negative. Without hesitation, Judge Worten sentenced Ernest Burkhart to life imprisonment in the state penitentiary at McAlester, Oklahoma. Appearing relieved that it was over, Burkhart smiled at friends in the courtroom. (At this time, District Attorney Roy St. Lewis asked the district court to permit William K. Hale and John Ramsey to be tried in federal court in Oklahoma City.) [62]

Blackie Thompson, a notorious outlaw serving a life term in state prison, was released under immunity to testify that William Hale had offered him $1,000 and a new Buick to blow up the Smith home. Thompson had refused. Ernest Burkhart, the weak link in the defense, finally confessed and testified against his uncle. He admitted that he had actually made the contract with the Smiths' killer. Acting on instructions from Hale, Ernest had approached John Ramsey and failed to talk him into killing the Smiths. He also talked with the "Kingpin of the Bootleggers," Henry Grammer, and failed to hire him for the job. He made the offer to another outlaw, Curly Johnson, and failed. He had tried to hire train and bank robber Al Spencer, but he, too, refused. Finally, he made an agreement with one Ace Kirby. For $3,000, Ace used nitroglycerin (perhaps up to ten quarts of the material reportedly stolen from Osage Torpedo Company) to blow up W. E. and Rita Smith and their housekeeper, a young white girl.[63] However, Ace Kirby could not be prosecuted. Some months earlier, he had been shot in half by a storekeeper's shotgun blast during an attempted robbery.[64] Testimony from the trial revealed that the explosion occurred at approximately 3:00 A.M. one morning, with the explosion leaving a hole 6 feet in diameter and 3.5 feet deep through concrete.[65]

The United States also charged William K. Hale and John Ramsey, a cowboy-farmer, with the killing of Henry Roan, a full-blood Osage (roll number 700), on January 31, 1923, additionally charging Hale "with aiding, abiding, counseling, commanded and procuring John Ramsey in so doing."[66] Marshal Dick Quinn and a group of federal officers transported Hale and Ramsey to the court at Guthrie, Oklahoma, where they would appear before the presiding judge, John H. Cotteral, and a grand jury.[67]

At this point, the Osage murders numbered seventeen. District Attorney Roy St. Lewis represented the federal government, and S. P. Freeling was the chief defense attorney for Hale. Ramsey denied his prior confession, in which he admitted that he had shot Roan at Hale's demand. The "King of the Osage" remained still, staring coldly, and when questioned, he denied the whole thing.

In 1926, the murder case went to trial in the state district court at Guthrie, Oklahoma, but two months later, a stalemated jury failed to reach a verdict against William K. Hale and John Ramsey. Realizing the possible danger posed by Hale and his power to terrorize others and aware that he might hire another killer, the Department of Justice in Washington transferred the trial from Guthrie to Oklahoma City, where Hale and Ramsey were again brought before a grand jury.[68]

Regarding the Roan killing, Ernest Burkhart testified that Hale had hired Ramsey to kill Henry Roan for the price of a new Ford automobile and $500. The "King of the Osage" took the stand and denied everything again. Hale claimed that he had been in Fort Worth attending the livestock show when the Smith home was blown up. He insisted, furthermore, he had no reason to want Roan killed. This time, the jury's verdict was guilty.

Hale, Ramsey, and Burkhart were sentenced to life imprisonment. Within days, the attorneys for Hale and Ramsey filed appeals. On January 19, 1926, Hale's attorneys, Freeling and J. I. Howard, filed an appeal on eight accounts to quash the indictment of Hale, and a

Tulsa attorney named J. W. Springer filed a separate appeal based on six accounts seeking to quash the indictment of Ramsey. Both sets of attorneys for Hale and Ramsey based their appeals on the assertion that the prosecuting side had violated procedure and that the state of Oklahoma instead of a federal court should have jurisdiction over the case.[69]

Hale appealed and was retried. Ramsey appealed and was retried. On October 20, the court date arrived. The government was represented by Roy St. Lewis, U.S. attorney; Oscar L. Luhring, assistant attorney general; Edwin Brown, assistant attorney general; Horace Dyer, assistant attorney general; and John T. Leahy, special assistant attorney general. The defense team consisted of J. I. Howard, W. S. Hamilton, Prince Freeling, and B. F. Weick representing Hale and J. M. Springer representing Ramsey. The honorable John C. Polock presided over the case. Both defendants pleaded not guilty.[70]

On the day of his murder, Henry Roan was wearing a light gray suit and some type of raincoat due to the usually cold weather during October in northern Oklahoma. He had $23.50 in his pocket and was wearing a watch and a small bracelet when J. R. Rhodes, a farmer and stock raiser, found his body slumped in the driver's seat of Roan's own Buick touring car. He had been shot in the back of the head with a 45-caliber bullet.[71]

Testimony given by the killer, John Ramsey, described the fatal happening and how it came about that Hale wanted him to murder Henry Roan. He stated that Hale went to Henry Grammer's ranch where Ramsey worked and sold whiskey and said he needed a job to be done. Hale asked Grammer to ask Ramsey if he would do it, and Ramsey replied to Grammer, "It depends on what the job [is]." Grammer said, "He [Hale] wanted an Indian bumped off." A few days passed, and Hale grew anxious about his request of Ramsey. He met Ramsey in Fairfax, where, Ramsey reported, "Hale told me he was going to buy me a car, and give me Five Hundred Dollars. ... So, I told this Indian [Roan] to meet me out on the road running thru Smith's pasture, that I would have some whiskey for him. ... He got out of the car and we sat on the running board of his car and drank what whiskey I had. The Indian then got in his car to leave, and I then shot him in the back of the head."[72]

But at his appeal, Ramsey gave a new account, claiming that Curly Johnson had actually killed Henry Roan. Ramsey stated that Burkhart's wife intended to get a divorce and marry Roan. In fact, however, Mollie Burkhart had been Roan's wife before she married Burkhart, and if she had divorced Burkhart and remarried Roan, Ernest Burkhart would have lost the wealth that Mollie had inherited from her mother and her murdered sisters.[73]

The prosecuting side then called William Hale to the witness stand and presented relevant documents as well. Hale denied any connection with the death of the rich Osage but said that Roan owed him a large sum of money. Roan wanted to make certain that the money was paid back, according to Hale, so the Osage agreed to have an insurance policy taken out for him worth $25,000, if by chance he should die before repaying Hale. Hale made the following statement in court, offering the letter to the Capitol Life Insurance Company as evidence.

> I had many different notes of his [Henry Roan's] in different amounts. He came to me at one time and told me that he would like to take an insurance policy to make me safe in what he owed me. He said within a year he would be able to pay me, all or at least a substantial part of what he owed me. I advanced to him, or told him I would advance to him money to pay the first premium. We calculated the amount he owed me, both on notes and on open accounts, and added a sufficient amount to pay the first year's premium on the policy, and he made me a new note for $25,000.00, to pay the total amount, or rather to take up the total amount by the new note. He then began to look about for the insurance on his life, as proposed by him. He secured the insurance from your company, thru an agent of yours.
>
> I will add further, that after Henry Roan made and delivered the $25,000.00 note that he became indebted to me in an additional sum of over $1600.00, for further live stock bought, and for money borrowed from me. So, as a matter of fact, at the time of his death, he owed me more than the $25,000.00.[74]

Hale also added that Roan had shot himself in the arm in 1921, perhaps to impress the court that the Osage victim was self-destructive.

The grand jury decided that Ramsey and Hale had violated Sections 273 and 275 of the U.S. Criminal Code "by willfully murdering Henry Roan."[75] On July 6, 1926, Hale and Ramsey were tried for the murder of Henry Roan in federal court in Guthrie, Oklahoma. After several weeks of testimony, the jury deliberated for forty-four hours and shocked many people with a deadlock, six voting for conviction and six for acquittal. In the fall of 1926, the case was retried in Oklahoma City, and after an eight-day trial, prosecutor St. Lewis succeeded, with the jury finding Hale and Ramsey guilty and sentencing them to ninety-nine years in prison. Hale appealed to the U.S. Eighth Circuit Court of Appeals, which overturned his verdict and granted him a new trial in federal court at Pawhuska, in Osage County. In January 1929, Hale was found guilty again and was sentenced to ninety-nine years at Fort Leavenworth Prison in Kansas.[76] As many as twenty killings of the Osage for their oil were uncovered, but not all of the murderers were brought to trial. In the case of William Hale and the "reign of terror," the federal government officials worked three years before they could indict Hale in 1929, but by that time, Hale had arranged the killings of all but two of his intended victims. J. T. Leahy represented the Osage, and the tribe contributed $20,000 of the $180,000 that it cost to investigate and conduct the trial.[77] Entering prison on May 30, 1929, Hale was paroled on July 31, 1947. The Osage National Council protested, to no avail. Four months later, Ramsey was released on parole, and Burkhart, who had turned state's evidence against his uncle and Ramsey, was released twelve years later, in October 1959.[78] Eventually, the "reign of terror" killings came to a halt, and peace came to the boomtowns of Carter Nine, Hogshooter, Pershing, Whizbang, and Wildhorse. But as one looked across the Osage land, the oil derricks continued to pump black crude near Burbank, Fairfax, and Shidler.

In many ways, for both the Osage and the rest of America, the Roaring Twenties was an age of recklessness. In their part of the country, the Osage spent huge amounts of money. An average Osage family of five had an income of $65,000 annually. Such wealth brought luxuries and extravagance; the Pierce Arrows that were popular among the Osage were sometimes discarded when they ran out of gas or got stuck in the mud. The only roads on the reservation took the rich Osage to Pawhuska, Hominy, Foraker, Bigheart, and Fairfax, yet one person went through ten automobiles in one year. Like automobiles, fancy houses were also purchased, and priceless china and silverware sat on shelves while the Osage ate with their fingers, as was their custom. Expensive vases were used to store vegetables rather than as decorative items, and grand pianos that served no useful purpose stood out on lawns in rain or shine.[79]

During the space of one afternoon in 1927, an Osage woman spent $12,000 for a fur coat, $3,000 for a diamond ring, $5,000 for an automobile, and another $7,000 for furniture, which she had shipped to California at the cost of another $600. In California, she had put $4,000 down as a deposit on a house, and during the same business transaction, she invested $12,000 in real estate in Florida.[80]

The rich Osage lived in a world of illusion without incentives, a world whose values seriously disrupted their kinship society and affected their entire worldview. Unimaginable wealth introduced the white society's cultural materialism to the Osage at a shocking pace. Still operating within a traditional value system, the Osage valued things differently. To them, the family and kinship relations in their communities superseded the cultural materialism of the white world. From an outsider's perspective, it seems the Osage did not truly appreciate the luxury goods they accumulated as they mixed with white society. Meanwhile, going unnoticed was the fact that the white culture, sudden wealth, and murders were destroying the Osage family unit and distorting the traditional values.

However, not all of the Osage lived in luxury. Serving as a government inspector in the 1920s, Dr. Charles A. Eastman, a Santee Sioux who held a medical degree, surveyed the conditions of the Osage and made his report. Of the 372 restricted adults he observed, 188 had court-appointed guardians and only 130 had permanent homes in Osage County in Oklahoma. The remainder made their homes with their parents or grandparents, and there were 283 minor allottees. Fifty-two of them had guardians, and there were 165 unallotted minors receiving payments through inheritance, of which 150 had guardians. In addition, 92 allottees who had legal, court-appointed guardians had received certificates of competency.[81]

Of the 130 Osage families in Eastman's survey, 15 adults had intermarried with whites. Twenty-one were widows or single, and 104 were married to other Osage. The total number of restricted adult Osage included in his survey was 234, leaving 138 restricted Osage who were either absent from the reservation or were minors. Of the latter group, some had married but had no homes; they did not work, and they lived with their parents and relatives. Dr. Eastman stated, "If their oil should fail the Osage people would be in a hard predicament, more so than any other Indian Tribe because they have lived expensively and have become accustomed to it." He concluded, "The Osage people have grown to be suspicious and snobbish because of their wealth. It is a matter of self defense. There are quite a number of them very anxious to get away from this State and go where they can live in peace."[82]

The Osage experienced an incredible increase in their yearly incomes, especially after the discovery of oil on their lands. For example, during the 1880s, they received $10.50 per year; in 1900, $200 annually; in 1910, $250; in 1915, $221.31; in 1920, the year of the first murder, ($8,090; and 1921, when four murders happened, $12,400. The U.S. Bureau of Investigation recorded that until June 30, 1931, approximately 2,000 Osage with headrights were paid a total net revenue of $241,546,289.82.[83]

Although the Osage survived Hale's murderous "reign of terror," one family and individuals related to them by marriage did not. The death of this family caused a missing link in the community during this tragic experience of murders. Although the windfall of money from oil was the obvious external factor in undermining the Osage, the family also came under attack, weakening the internal cohesion of the people.

Externally, the Osage had to deal with a different system of cultural values and philosophica░░░░░░░░░░░░░░░░░░░░idustry thrust the Osage into confron░░░░░░░░░░░░░░░░░░░░r lands and believing that they sho░░░░░░░░░░░░░░░░░░░system whether they liked it or not. As the Great Depression hit the Osage and the rest of the country in 1929, Commissioner of Indian Affairs C. J. Rhoads accepted the advice of Superintendent J. George Wright at the Osage Agency, calling for a regulation that would allow adult Osage of less than half blood to write for permission to withdraw their surplus funds to meet their needs.[84]

Undoubtedly, the Osage were not ready for the shrewd capitalism that impacted their lives, followed by the economic suffering due to the depression. Their earlier riches would be remembered when there was a resurgence in the oil industry in the 1970s and 1980s. In 1982, 11,200,000 barrels of oil and 8,600 million cubic feet of gas were produced annually from the Osage land, but the tribe members owned less than 200,000 acres of the surface in Osage County.[85]

The sad story of the Osage in the 1920s is legendary, and it is a vivid reminder of the worst that can come from the greed encouraged by American capitalism—murder for profit. It also is a lesson in what can happen when Native Americans are robbed of family, one of the fundamental elements of their society. Stripped of their traditional strength and their interdependence on each other, the family members were easy prey for predators like William K. Hale.

NOTES

1. Terry P. Wilson, *The Underground Reservation: Osage Oil* (Lincoln and London: University of Nebraska Press, 1985), pp. 8–9.
2. Charles Kappler, comp. and ed., *Indian Treaties, 1778–1883*, 3d ed. (New York: Interland Publishing, 1975), pp. 95, 201, and 246.
3. Wilson, *Underground Reservation*, p. 17; also, for the general incidents of the Osage tribe in Oklahoma, see Letters Received (Miscellaneous Correspondence), 1860–1923, Osage Agency, Record Group 75, Federal Archives and Records Center, Fort Worth, Texas.
4. *Osage Indian Tribe Centennial Celebration, 1872–1972*, September 30, 1972, Commemorating the Hundredth Anniversary for the Tribe's Removal From Kansas to the Osage Reservation, Indian Territory, Pawhuska, Oklahoma, Osage File, Oklahoma Historical Society, Oklahoma City.
5. Wilson, *Underground Reservation*, p. 20.
6. Paul McGuire, *Osage County, Osage Indians: History, People* (Pawhuska, Okla.: Adrin, 1969).
7. Gerald Forbes, "History of the Osage Blanket Lease," *Chronicles of Oklahoma* 19, no. 1 (March 1941): 70–71.

8. Ibid., p. 71.
9. Ibid.
10. Ibid., p. 72.
11. Ibid.
12. Ibid., p. 73.
13. Ibid.
14. Wilson, *Underground Reservation*, p. 119.
15. *Dawes Allotment Act*, 1887, *U.S. Statutes at Large* 22, 245, 273.
16. Memorial signed by Ni Kah Ke Pap Nah, James Bigheart, and A. L. Chouteau, Osage Delegates to the Honorable Committee on Territories of the House of Representatives, January 25, 1888 (Washington, D.C.: 1888), Osage File, no box no., Oklahoma Historical Society, Oklahoma City.
17. Berlin B. Chapman, "Dissolution of the Osage Reservation, Part One," *Chronicles of Oklahoma* 20, no. 3 (September-December 1942): 244–245.
18. Ibid., p. 245.
19. *Certified Roll of Members of the Osage Tribe of Indians of Oklahoma of Less Than One Half Indian Blood, of One Half Indian Blood or More (and Members According to Band)*, Approved by F. M. Goodwin, Assistant Secretary of the Interior, September 24, 1921, for the U.S. Government, Osage File, no box no., Oklahoma Historical Society, Oklahoma City.
20. Chapman, "Dissolution," p. 251.
21. *The Constitution and Laws of the Osage Nation*, Pawhuska, Osage Nation, 1881 and 1882 (Washington, D.C.: R. O. Polknshorn, 1883).
22. Wilson, *Underground Reservation*, p. 73.
23. "Constitution and Laws of Osage Nation," p. 99.
24. Ibid., p. 34.
25. Berlin B. Chapman, "Dissolution of the Osage Reservation, Part Two, "*Chronicles of Oklahoma* 20, no. 4 (September-December 1942): 377, and David L. Baldwin, "Oklahoma Osage Top Oil Production, Systems Management," *The CERT Report* 4, no. 11 (September 13, 1982): 7.
26. Ibid., p. 78.
27. Berlin B. Chapman, "Dissolution of the Osage Reservation, Part Four," *Chronicles of Oklahoma* 21, no. 2 (June 1943): 175.
28. The eleven bands of the Osage according to the census compiled by Superintendent Hugh Pilzer in 1910 were: Big Chief, consisting of 121 members; Mon-in-ka-neon-in, with 49 members; Ni-ka-wa-zhi-to-ga, with 89 members; Big Hill, with 26; White Hair, with 29; Tall Chief, with 16; Ku-zhi-wa-tse, with 22; Black Dog, with 23; Saucy Chief's Band, with 102; Beaver, with 57; and Strike Axe, with 56 members. File Number 3160 Francis La Flesche, copy of 1910 Osage Census, n.d., National Anthropological Archives, Washington, D.C.
29. William J. Broad, "The Osage Oil Cover-Up," *Science* 208, no. 4439 (April 4, 1980): 33.
30. Forbes, "History of Blanket Lease," p. 74.
31. Bill Burchardt, "Osage Oil," *Chronicles of Oklahoma* 41, no. 3 (Autumn 1963): 257.
32. Lewis Meriam, Ray A. Brown, Henry Roe Cloud, Edward Everett Dale, Emma Duke, Herbert R. Edwards, Fayette Avery McKenzie, Mary Louise

Mark, W. Carson Ryan Jr., and William J. Spillman, *The Problem of Indian Administration* (Baltimore, Md.: Johns Hopkins Press, 1928), pp. 446–451.

33. Broad, "Osage Cover-Up," p. 33.
34. Wilson, *Underground Reservation*, p. 107, and Forbes, "History of Blanket Lease," p. 75.
35. Wilson, *Underground Reservation*, p. 110.
36. Ibid., pp. 110–111.
37. Ibid., p. 136.
38. Forbes, "History of Blanket Lease," p. 76.
39. A. W. Ambrose of Bureau of Mines to Interior Secretary Albert Fall, July 14, 1922, Item 6, Folder "Oil-Indian," Box 7, Albert Fall Papers, Special Collection, Zimmerman Library, University of New Mexico, Albuquerque.
40. Forbes, "History of Blanket Lease," p. 78.
41. Interior Secretary Albert Fall to Commissioner of Indian Affairs Charles H. Burke, November 29, 1922, Item 6, "Oil-Indian," Box 7, Albert Fall Papers, Special Collection, Zimmerman Library, University of New Mexico, Albuquerque.
42. Burchardt, "Osage Oil," p. 258.
43. Ibid.
44. The Federal Bureau of Investigation was founded in 1908 as the U.S. Bureau of Investigation; its name was changed in 1935.
45. "Unique Deception Methods Used by Federal Agents in Solving Mysterious Cases Revealed Here," *Butte Daily Post*, September 30, 1938, Reel 1, section 1, microfilm, FBI Files Osage Murders, University of Wisconsin Library, Milwaukee.
46. Court Report by Calvin S. Weakley, August 13–18, 1923, at Oklahoma City, Bill Smith et al., Case, O. C. 7060, Reel 1, section 1, microfilm, FBI Files Osage Murder, University of Wisconsin Library, Milwaukee.
47. Dorothy Emery, "Fiendish Killing in Ravine Told by Murderer," *Tulsa Tribune*, June 3, 1926, Folder "Clippings," Box 1, Records of the Bureau of Indian Affairs, Records for the Five Civilized Tribes Agency, Records of the Office of the Superintendent, Office Files of Various Superintendents, 1920s, Record Group 75, Entry number 317, Federal Archives and Records Center, Fort Worth, Texas.
48. Ibid.
49. Memorandum for the Director of the Department of Justice, March 12, 1925, Reel 1, section 5, microfilm, FBI Files Osage Murders, University of Wisconsin Library, Milwaukee.
50. Ibid.
51. Burchardt, "Osage Oil," p. 261.
52. Broad, "Osage Cover-Up," p. 33.
53. Title of Case W. E. (Bill Smith, et. als., Murder of _____: [sic]) Osage County, O. C. 7060, report made at Oklahoma City, December 26, 1923, Reel 1, section 2, microfilm, FBI Files Osage Murders, University of Wisconsin Library, Milwaukee.
54. Preliminary Report, by T. F. Weiss, September 1, 1923, Reel 1, section 2,

p. 1, microfilm, FBI Files Osage Murders, University of Wisconsin Library, Milwaukee.

55. Letter From M. K. Sniffen of Indian Rights Association to FBI, December 1, 1924, FBI Files Osage Murders, University of Wisconsin Library, Milwaukee.

56. C. B. Glasscock, *Then Came Oil: The Story of the Last Frontier* (Indianapolis and New York: Bobbs-Merrill, 1938), p. 270.

57. Court Report by Calvin S. Weakley, p. 4.

58. Glasscock, *Then Came Oil*, p. 270.

59. Ibid.

60. "Unique Deception Methods Used."

61. Glasscock, *Then Came Oil*, p. 271.

62. "Confession to Slaying Accepted," *Muskogee Times-Democrat*, June 21, 1926, Folder "Clippings," Box 1, Records for the Bureau of Indian Affairs, Records of the Five Civilized Tribes Agency, Records of the Office of the Superintendent, Office Files of Various Superintendents, 1920s, Box 1, RG 75, Entry 317, Federal Archives and Records Center, Fort Worth, Texas.

63. "Unique Deception Methods Used."

64. Burchardt, "Osage Oil," p. 265.

65. "Unique Deception Methods Used."

66. *U.S. v. John Ramsey and William K. Hale*, No. 5660. Criminal, in the District Court of the United States for the Western District of Oklahoma, January 25, 1926, signed by District Judge John H. Cotteral, Box 232, Record Group 21, Entry E.40-W-16, U.S. District Courts Western District of Oklahoma, Oklahoma City, Criminal Cases Files, 1907, Federal Archives and Records Center, Fort Worth, Texas.

67. Ibid.

68. Glasscock, *Then Came Oil*, p. 271.

69. See motions for quash and *demurrer* in Folder, Criminal 5660, Box 232, Record Group 21, Entry number E.40-W-16, U.S. District Courts Western District of Oklahoma, Oklahoma City, Criminal Case Files, 1907, Federal Archives and Records Center, Fort Worth, Texas.

70. Ibid. See pp. 1–2, vol. 1, Filed February 14, 1927, Bill of Exceptions, *U.S. Plaintiff v. John Ramsey and William Hale, Defendants*, No. 5728, in the District Court of the United States for the Western District of Oklahoma, Box 236, Entry Number E.40-W-16, RG 21, U.S. District Courts, Western District of Oklahoma, Oklahoma City, Criminal Case Files, 1907-, Federal Archives and Records Center, Fort Worth, Texas.

71. See ibid., pp. 45, 46, 52, 55, and 85.

72. Government's Exhibit No. 9, signed by John Ramsey, witnessed by Edwin Brown, statement to F. S. Smith and T. B. White, Chief of Bureau of Investigation for Oklahoma and Arkansas, Government's Exhibit No. 9., p. 200., vol. 1, Filed February 14, 1927, Bill of Exceptions, *U.S., Plaintiff v. John Ramsey and William Hale, Defendants*, No. 5728, in the District Court of the United States for the Western District of Oklahoma, Box 236, Entry Number E.40-W-16, RG 21, U.S. District Courts, Western District of Oklahoma, Oklahoma City, Criminal Case Files, 1907-, Federal

Archives and Records Center, Fort Worth, Texas; refer also to the testimony of Federal Agent Frank Smith regarding Ramsey killing Roan in the court records: ." 'I shot him in the back of the head.' He said he shot him with a 45 automatic. I asked him then where he got the automatic, and he said he got it at Henry Grammer's ranch, that Henry had an arsenal there, he had all kinds of guns"; see p. 239, vol. 1, Filed February 14, 1927, Bill of Exceptions, *U.S., Plaintiff v. John Ramsey and William Hale, Defendants*, No. 5728, in the District Court of the United States for the Western District of Oklahoma, Box 236, Entry Number E.40-W–16, RG 21, U.S. District Courts, Western District of Oklahoma, Oklahoma City, Criminal Case Files, 1907–, Federal Archives and Records Center, Fort Worth, Texas.

73. Burchardt, "Osage Oil," p. 265.
74. Government Exhibit No. 17, W. K. Hale to the Capitol Life Insurance Company, Denver, Colorado, August 22, 1923, Attention Mr. William E. Hutton, pp. 756–758, Part 2, Filed February 14, 1927, Bill of Exceptions, *U.S., Plaintiff v. John Ramsey and William Hale, Defendants*, No. 5728, in the District Court of the United States for the Western District of Oklahoma, Box 236, Entry Number E.40-W–16, RG 21, U.S. District Courts, Western District of Oklahoma, Oklahoma City, Criminal Case Files, 1907-, Federal Archives and Records Center, Fort Worth, Texas.
75. Indictment, Viol. Secs. 273 and 275, Criminal Code, by willfully murdering Henry Roan, an Osage Indian in the Indian Country, No. 5659, U.S. District Courts, Western District of Oklahoma, Oklahoma City, Criminal Case Files, 1907, Federal Archives and Records Center, Fort Worth, Texas.
76. Kenny A. Franks, *The Osage Oil Boom* (Oklahoma City: Oklahoma Heritage Association, 1989), p. 125.
77. Wilson, *Underground Reservation*, p. 146.
78. Franks, *Osage Oil Boom*, p. 127.
79. Broad, "Osage Cover Up," p. 33.
80. Burchardt, "Osage Oil," p. 265.
81. Raymond Wilson, "Dr. Charles A. Eastman's Report on the Economic Conditions of the Osage Indians in Oklahoma, 1924," *Chronicles of Oklahoma* 55, no. 3 (Fall 1977): 344–345.
82. Wilson, "Eastman Report," p. 345.
83. FBI Memorandum, October 1932, Reel 3, section 20, microfilm, FBI Files Osage Murders, University of Wisconsin, Milwaukee.
84. C. J. Rhoads to J. George Wright, January 7, 1930, Elmer Thomas Papers, Box 2, Folder 44, Carl Albert Congressional Research and Studies Center, University of Oklahoma, Norman.
85. David L. Baldwin, "Oklahoma Osage Top Oil Production, Systems Management," *The CERT Report* 4, no. 11 (September 13, 1982): 7–9.

3

STRUGGLE FOR PUEBLO WATER
RIGHTS IN THE SOUTHWEST

I ndian communities in the Southwest have depended on water from
the Río Grande since prehistoric times. Called "the Great River"
by the Spanish, the 445-mile Río Grande is the second longest
river in the United States and serves for a lengthy distance as the
international boundary between the United States and Mexico. Following the Paleo-Indian cultural periods of Sandia, Clovis, and Folsom
of the big game hunting tradition, later domestic traditions of Native
Americans became dependent on to the assured supply of water from
the Rio Grande. In subsequent centuries, early Native Indians developed horticulture to advance their way of life, providing approximately
twenty-five percent of their food supply.[1] Descendants of these people
developed in the Desert Archaic tradition commonly known as the
Hohokam, Mogollon, and Anasazi as they became permanent settlers.
These three peoples are credited with developing agriculture in the
Southwest and introducing irrigation, thus freeing more time for developing art, philosophy, and civilization in general. Water was precious and essential the descendants, enabling most of the Pueblo people
to live in communities originally established along the San Juan River
and its tributaries. The Pueblo Indians also had to learn to fight for
their irrigated lands against other Indians, the Spanish, the Mexicans, and white settlers.

Drought occurred periodically, and the Pueblo communities were
eventually forced to move south and east. Although some remained in
the San Juan area, the Zuni, Laguna, and Acoma relocated to an area
that would become New Mexico. Some of the Pueblo people joined

4. Pueblo lands. From the author's collection.

other Indians already living along the Río Grande. This bountiful river favored them, allowing them to grow corn, squash, and beans to feed their people. Their communities flourished with the irrigated fields of corn. Life focused on artwork, philosophy, and religion, with an emphasis on the important relationship of deities and the rain that blessed the people with life-sustaining water. All was well until the Spanish conquistadors invaded the Pueblo homelands and dominated them between 1500 and 1700). Then came the Mexicans in the 1800s, followed by the Texans, other raiding tribes, and finally the settlers of the United States, who succeeded in obtaining statehood for New Mexico and Arizona in 1912.

The Pueblo communities lived peacefully again until Holm O. Bursum of Socorro, New Mexico, became a U.S. senator in 1921. New Mexico's governor, Merritt C. Mechem, a former judge, appointed Bursum to replace Senator Albert Fall after President Warren G. Harding asked Fall to join his cabinet as secretary of the interior. During the same year, Senator Bursum introduced a bill to settle land claims of non-Indians within Pueblo boundaries.

Born in Fort Dodge, Iowa, in 1867, Bursum was described by one newspaper in New Mexico as a man who fought continually for cattlemen, ranchers, and miners. When Bursum's senatorial career began, so too did the problems of the Pueblo communities, provoking a major political effort from the Pueblo communities and inspiring many Americans across the nation to fight to save the Pueblo lands. The Pueblo communities remained intact against congressional action to legislate their lands.

The "community" or the "village" of the Pueblo people is the focus of their society. Among the native populations of the Americas, the Pueblo communities have the longest continuity, with the commu-

5. Senator Holm O. Bursum of New Mexico. Courtesy, University of New Mexico Zimmerman Library, Special Collections.

nities of "Old Oraibi" and "Acoma" being the oldest continuing settlements north of the Río Grande. These two communities represented the third basic element of native life in America. They exemplified the height of the socialization of native people, as related and unrelated families joined in a group effort to survive the rigors of life in the semidesert environment of the Southwest. Cooperation, based on kinship solidarity, proved essential to the communities in protecting and providing for the people. Group consensus allowed each community to respond as a society, which then decided norms, developed ceremonies, and established laws for organizational success. At times, threats from the outside and common causes led the communities to cooperate with others politically to form a confederacy, as the Pueblo did against the Spanish in 1680 and again in the 1920s to protect their lands and water rights. Above human politics, the Pueblo recognized a relationship with the dry, arid desert and the precious water from the Rio Grande and adapted to the environmental conditions to perpetuate their traditional lifestyle.

The Rio Grande that nurtured the homeland of the Pueblo communities was known by various names in the past. In 1540, early explorers called the river the Tiguex. In 1598, Don Juan de Oñate referred to it as the Spanish Rio Bravo, and it was the Grande according to General James Wilkinson in 1806.

During the fifteenth century, the people of the Great River were named the Pueblo (meaning villages) by the Spanish, as the foreign imperialists came into contact with other natives in Mexico, Central America, and South America. The Spanish conquistadors ruthlessly invaded the various regions of the Western Hemisphere, laying waste to the villages of all native groups in the Southwest until the Pueblo communities united in opposition under the leadership of Popé, a medicine man from San Juan Pueblo. When they briefly halted the Spanish advance in 1680, they provoked the wrath of their enemy, and the soldiers viciously decimated the Pueblo. Under the authority of the king of Spain, those who survived were given Spanish citizenship and received land grants of four square leagues, possibly from Don Domingo Cruzate in September 1689. On December 29, 1693, Don Diego de Vargas attacked and ordered the execution of 70 Pueblo men, and 400 women and children were sold into slavery. With the territory firmly under Spanish control, the king of Spain and the Council of State confirmed the earlier land grants and increased each total grant to 1,100 varas (one vara equaled 33 inches) per community. The land of the Pueblo became New Spain, a political entity lasting from 1535 to 1810, with the "Recopilación de Leyes de las Indias" (Compilation of Laws for Indians) serving as the code of law for Spanish America.[2]

During the Spanish occupation, the Apache raided the Pueblo communities, bringing further destruction and loss of lives. From an original estimate of 70 to 100 communities, the Pueblo were reduced to approximately 20 communities. This travesty left the Zuni, Acoma, and Laguna west of the Rio Grande; the Pecos Pueblo east of the Rio Grande on the Pecos River; and the remaining 16 communities—including the Isleta, Sandia, Jemez, Santa Ana, Zia, San Felipe, Santo

Domingo, Santa Clara, Cochiti, Tesuque, Pojoaque, Nambe, San Ildefonso, San Juan, Picuris, and Taos—along the upper Río Grande.

As early as 1551, Spanish officials developed a series of laws affecting the Pueblo communities, and the Spanish crown announced various policies in 1573, 1618, 1687, 1695, 1781, and 1811.[3] As wards of the crown, the Pueblo people would have title to all lands used and occupied by them on a community basis. Only a viceroy, governor, or captain general could grant additional lands to the Pueblo and certify land sales made by them.[4] Under Spanish law, the Pueblo nations possessed superior rights to all water that crossed or bordered their lands, and non-Pueblos could not legally reside on Pueblo lands. Ironically, the Spanish granted the Pueblo communities their own former lands, as well as water rights that had been theirs for centuries before the Spanish arrived.

Spanish domination continued until the Mexican Revolution in 1821 produced a change in status for the Pueblo Indians. Three years later, Mexico granted citizenship to the Pueblo people under the Plan of Iguala of 1821.[5] Citizenship, however, brought little benefit for the Pueblo since the Mexican government paternally regulated their communities as a part of Mexico. Furthermore, this change of national jurisdiction failed to thwart non-Pueblos, who increasingly trespassed and remained on Pueblo lands. As the Pueblo lost their lands to the Mexicans, Americans called Texans began to settle in the Southwest.

In the summer of 1846, the United States and Mexico went to war, and General Stephen Watts Kearney and his soldiers ultimately defeated the Mexican forces. With his Army of the West, Kearney then occupied the area that would become New Mexico in August and set up a territorial government consisting of courts, judges, and a legislature. Continued American occupation led to the signing of the Treaty of Guadalupe Hidalgo in 1848, stipulating that Mexico surrender claims in toto to territory east of the Rio Grande and cede New Mexico and upper California to the United States for $15 million. Under this arrangement, the United States agreed to recognize and protect the Indian rights that were previously recognized under Spanish and Mexican rule.[6]

Section 8 of the treaty provided that Mexican citizens living in the area that would become New Mexico had the option of retaining their Mexican citizenship, but if they failed to apply to retain that citizenship within a year, they would become citizens of the United States. The Pueblo people did not attempt to retain their Mexican citizenship; thus, in legal limbo, they were not wards of the U.S. government and had no federal trust protection. The Pueblo communities held the status of conquered nations, being passed from one conqueror to another. Their sovereignty, which was key to their water and land rights, remained undetermined. But according to the Treaty of Guadalupe Hidalgo, the Pueblo held property rights over some 700,000 acres, which was recognized by the United States.[7]

Nonetheless, life in the Pueblo communities continued as usual, and in 1851, the U.S. Congress extended the protection of the Indian Trade and Intercourse Act of 1834 to the tribes of the newly formed Territory of New Mexico (established in 1850), consisting of present-day New Mexico, Arizona, and a portion of Colorado.[8] Within three years, the United States established further control over the Southwest. Another treaty, signed in 1853, created the Gadsden Purchase, and the United States paid Mexico $10 million for all of the territory along the current southern boundary of the United States from the Río Grande to the Colorado River. Now the Pueblo definitely had a new landlord—the United States, whose surveyor general surveyed and identified certain lands belonging to the Pueblo people under an act passed on December 22, 1858.[9] Based on aboriginal rights, the Pueblo people continued to possess the reserve rights (first rights to the land and its natural resources) that the Spanish and Mexican governments had recognized, and now the United States confirmed the same rights. This legal point was confirmed after 1854 when the surveyor general, authorized by the U.S. Congress, surveyed New Mexican Indian lands and confirmed Pueblo sovereign rights. Nonetheless, ignoring whatever legal rights the Pueblo possessed, trespassers and squatters intruded upon their lands throughout this period, and they seized the very best lands that generations of the Pueblo people had irrigated since the Paleo-Indian era.

On August 1, 1861, the United States efficiently shaped all of New Mexico south of the thirty-fourth parallel into the organized Territory of Arizona. As a gesture of peace and goodwill, President Abraham Lincoln gave the nineteen Pueblo leaders silver-headed canes, exemplifying the positive rapport between the Native communities and the United States. Lincoln pledged that the land rights, liberties, religions, and customs of the Pueblo people would forever be respected by the United States and that their treaties would never be broken.[10] This relationship faced a challenge in 1876 when the federal government removed a Mexican citizen from Taos Pueblo on the basis of the Indian Trade and Intercourse Act of 1834, resulting in a court case known as *U.S. v. Joseph*. The 1834 act called for only the United States to trade with Indians within the United States. The territorial supreme court of New Mexico ruled that the Intercourse Act did not apply to the Pueblo Indians since the Pueblo were not under U.S. jurisdiction.[11] In *U.S. v. Joseph*, the court ruled that the Pueblo people held dual citizenship in the United States and Mexico but that general title to Indians lands remained in the possession of the United States, except in the case of the Pueblo. Furthermore, the court stated that "if the defendant is on the lands of the Pueblo without the consent of the inhabitants, he may be ejected, or punished civilly by a suit for trespass"; the defendant could be there legally if granted permission by consent or license, according to the court.[12]

Following the American Civil War, the competition for Pueblo lands intensified while Indians and Americans fought over Indian lands during the 1870s and in the well-known *Joseph* case. An estimated 3,000 Hispanics and white Americans made claims to former Pueblo lands, mostly the irrigated lands. The opportunists wanted the best available lands for farms, ranches, and town sites. Both Hispanics and white Americans (and the state of New Mexico after 1912) opposed the legal protection of the Pueblo and the movement to return the lands to the Pueblo people; indeed, they would not surrender the lands without a fight. From their perspective, many non-Pueblo landowners had purchased the lands in good faith, and some of their families had lived on the lands for two or more generations.

The illegal claims to Pueblo lands were based on the previous Supreme Court ruling in *United States v. Joseph* (1876), establishing that the Pueblo, due to their advanced culture, were not actual wards of the government and thus did not have the protection of sovereign rights from the United States.[13] In effect, the ruling stated that recognition of their sovereignty allowed them to have complete title to their lands and that they could dispose of them however they pleased.

This legal view of Pueblo sovereignty jeopardized the Indians' land and water rights. The Spanish had historically protected their sovereign rights, upholding the doctrine that Pueblo lands were inalienable, and they had provided free legal services when needed. By the 1870s, however, though the Pueblo had their sovereignty, they had no protection. Furthermore, if their sovereign rights were not reinforced, nothing could prevent individual Pueblo from selling land that had been held in common since time immemorial. As a result of this fiasco, thirty percent or more of the best Pueblo land passed into the hands of white squatters.

For fifteen years, ensuing court cases followed the precedent of the *Joseph* decision until 1891, when the attorney general ruled that federal laws regulating Indian traders did not apply to the Pueblo land.[14] Returning the Pueblo to legal limbo, the attorney general made their sovereign status and legal rights vulnerable. In 1905, the territorial supreme court of New Mexico decreed that, based on the *Joseph* decision, the Pueblo would have to pay taxes on their properties, but Congress rescued the Pueblo and passed an act granting them special tax exemption on their lands.[15] However, instead of benefiting the Pueblo communities, the exemption in fact induced many non-Pueblos to illegally settle on Pueblo lands.

Local pro-Pueblo opinion increased during the ensuing years, recognizing that the Pueblo communities needed federal protection. In 1910, the U.S. Congress passed the New Mexico Enabling Act, which stated that "the terms 'Indian' and 'Indian country' shall include the Pueblo Indians of New Mexico and the lands now owned and occupied by them."[16] The United States continued to flex its plenary authority under its own constitution with new laws designed to undermine the Pueblo communities.

The statehood movement in New Mexico Territory only added to the growing concerns of the Pueblo people. Under the Enabling Act of 1910, New Mexico Territory accepted the cession of all jurisdiction over Indian lands, and jurisdiction over the Pueblo communities was a part of the movement for statehood for both New Mexico and Arizona Territories, which culminated in their recognition as states in January 1912. Overall, from 1851 to 1913, the Pueblo people lost as much as eighty to ninety percent of their land to non-Pueblos seeking the irrigated areas that the Pueblo had developed over the centuries.[17]

An important court decision in 1914 led to a further decline of Pueblo sovereignty. The question of Pueblo rights arose when local officials arrested a Spanish American named Joseph Sandoval for selling liquor at Santa Clara and San Juan Pueblos. The decision went against Sandoval and in favor of federal jurisdiction of Pueblo lands in New Mexico.[18] In 1913, the Supreme Court reversed the *Joseph* ruling in *U.S. v. Sandoval* and decreed that the Pueblo people were Indians by race, custom, and government and that the United States had appropriated funds to improve Pueblo conditions, with Congress exempting them from taxation. Furthermore, the United States was, in fact, responsible for the well-being of the Pueblo people, just as it was the guardian for other Indians in America. The court ruled that U.S. guardianship should have been extended since 1848 and thus found that the original Pueblo lands were protected from illegal purchasers and squatters. At this point, the Pueblo held the same legal status as other Indians, and they became wards of the United States.[19]

This turn of legal events caused considerable havoc, much like that which had occurred during the Spanish dominion when both Spanish and Mexican opportunists claimed the same lands as the Pueblo.[20] The *Sandoval* decision established two points. First, the Pueblo communities would be protected in a paternalistic fashion from opportunists interested in their lands. This new federal responsibility to the

Pueblo meant that the government would supervise and stay in contact with the communities to safeguard their rights and their lands. Second, *Sandoval* usurped the legal sovereignty of the Pueblo communities. Although these communities had been legally affected by the laws and policies of the Spanish, Mexican, and U.S. governments in the past, this latest decision violated the natural right of the Pueblo communities to govern themselves as they had before the arrival of Europeans. The *Sandoval* ruling meant that the Pueblo could no longer sell their land, and it invalidated all sales since 1848 and called for the return of all land and water to them. The *Sandoval* decision had two major effects: Although it was a major victory for the Pueblo communities in terms of assuring the return of their lands and water, it also prompted a backlash from non-Pueblos who held such lands and water. Reestablishing the legal status of Pueblo lands, the decision affected approximately 12,000 people holding 3,000 claims; some of these people held titles to the lands. Though this large number of claims involved only about ten percent of all Pueblo lands, it represented practically all of the available water for agricultural purposes.

Although the court ruled that the federal government had to enforce the return of the lands and water rights to the Pueblo, subsequent suits and actions from the Department of the Interior kept the whole matter and its players embroiled in hostilities. During this time, poor living conditions forced residents of Tesque, San Idelfonso, San Juan, and some of the other Pueblo communities to accept government rations. They had lost most of their best cultivated land, and a drought added to their deprivation and starving conditions.

In 1921, violence broke out between the Pueblo, white Americans, and Hispanics when drought conditions compelled the Pueblo to demand their legal rights to the land; the same circumstances continued the following year. Meanwhile, settlers who wanted to sell their lands or mortgage them found their properties almost worthless if they were located next to Indian lands. The settlers' inability to sell, lease, or mortgage their properties added to the building friction with the Pueblo communities.[21]

In 1922, President Harding appointed Albert B. Fall, one of New Mexico's first senators, as his secretary of the interior. Fall had ambitions of solving the Pueblo land crises, which would obviously gain the confidence of his supporters and win him additional political backing. Controversy emerged over Pueblo lands when the new senator from New Mexico, Holm Bursum, introduced a bill representing the land interests of his non-Indian constituents. This would lead to the emergence of a notorious measure during the following year. Bursum's bill sought to settle the claims of white settlers on Pueblo land at a heavy loss to the Indians. The full details of the bill and the ulterior motive behind it became public and prompted the Pueblo Indians and other concerned individuals to oppose the Bursum bill. Soon, the injustice to the Pueblo would become national news.[22]

Seeking the voting power of the Hispanics and white Americans, Fall chose his course against the Pueblo. First, he requested Colonel Ralph E. Twitchell, a New Mexican scholar on Spanish history, to prepare a historical and legal report on Pueblo land titles (which was not completed until the spring of 1922). In May, impatient for the results of the report, Secretary Fall requested Senator Bursum to draft a bill to confirm all purchases of Pueblo lands since 1902.

In 1917, five years after statehood was granted to New Mexico, the federal government had conducted an expensive survey of Pueblo Indian lands. Referred to as the Joy Survey, this effort to define the borders of Pueblo lands involved a congressional interpretation of title to all lands legitimately or irrevocably out of Pueblo possession.[23] White settlers before 1917 were protected trespassers who settled on Pueblo lands. The status of land ownership and that of the Pueblo lands soon became even more important legally. On September 2, 1919, agent S. N. Brosius reported the unfavorable situation involving the Pueblo to the executive committee of the Indian Rights Association in Philadelphia.[24]

Bursum introduced the bill that Fall had asked him to draft on May 31, 1921, and it drew immediate opposition. Members of the Indian Rights Association visited Secretary Fall to protest on behalf of the Pueblo communities.[25] Hastily drawn up, the bill halted the eviction of settlers, had too short a statute of limitations, and was generally ineffective. At the request of Secretary Fall, the special assistant to Attorney General Twitchell addressed the weaknesses of the first Bursum bill to the Senate committee assigned to study it, and the bill was tabled without further action. A second Bursum bill, introduced on July 10, 1921, also failed due to several weaknesses. This bill called for two members of a proposed commission to be from New Mexico and Arizona. Twitchell suggested that because the commissioners from the two states would face opposition from the Pueblo and their supporters the members of the commission should come from outside of Arizona and New Mexico.[26]

After receiving his appointment as interior secretary, Albert Fall began to arrange certain oil leases for the benefit of specific individuals. As the secretary of the interior, he held immense power over the government's leasing of oil lands. For example, in May 1921, an executive order transferred the administration of the naval oil reserves from the Navy Department to the Interior Department, allowing Fall to lease Elk Hills in California to Pan-American Petroleum Company under E. L. Doheny, president of the company. Next, on April 7, 1922, Secretary Fall leased the Teapot Dome area in Wyoming to Mammoth Oil Company under H. F. Sinclair, who was the company's president. (This second scandal eventually led to Fall's 1931 conviction of bribery and a term in the federal penitentiary.)

During these nervous months while rumors of the Teapot Dome fraud circulated, Commissioner of Indian Affairs Charles H. Burke prepared to leave for New Mexico, where he would meet with several Indians at Santa Clara Pueblo. He would also get together with Twitchell and Santa Fe attorney A. B. Renehan, who had represented Sandoval in the *Sandoval* case, as well as 155 non-Indians involved in a suit to settle title within the Santa Clara and San Idelfonso Pueblo grants. Twitchell and Renehan returned with Burke to Washington for a meeting with Fall and Senator Bursum to draft another bill. Senator Bursum introduced this measure, the infamous Bursum bill (S.R. 3855), to the Senate on July 20, 1922, per the instructions of Secretary Fall. This draft was described as "a Bill to ascertain and settle claims of persons not Indians within Pueblo Indian land, land grants, and reservations in the State of New Mexico."[27]

The bill went to the appropriate Senate committee for discussion and was returned to the Senate floor on September 11, 1922, without a public hearing. Senator Bursum spoke to urge support for his bill. He explained that it provided the rules for suits to be filed in state courts in New Mexico, favoring non-Indian interests against the Pueblo communities. The Pueblo, he said, would be compensated with public agricultural lands near their communities or with money.

B. C. Hernandez of the Treasury Department for the District of New Mexico, a supporter of Bursum's bill, argued that the earlier Spanish rulings had encompassed all people living within the land grants. Thus, Hernandez reasoned that the United States had total jurisdiction over Pueblo lands. Many non-Indians would benefit, guaranteeing that New Mexico would vote Republican in the 1924 presidential election, according to Hernandez.[28] A different opinion claimed that the issue was too political and that the Republicans were at the bottom of the Pueblo lands controversy and would cause harm to the Indians and to New Mexico.[29] The disagreement over the Bursum bill grew more political and soon overshadowed the interests of the Indians and the irrigated lands involved in the original dispute.

The Senate approved the Bursum bill and sent it to the House,[30] despite the fact that Senator Bursum admitted no Indians had been asked to participate in drafting it. Meanwhile, the Pueblo people knew nothing of this action in Congress.[31] Surprised upon learning about the bill, the Pueblo communities began to mount an opposition, and the injustice inherent in the measure led many concerned persons to support the Indians. Editorials in the *Santa Fe New Mexican* newspaper motivated artists and intellectuals in the Santa Fe area and in Taos to support the Pueblo communities.[32]

A further provision of the Bursum bill delivered yet another blow to the Indians, stating that the future of Pueblo water rights would fall under the jurisdiction of New Mexico. The wording of the provision implied that the Pueblo communities themselves would come under the state's jurisdiction. Such an action threatened the sovereignty of the communities and their "reserved right" for water on their reservations as established in the famous *Winters* case of 1908.

Bursum's bill threatened disaster for the Pueblo, with large losses of lands.[33] The senator had hoped to push the bill quietly through congressional channels, and, in fact, the Pueblo almost missed the hearings on the bill in Washington. Bursum had conspired, with Secretary Fall's approval, to keep the issue out of the press, and local officials kept quiet so that the bill might become law without the Pueblo learning about it.

Indian Country came alive with hostility in the Southwest. Most of the writers and artists who supported the Pueblo lived in Santa Fe and Taos. The magnetic appeal of the Southwest, especially Taos, had lured artists such as Ernest L. Blumenschien and Bert Phillips to the area in 1908, and by 1914, members of the growing colony of artists and writers formed the Taos Society of Artists. Other artists and writers followed, among them Mabel Dodge Sterne, who once ran a salon in Greenwich Village. Arriving in 1917, she described the mystical Southwest in letters to her friends, arousing their curiosity about the landscape and the native culture of this area. She convinced others to visit, including John Collier, a poet from New York, and D. H. Lawrence, the British novelist. These avant-garde writers, artists, and intellectuals soon developed a respect for the Pueblo communities and an affinity for them.

As tension grew, Stella Atwood of Riverside, California, hired John Collier as a research agent for the General Federation of Women's Clubs. Learning about the Bursum bill, an upset Collier protested to Congress. Mabel Sterne's husband, Tony Luhan, a Taos Indian, served as an interpreter to help spread news of the threat among the Pueblo people. Holding meetings late into the night, Collier met with Pueblo elders to explain the possible dangers of the Bursum bill.

An intense Collier visited other Pueblo communities, warning the people of the Bursum bill's dangerous provisions, and they listened intently. Always a passive people of peace, groups from each community at Santo Domingo, north of Albuquerque, formed the All-Pueblo Council. Once together, the Pueblo communities pledged to fight the Bursum bill with all of their resources.

During these tense weeks, the artists and writers at Taos and Santa Fe issued a statement entitled the "Proclamation to the American Public" in defense of American Indian rights. United behind the slogan "Let's Save the Pueblos," the support group used its writing talent to convince newspapers and magazines throughout the country that the Pueblos were right, via letters and articles denouncing the injustice to the Pueblo people. Joining the momentum, the General Federation of Women's Clubs, with a national membership of two million, worked on behalf of the Pueblo communities. Stella Atwood, president of the club, raised money, contacted lawyers, and set up a lobby system in Washington. Her club members flooded their representatives with telegrams and letters. Atwood and the federation soon made the Pueblo case a national issue.[34] Support for the Pueblo generated additional support from the American Indian Defense Association and the Indian Rights Association.

During October 1922, *Sunset Magazine* took up the Pueblo cause with a series of scathing articles written by John Collier and others to encourage public interest and urge support for the Pueblo. The magazine's editors distributed copies to every member of Congress and other government officials who might help the cause.[35] Other magazines, such as *Outlook*, the *New Republic*, and the *Nation*, also published articles by authors who supported the Pueblo communities.[36] In New Mexico, the *Santa Fe New Mexican* newspaper led the criticism against Bursum and Fall; Bronson Cutting, a progressive Republican and owner of the newspaper, was a political opponent of the two men.

On the morning of November 5, 1922, 121 representatives of all the Pueblo met with John Collier, Margaret McKittrick, Elizabeth Sergeant, Francis Wilson, and several Franciscan fathers at Santo Domingo and drafted an appeal to the American people to defeat the Bursum bill. Denouncing the bill as a threat to their existence, the Indians raised $3,500 to send a delegation of seventeen Pueblo officials to Washington to present their case in January 1923. As symbols of their sovereign authority, the Pueblo delegates carried the canes that Lincoln had given to them in recognition of the sovereign rights granted by the Spanish. The delegates traveled to cities, spoke before sympathetic audiences, and won support. In Washington, they faced off with members of Congress who still needed to be convinced to vote against the Bursum bill. As an alternative to Bursum's measure, the Pueblo delegation supported a proposed bill from the senior senator from New Mexico, Andrieus A. Jones, which received less attention due to the angry protest against the Bursum legislation.[37]

The General Federation of Women's Clubs also hired Francis Wilson, an attorney in Santa Fe who had represented the government in the *Sandoval* case, to help defeat the bill. Wilson wrote William Borah, an influential senator from Idaho and member of the Senate Committee on Public Lands and Surveys, and described the problems of the bill. Borah gathered support and called for hearings before the committee in January.[38] As a part of the growing national support for the Pueblo Indians, the Eastern Association of Indian Affairs in New York City raised $2,300. Members of the House of Representatives unanimously recalled the bill, with the explanation that its purpose had been misrepresented to them.

Undaunted by the stiff opposition, Senator Bursum introduced S.R. 726 on December 10, 1923, to the Senate during the Sixty-eighth Congress. This bill, which had the same intent as the original measure, was read twice and referred to the Committee on Public Lands and Surveys, then to the secretary of the interior, who suggested some changes. The bill reappeared with amendments as S.R. 2932 "to quiet the title to lands within Pueblo Indian land grants, and for other purposes."[39]

Unsure of the legality of the measure, especially after the defeat of S.R. 3855, Bursum requested a legal interpretation from Attorney General Harry Daughtery. On January 8, 1924, the attorney general sent Bursum an unofficial and confidential memorandum, together with a legal opinion from the Department of Justice. If the land was "fee patent" to quiet the title to lands within the Pueblo land grants, the bill was unconstitutional, according to the Justice Department.[40]

Following the senator's introduction of S.R. 3855, letters poured into his office supporting both sides of the issue. A number of irate individuals claimed that those who backed the Pueblo Indians were "ignorant" of the actual situation, which they contended was only an attempt to ascertain the legal ownership of land involving the Pueblo communities. Senator Bursum berated one woman who was against bill: "The trouble is that your Women's Clubs do not stop to analyze the real purpose and effect of the bill which was a compromise agreed upon by the Indian Bureau and the settlers as a proper means of settling all disputes, and to extend justice and equity to everyone concerned. The bill also provided for giving the Indians more land than they now have, take it all around, I should say the bill is as advantageous to the Indians as it is to the non-Indians."[41] Supporters of the Pueblo became especially alarmed upon learning that no one had scheduled a public hearing for S.R. 3855, and they asked for the bill to be dismissed.

Upset about the recall of the Bursum bill, Secretary Fall threatened to use his political influence to move the measure into law, but by December, the incident became linked to the notorious Teapot Dome fraud. With his wrongdoing in that matter exposed, Fall quickly lost influence in the plagued Harding administration. He considered resigning from the cabinet, and in January, the president announced that Fall would leave office in March for personal reasons. Fall, however, continued to support the Bursum bill and testified before Senate and House committee hearings on its behalf.

During these troubled weeks, John Collier and a small group of Pueblo supporters met in Bursum's office in Washington to discuss the legislation. The senator said that he was "anxious to reach some solution" but wanted to consult with other interested parties to prevent conflicts of interest. Agitated about the situation, Collier seemed in a hurry to settle the controversy and persuaded senior senator Andrieus Jones to introduce his own bill. Bursum claimed that Congress would not pass such a bill, calling for the creation of an independent tribunal at a cost of $400,000, since it already had a system to settle land claims disputes.[42]

Prior to the Senate committee hearings, Francis Wilson drafted an alternative bill, and the senior senator from New Mexico introduced it, with Pueblo support. Known as the Jones-Leatherwood bill, the compromise measure proposed a three-person commission, appointed by the president with congressional approval, to examine claims and grant or reject land titles. The Pueblo communities supported the bill because it called for a self-sustained system for the reclamation of arid tracts owned by the Pueblo and for a court to adjudicate the claims of squatters on their lands.[43] This bill involved extensive irrigation projects for the Pueblo communities. The Senate Committee on Public Lands and Surveys and the House Indian Affairs Committee began their hearings in January and February on both bills. The Jones-Leatherwood bill drew criticism from supporters of the Bursum bill, who claimed that more than $400,000 would be needed for the proposed special court, including two attorneys at a salary of $6,000 each (one to be named by the Indians) and related expenses.[44] One critic claimed that the bill would "supply a good paying position to John Collier," as he had already benefited from the generosity of Mrs. Sterne and the sympathetic Federated Women's Club.[45]

United in their protest, Collier, Atwood, Wilson, and Pablo Abeyta, an Isleta Pueblo Indian, testified against the Bursum bill and in support of the Jones-Leatherwood measure. In speaking before both the Senate Committee on Public Lands and Surveys and the House Indian Affairs Committee, Wilson focused on the elements in the Bursum measure that threatened Pueblo life. Secretary Fall also testified before the committees and explained that the Bursum bill was necessary. He also criticized the Jones-Leatherwood bill for its high expenses and refused to be questioned by Wilson, the attorney for the other side.[46]

The hearings in the House of Representatives were anti-Pueblo in tone and began with a personal attack on Stella Atwood that brought her to tears. Wilson took the stand, and Republican representative Homer Snyder of New York, chairman of the House Committee on Indian Affairs, challenged Wilson's view of the Pueblo people. As a result of the criticism of both bills, a compromise measure called the Lenroot bill was drafted in the Senate Committee on Public Lands and Surveys during February. The bill called for the president to appoint a lands board of three members with the authority to investigate and grant title to lands in dispute. Non-Pueblos who had title to land for twenty years and settlers without title who had occupied the land for thirty years were granted titles of ownership.[47]

Wilson accepted the bill, thinking that it did provide justice for the non-Pueblos who had been on the land for a lengthy time. Collier, however, critically disagreed with Wilson and objected to the bill, arguing that it allowed trespassing on Pueblo lands and the obtaining of land titles without compensating the Pueblo people. With the criticism shifting to the legislation, Senator Bursum rewrote his bill and reintroduced it in the Senate. Taking a strong pro-Pueblo stand, an inspired John Collier wrote an alternative bill, and Senator Charles Curtis of Kansas agreed to introduce it. Shortly afterward, Collier returned to New Mexico to avoid further division with Wilson and diminishing support for the Pueblo cause. During this trip, Collier planned his next move. He urged support for his bill and arranged for another delegation of Pueblo to go to Washington to testify on its behalf.

Meanwhile, turmoil engulfed the plagued Harding administration as critics scrutinized every federal move. In March, Dr. Hubert Work replaced Secretary Fall in the Interior Department, which oversaw the activities of the Bureau of Indian Affairs. With national publicity criticizing federal actions, the Pueblo controversy compelled Work to create an advisory committee. Consisting of 100 people—Indians, conservatives, scientists, reformers, and missionaries, and luminaries such as Bernard Baruch, Oswald Villard, and William Jennings Bryan—this group agreed to investigate Indian conditions and make recommendations. With the federal government in chaos, a worried President Harding fell ill during the summer of 1923, and died on August 2.

Trouble was still brewing in Washington and in Indian affairs as Calvin Coolidge, the vice president who hailed from Vermont, ascended to the presidency.

Both the government and representatives from the Pueblo side hoped to resolve the Pueblo lands controversy, and attorneys for the settlers and the Indians met with the Senate Committee on Public Lands and Surveys to draft a compromise bill called the Pueblo Lands Act, establishing a lands board made up of the interior secretary, the attorney general, and a third member appointed by the president. The bill passed in the Senate on May 13 and in the House on June 5. President Coolidge signed the bill into law on June 9, 1924, as Public Law 253. The Pueblo Lands Board then began hearing claims and making decisions, many of which were challenged in court. The board worked into the next decade as a protector of the Pueblo Indians and their lands.[48]

The new legislation specifically gave the board authority to determine the boundaries of the Pueblo lands and the status of all land within those boundaries. The board also held the power to determine which lands within the Pueblo grants had been assumed by non-Pueblos for a sufficient length of time to establish non-Pueblo ownership in place of Pueblo ownership; in these cases, the lands would be quitclaimed to the non-Pueblos by the court.

The Pueblo Lands Act also called for the board's commissioners to be appointed by a court. Empowered with considerable authority, the board determined the land and water rights seized from the Pueblo and decided if the lands could have been recovered for the Pueblo Indians by the United States via prosecution. In such situations, the board had to determine the fair market value of the lands. If a valid Spanish or Mexican grant conflicted with a Pueblo land grant, the disagreement would be reported to Congress. The report from the board held the authority of a final judgment unless a review de novo was sought in the U.S. district court.

Starting with a full load of cases, the board held hearings between 1925 and 1930 and issued a series of individual reports for each Pueblo community. These reports specified the land and water rights of the Pueblo as a safeguard to protect Pueblo property. The titles of the lands claimed by the Pueblo fell under the jurisdiction of the federal court, and no interest in Pueblo land could be obtained legally without congressional approval. Compensation paid for lands taken from non-Pueblo individuals was to be applied to obtain "lands and water rights" to replace those lands lost and to construct reservoirs and irrigation projects for the benefit of the remaining Indian lands. Several years later, Congress passed the Pueblo Lands Act of 1933 to supplement the 1924 act; this new law also increased the compensation to the Pueblo.[49]

Section 9 of the Pueblo Lands Act of 1933 proved to be imperative to defining the water rights of the Pueblo Indians. It held: "Nothing herein contained shall in any manner be construed to deprive any of the Pueblo Indians of a 'prior right' to the use of water from streams running through or bordering on their respective Pueblos for domestic, stock-water, and irrigation purposes for the lands remaining in Indian ownership, and such water rights shall not be subject to loss by nonuse or abandonment thereof as long as title to said land shall remain in the Indians."[50]

Although the legislative measures of 1924 and 1933 restored much of the land to the Pueblo people, the state of New Mexico viewed the measures as taking land away from many of its citizens. On the other side, the Pueblo complained that the board operated using fixed values of $35 per acre even though much of the good valley land had been appraised by the board itself at more than $100 per acre.[51] In the context of the monetary value system of American capitalism, the Pueblo communities believed their land was worth much more. In the context of their own value system, the land of their ancestors was considered invaluable, especially to their future generations.

By the mid-1930s, the immediate conflict was over, but the competition for land has continued to this day—a competition that is made even more significant by the limited water and the dry environment of the area. The southwestern part of the United States continually thirsts for water to supply its increasing needs. This desire has become seriously evident since the mid-1980s, and water on the lands of the Pueblo communities is becoming increasingly attractive for white farmers, for energy companies that need it to send coal through huge pipes to faraway cities, and for basic industrial uses in the Southwest. As a result, the Pueblo communities have to fight aggressively in the courts, much as they fought in war centuries ago, to protect their precious water supplies. Ironically, past politics overshadowed the inherent strength of the Pueblo communities and the importance of water in the Southwest, and the mainstream society's version of history has only reinforced this.

The Río Grande and the Colorado River supply most of the natural water in the southwestern region of the United States. Due to the arid climate, with temperatures frequently soaring above the 100-degree mark, water has always been a precious commodity. History has recorded the efforts of numerous peoples and nations to capture the precious water belonging to the Pueblo communities. The Spanish arrived as the first European conquerors to invade the Pueblo Southwest in quest of jewels, silver, and gold. As conquistadors led Spanish armies against the Pueblo communities, the Spanish crown exercised its presumed power over the Pueblo and their lands. Although the Spanish were not immediately interested in the water supplies, they claimed Pueblo land and placed it under Spanish authority. The same story of greed was repeated when the Mexicans and the Americans controlled the Southwest. Yet in spite of all the imperialistic drives for land and water resources in the Southwest, the Pueblo communities continued to preserve their sovereignty, which they found essential to protecting their lands and water rights.

In the early-twentieth-century controversy over these matters, as the Bursum bill became a political focus involving Republican influence, the true origin of the issues of water and irrigated lands within Pueblo domain were overshadowed. Nonetheless, the Pueblo communities endured—proving the strength of the internal cohesiveness of these Indian people and demonstrating anew that "community" is an essential element for survival. The individual, family, and community composed the tribe or nation that determined native identity.

Before long, however, another generation of Indians in the Klamath Tribe of the Pacific Northwest would also struggle to protect its own vital natural resource—timber—and its identity against the threat posed by a federal policy called termination.

NOTES

1. Bertha P. Dutton, *American Indians in the Southwest* (Albuquerque: University of New Mexico Press, 1983), p. 9.
2. "Nefas and Narrandum," *Taos Valley News*, March 4, 1923, Folder 4, Box 8, Holm O. Bursum Papers, Special Collections, University of New Mexico Library, Albuquerque.
3. According to the "Recopilación," the Spanish crown expected the Pueblo people and other Indians under its jurisdiction to pay tribute and to provide a certain amount of labor in the form of a taxation system. More specifically, the *mercedes* (viceroys) of New Spain, in the name of the king, were assigned responsibility over mills, salt deposits, lime deposits, streams, and rivers. In all, the "Ramo de Mercedes" in the "Archivo General de la Nacion" contains eighty-three volumes of property grants, summaries of disputed property rights, and grant petitions for the "Audiencia de Mexico" area for the period 1542 to 1620. See William B. Taylor, "Land and Water Rights in the Viceroyalty of New Spain," *New Mexico Historical Review* 50, no. 3 (July 1975): 189.
4. Felix Cohen, *Handbook of Federal Indian Law*, reprint ed. (Albuquerque: University of New Mexico Press, 1986), p. 383.
5. Myra Ellen Jenkins, "The Baltazar Baca Grant: History of an Encroach-

ment," reprint from *El Palacio*, vol. 68 (Spring–Summer 1961): 50.

6. Cohen, *Handbook*, p. 384.

7. Bursum bill, introduced in the U.S. Senate during 1921. Refer to "Extension of Remarks of Hon. Alice M. Robertson, of Oklahoma in the House of Representatives," *Congressional Record*, 67, 4th sess., March 4, 1923.

8. Dutton, *American Indians in the Southwest*, p. 10.

9. *U.S. Trade and Intercourse Act*, June 30, 1834, *U.S. Statutes at Large* 4(1834): 729.

10. Judson King, "President Lincoln's Nineteen Silver-Header Canes," *National Popular Government League*, Bulletin No. 145, February 12, 1931, Box 2, Folder 37, Elmer Thomas Papers, Legislative Series, Carl Albert Congressional Center, University of Oklahoma, Norman.

11. *U.S. Trade and Intercourse Act*, 735–738.

12. In a previous case known as *U.S. v. Lucero*, the New Mexico territorial government filed a petition asking the U.S. Supreme Court to hear the case; see *United States v. Lucero*, 1 N.M. 440 (1860).

13. Treaty of Guadalupe Hidalgo, February 2, 1848, United States–Mexico, 9 Stat. 922, T.S. No. 207; for a comprehensive study of the international agreement, see Richard Griswold del Castillo, *The Treaty of Guadalupe Hidalgo: A Legacy of Conflict* (Norman: University of Oklahoma Press, 1990).

14. *United States v. Joseph*, 94 *U.S. Statutes at Large* (1876): 617, 618.

15. Willard H. Rollins, "Indian Land and Water: The Pueblos of New Mexico (1838–1924)," *American Indian Culture and Research Journal* 7, no. 1 (1983): 7.

16. *Territory of New Mexico v. Delinquent Taxpayers*, 12 N.M. 139, 76, Pac. 316 (1904), and *Act of March 3, 1905*, 33 *U.S. Statutes at Large*, 1084.

17. Act of June 20, 1910, 36 *U.S. Statutes at Large*, 557.

18. *United States v. Joseph*, 94 *U.S. Statutes at Large*, (1876): 614.

19. Charles T. DuMars, Marilyn O'Leary, and Albert E. Utton, *Pueblo Indian Water Rights, Struggle for a Precious Resource* (Tucson: University of Arizona Press, 1984), p. 56.

20. Kenneth R. Philp, "Albert B. Fall and the Protest From the Pueblos, 1921–23," *Arizona and the West* 12, no. 3 (Autumn 1970): 239.

21. *United States v. Sandoval*, 231 *U.S. Statutes at Large* (1913): 28.

22. Ibid.

23. Clara D. True to S. M. Brosius, March 2, 1919, Indian Rights Association Papers, Reel 34, microfilm, Marquette University Library, Milwaukee, Wisconsin.

24. S. N. Brosius to Executive Committee of Indian Rights Association, [report], September 2, 1919, Indian Rights Association Papers, Reel 34, microfilm, Newberry Library, Chicago.

25. U.S. *Congressional Record*, 67th Con., 4th sess., 1923, 64, part 1, 571, 307.

26. Donald R. Moorman, "A Political Biography of Holm O. Bursum: 1899–1924," Ph.D. diss. University of New Mexico, Albuquerque, 1962, p. 309.

27. U.S. Congress, "Hearings Before the Subcommittee of the Senate Committee of Public Lands and Surveys on Senate Bill 3865 [S.R. 3855] and Senate Bill 4223," 67th Cong., 4th sess., January 15 to February 1, 1923, p. 52.

28. B. C. Hernandez, Treasury Department for District of New Mexico, to Senator Holm O. Bursum, November 22, 1922, Folder 2, "Indian Lands Bills 1922," Box 12, Holm Bursum Papers, Special Collections, University of New Mexico Library, Albuquerque.

29. Mrs. George Prichard to Senator Holm O. Bursum, March 23, 1923, Folder 2 "Correspondence Indian Bills 1922," Box 13, Holm Bursum Papers, Special Collections, University of New Mexico Library, Albuquerque.

30. Senate hearings, 67th Cong., 4th sess., 6–7.

31. "Remarks of Alice Robertson," *Congressional Record*, 67th Congress, 4th sess., March 4, 1923. Members of the House Committee on Indian Affairs in 1923 included: Homer P. Snyder, New York, chairman; Philip P. Campbell, Kansas; Royal C. Johnson, South Dakota; Frederick W. Dallinger, Massachusetts; Albert W. Jefferies, Nebraska; R. Clint Cole, Ohio; John Reber, Pennsylvania; Alice M. Robertson, Oklahoma; E. O. Leatherwood, Utah; Nestor Montoya, New Mexico; L. M. Gensman, Oklahoma; Sidney C. Roach, Missouri; Washington J. McCormick, Montana; Olger B. Burtness, North Dakota; Dan A. Sutherland, Alaska; Carl Hayden, Arizona; William J. Sears, Florida; Zebulon Weaver, North Carolina; F. B. Swank, Oklahoma; Ross A. Collins, Mississippi; Hampton P. Fulmer, South Carolina; Morgan G. Sanders, Texas; and H. E. Devendorf, clerk.

32. Marc Simmons, *New Mexico, A Bicentennial History* (New York: W. W. Norton, 1977), p. 174.

33. List of Acres Owned by Pueblo Communities in New Mexico

Name of Pueblo	Spanish Grant	U.S. Grant	Total Acres
Acoma	95,791.66		96,662.77
Acoma (Santa Ana tract)	871.33		17,544.77
San Juan	17,544.77		17,460.69
Picturis	17,460.69		17,460.69
San Filipe	33,692.00	13,816.00	47,508.00
Jemez	17,510.15	17,000.00	34,510.15
Taos	17,360.55		17,360.55
Santa Clara	17,368.52	21,960.00	39,328.52
Tesuque	17,471.12		17,471.12
San Ildefonso	17,292.64		17,292.64
Pojoaque (extinct)	13,520.38		13,520.38
Zia	17,514.63		17,514.63
Sandia	24,187.29		24,187.29
Isleta	110,080.31		110,080.31
Nambe	13,590.43	6,000.00	19,590.43
Santa Ana	17,360.56		17,360.56
Zuni	17,581.25		17,581.25
Laguna and annexes	257,731.54		257,731.54
		Total Acres	782,705.82

Source: Surveyor General's Office, Santa Fe, Mexico, December 27, 1922; Amando Chavez to Senator Holm O. Bursum, Folder 2, "Correspondence Indian Bills 1922," Box 13, Holm Bursum Papers, Special Collections, University of New Mexico Library, Albuquerque.

34. "Indian Bill Will Destroy Pueblo Life, Say Indians in Memorial to Country," *Santa Fe New Mexican*, November 6, 1922, pp. 1 and 6.
35. "Remarks of Alice Robertson," *Congressional Record*, 67th Congress, 4th sess., March 4, 1923.
36. Philp, "Albert Fall and Pueblo Protest," p. 244.
37. Philp, *Collier's Crusade for Indian Reform*, p. 45.
38. "Remarks of Alice Robertson."
39. The procedural history of the Pueblo Lands Act is as follows: S.R. 726 was introduced by Senator Bursum on December 10, 1923, in the Senate (68th Cong., 1st sess.), and the bill was read twice and referred to the Committee on Public Lands and Surveys. S.R. 726 was then referred by the committee to the secretary of the interior, who suggested some changes, and it reappeared with amendments as S.R. 2932. Senator Bursum reintroduced it on March 25, 1924 (68th Cong., 1st sess.), and it was read twice and referred to the Committee on Public Lands and Surveys as S.R. 2932—to quiet the title to lands within Pueblo Indian land grants and for other purposes. Reported out of the Senate Committee on Public Lands with amendments on May 3, 1924 (S.R. 492), it was amended and passed by the Senate on May 13, 1924; referred to the House Committee on Indian Affairs on May 14, 1924, reported out of the House Committee on Indian Affairs on May 19, 1924 (H.R. 787), passed by the House on June 5, 1924, and approved by the president of the United States on June 7, 1924—Public Law No. 253, during the 68th Congress, 1st session.
40. Attorney General Harry Daughtery to Senator Holm O. Bursum, unofficial confidential memorandum, with legal opinion from Justice Department, January 8, 1924, Folder, Box 4, Holm Bursum Papers, Special Collections, University of New Mexico Library, Albuquerque.
41. Senator Holm O. Bursum to Mrs. Betsy J. Edwards, January 3, 1923, Folder 2, "Correspondence Indian Bills 1922," Box 13, Holm Bursum Papers, Special Collections, University of New Mexico Library, Albuquerque.
42. Senator Holm O. Bursum to Judge C. J. Roberts, January 2, 1923, Folder "Correspondence Indian Bills 1922," Box 13, Holm Bursum Papers, Special Collections, University of New Mexico Library, Albuquerque.
43. "Delegation of Pueblos to Petition Congress," *New York Tribune*, January 7, 1923, Folder 4, Box 8, Holm Bursum Papers, Special Collections, University of New Mexico Library, Albuquerque.
44. John A. Harper to *Albuquerque Journal*, telegram, January 13, 1923, Folder "Correspondence Indian Bills 1922," Box 13, Holm Bursum Papers, Special Collections, University of New Mexico Library, Albuquerque.
45. Dr. T. P. Martin to Senator Holm O. Bursum, January 15, 1923, Folder 7 "Correspondence Indian Bills 1922," Box 13, Holm Bursum Papers, Special Collections, University of New Mexico Library, Albuquerque.
46. Rollins, "Indian Lands and Water," p. 15.
47. Pueblo Lands Board Appropriation Act, May 31, 1933, *U.S. Statutes at Large*, 48 pt. 1:108–111.
48. Rollins, "Indian Lands and Water," p. 17.

49. U.S. *Senate Journal*, 68th Congress, 1st sess., 1923–1924, 341–342.
50. *Pueblo Lands Board Appropriation Act*, 108–111.
51. DuMars, O'Leary, and Utton, *Pueblo Indian Water Rights*, p. 65.

4

TERMINATION OF THE KLAMATH AND TIMBERLANDS IN THE PACIFIC NORTHWEST

Located in southeastern Oregon, the Klamath Reservation is blessed with thick, green stands of timber and embraced by the Cascades sloping from the Rocky Mountains. Tall ponderosa pines and white fir trees drape the land belonging to the Klamath in a natural basin of marshes and streams alive with fish, mussels, and waterfowl. This southern part of Oregon contains the Klamath Basin, named after a people whose lives, ironically, were both blessed and cursed by the plethora of trees.

In the 1940s and 1950s, local people from outside of the reservation wanted to harvest the timber of the Klamath when the federal government considered removing trust restrictions over the tribal lands. The external pressure created strife among the tribal members and numerous problems for the Klamath Tribe, the wealthiest timberlands tribe in Indian Country. Confusion divided the Klamath until almost a generation later, when they were forced to draw upon their ancestral strength to save their identity.

The Klamath Tribe is a collection of villages or communities in the Klamath Basin. The "tribe" or "nation" is the ultimate unit of kinship relations among traditional Indian people. The "nation" represents the identity of the people. The Klamath Nation consists of all the previous fundamental elements of person, family, clan or society, and community and is sanctioned by the final element of spirituality. The Klamath Nation, like many Indian nations during the twentieth century, has withstood the extreme pressures of federal policy and the alienation imposed by American capitalism.

As a group-oriented people, the Klamath, their neighbors the Modoc, and many other Native nations have survived the onslaught of genocide, disease, and the government's termination of their legal trust status. The latter resulted from the local interest in exploiting the Klamath for their timberlands. Following World War II, the federal government introduced a new policy of terminating trust relations with the Klamath and several other tribes as a first step in assimilating Indians into the mainstream society. The U.S. Congress legislatively terminated the Klamath, but their response ultimately proved their resiliency. The integral elements of "person," "family," and "community" were seriously weakened, but the strength of the last elemental quality of Native identity—the "tribe" or "nation"—enabled the Klamath to overcome the termination policy of the Eisenhower administration and the traps of mainstream capitalism.

The Klamath originally lived as an association of smaller tribes or tribelets consisting of numerous villages. The A'ukckni (meaning Klamath Marsh), the largest and most influential group with approximately one-half of the total Klamath population, lived in twenty-nine or more communities. The Kowa'cdikni, of a village on Agency Lake, were perhaps an extension of the Klamath Marsh tribelet and became known as the Agency Lake people. The Du'kwakni, of the delta of the Williamson River, were scattered in five communities and were known locally as the Williamson River people. The Gu'mbotkni of Pelican Bay and the marsh to the north, who lived in seven or more communities, were called the Pelican Bay people, and the Iu'lalonkni, of Klamath Falls (Link River), became known as the Klamath Falls people. Thirteen additional communities lived along the eastern shore of Klamath Lake.[1] The remaining group was the Upland Klamath of the Sprague River valley.[2] These groups were related strictly according to kinship. No political mechanism united the Klamath, and at times, the communities even went to war against each other. Early Klamath social organization was fundamentally simple, and the culture reflected the influence of the Northwest Coast. The Klamath trapped beaver, otter, and rabbit and used nets to fish and take waterfowl. On many occasions, they hunted with the friendly Modoc for antelope, mule deer, and mountain sheep. A rainy climate assured flourishing forests and a steady supply of food. This comfortable, sedentary people placed little emphasis on rank and wealth, and the respected officials were the primary leader and the shaman.

The Klamath experienced major external influences when trade with other tribes developed in the Dalles after 1800, which, in turn, brought wealth, slave-holding, and social status when white settlers began to arrive. Within the next score of years, drastic sociopolitical changes affected the Klamath Tribe as whites settled in the Lost River valley and around Little Klamath Lake. Pressure from the white settlement led to land negotiations, and the Treaty of 1864 established the Klamath Reservation.[3] Learning to cope with a restricted way of life, the people constructed a small sawmill in 1870. Their objective was to supply lumber for constructing agency buildings and "box houses" for tribal officials as an example for the rest of the people.[4] Thus, the Klamath had entered the timber industry and begun selling lumber to Fort Klamath and throughout the area by 1873. Two years later, however, the commissioner of Indian affairs stated that the Supreme Court had ruled in 1873 that reservation timber was the property of the United States and that, therefore, the Klamath were selling their timber illegally.[5]

Further interest in timber increased the momentum to allot tribal lands in the Pacific Northwest, and the Klamath received allotments of 80 acres of farmland or 160 acres of grazing land per person in 1895. The government issued the last allotment in 1906. From an original 1,624 allotments involving 247,515 acres, only 1,130 allotments or less, amounting to 133,000 acres, remained as tribal land by the end of allotment in 1934.[6] The Klamath never experienced the affluence that many attained during the Roaring Twenties, and conditions only worsened during the Great Depression and in the late 1930s.

When the United States entered World War II, many Klamath fought in the armed services or participated in the war effort at home. A stream of tribal members left the reservation to work in factories during the war years and in small towns and cities after 1945. Enjoying the simple materialism and entertainment of white society, some tribal members desired to improve their lifestyles and live like Anglo-Americans. Having fought in the war or experienced life in the mainstream society, the Klamath seemed ready to integrate into America's capitalistic culture. With their daily contact with non-Indians, most relocated Klamath people began drifting away from the unity of the tribe and the reservation, and a long period of political strife ensued, pitting the progressive tribe members against the traditionalists. During the 1940s, the two fundamental interest groups divided the Klamath Tribe. Some members wanted to assimilate into the mainstream and regarded governmental trust restrictions as obstacles in their new lives. Wade Crawford, who had been appointed by BIA Commissioner John Collier as superintendent of the reservation in 1933 and served four years, led the faction that held this progressive, anti-traditional view. Removed from the superintendency in 1937 due to his unpopularity, a sardonic Crawford advocated the distribution of tribal assets on a per capita basis and the termination of the tribal government.[7] Crawford hoped to obtain support from absentee Klamath, and in 1945, he traveled to Washington as a tribal delegate to lobby Congress to enact a bill for termination.[8] On the opposing side, conservative, traditional tribal members believed that the tribe should be maintained and that tribal lands should be kept, even under trust restrictions if necessary. The antitermination group included Boyd Jackson, Dice Crain, Jesse Lee Kirk, and most members of the tribe, who actually objected to any new legislation from the federal government. Clinging to their traditional past, they faced a host of enemies—the federal government, the Wade faction, non-Klamath terminationists, and the lumber companies.

On June 5, 1947, the Klamath Business Committee debated S.R. 1222, which proposed the liquidation of the trust status for Klamath lands. The conservative faction opposing withdrawal of the trust prevailed and met again on July 31 to pass a tribal resolution against termination of the trust status. An estimated 303 families, encompassing 780 adults and children, lived on the reservation at that time. About one-tenth of the reservation was privately owned by Indians, and some 860,000 acres were held in common by the tribe; whites ultimately managed to obtain almost ninety-five percent of the 106,350 acres belonging to individual Klamath. The total standing timber on tribal lands was more than 3,780,000 board feet, with ninety-two percent of the ponderosa pine valued at more than $80 million.[9]

Crawford advocated an end to the termination discussions, and he supported a federal purchase of tribal lands to establish a national forest, plus the liquidation of additional properties. The Jackson group voiced opposition to any such legislation in hearings held in Washington and on the reservation during the early 1950s. A suggested compromise resulting from the continued discussion called for Superintendent Bert G. Courtright to draft a bill for the voluntary withdrawal of the Klamath from trust status, with each member to be paid a portion of their share in the tribal lands.[10] During the discussion, Sheldon Kirk, chairman of the tribe's General Council, intervened to form a special committee of those tribal members who wanted to retain the Klamath Reservation. The committee had eight other members—Boyd Jackson and some of his supporters. Believing that traditionalism was a thing of the past, the committee worked hard on a new tribal constitution to achieve self-government over the next two decades. In 1950, the tribe adopted the constitution but only after the provision for voluntary termination for individual tribal members became a part of it.[11] During the 1950s, the Klamath received per capita payments of $800 annually. An estimated thirty-seven percent of the tribe depended solely on this amount to live, fifty-six percent earned additional income as unskilled laborers, and only five percent held professional or technical jobs. Extra employment increased the average total income per Klamath family to $4,000 annually.[12] Given these percentages, it is clear that the Klamath would have difficulty earning their way in the white people's competitive world.

Determined to assimilate the Klamath, the federal government and the Jackson group collaborated on termination. In early May, tribal representative Boyd Jackson met with Commissioner of Indian Affairs William Brophy and Associate Commissioner William Zimmerman to vocalize support for Senate Bill 794, a measure to assist the elderly Klamath who received allotments. Known as the Klamath welfare bill, the measure offered financial assistance to the Klamath who required funding to develop their properties.[13] Congress discussed the bill but deferred further action due to indecision on how to terminate the trust relationship between the Klamath Tribe and the United States.

Facing a stalemate, Congress entertained other bills calling for termination of trust restrictions for all Indians. Caught in the congressional momentum, the Klamath and the Menominee of Wisconsin, both woodland tribes, were used by the federal government as the leading examples to other tribes of Native groups with no federal restrictions. Congress pushed forward with additional Klamath legislation. Two similar bills, J.R. 2165 and H.R. 1113, supported the termination position of the federal government and drew the attention of the Klamath. Wade Crawford testified that "there are different [Indian] groups—different classes, throughout the United States. It is impossible to draw legislation ... that would correct all the wrongs and give the Indians what they want and need on the different reservations ... to bring the Indians into full citizenship."[14] A determined Crawford advised that if Indians in different age-groups were surveyed regarding trust removal, the results would indicate that other advanced Indians like the Klamath could be successfully assimilated. Reviewing his own tribe, he suggested that young people from 18 to 35 or 40 years of age would be the best candidates for assimilation. Crawford believed that this age-group could adopt the values of the American mainstream and that the changing lifestyle of the Klamath's off-reservation experience suggested assimilation would succeed.

Supporting the proassimilation Klamath, Senator Wayne Morse of Oregon introduced a bill on their behalf. On May 2, 1947, he submitted Senate Bill 1222 in Congress "to remove restrictions on the properties and monies belonging to the individual enrolled members of the Klamath Indian reservation ... to confer complete citizenship upon such Indians."[15] Following World War II, the Klamath Reservation consisted of the Modoc, the Klamath, and the Yahooskin Band of Snake Indians who lived in southern Oregon. Senator Morse proposed that all tribal members be "permitted as rapidly as possible to assume all the rights and prerogatives, the privileges of all of the citizens."[16] Some members had already partially assimilated into the American mainstream and attended school and socialized with whites who lived near the reservation, so the federal government assumed that the Klamath and other tribes who were familiar with white ways could take total control of their own affairs.

Crawford and a few ardent proassimilationists had influenced Senator Morse to act on behalf of the entire tribe. However, although the Klamath had superficially entered the materialistic world of the white man, they were not psychologically prepared for that world. Like their ancestors who had traded with whites long ago, the people temporarily enjoyed the alien materialism and decided to pursue it without regard for the educational and occupational qualifications that would be required for success in the white culture.

Nonetheless, in the aftermath of World War II, the prevailing attitude was that the Klamath were capable of living in the mainstream. On March 29, 1948, President Harry Truman signed House resolution 2502, creating a new act authorizing individual payments of $500 to Klamath tribal members from the tribe's capital reserve fund. The Treasury Department paid another $200 to each Klamath veteran of World War II. The amount of money withdrawn from the Klamath's account prompted President Truman to advise the tribe on wise spending. "I urge the Klamath Indians to give deep thought to the use of their resources, both individual and tribal, in ways that will insure their future security and progress," said the president.[17]

Truman referred to the Klamath's natural resource of timber, indigenous to the area and available in abundance—the vast resource upon which all the policy discussions and the Klamath's appetite for materialism were predicated. With the termination of the trust status regarding these properties and the restrictions lifted from moneys, the Klamath would hold complete control over what they owned. Technically, they were ready to enter the free enterprise system, but realistically, they lacked the sociocultural experience to think capitalistically and execute competitively.

The election of Republican Dwight D. Eisenhower as president in 1952 only added to the momentum to terminate the Klamath and other Indian tribes. Forced with accepting termination, tribal members disagreed over the procedure to realize that goal and wondered what their ultimate fate would be. During fiscal year 1953, the federal government held consultations about reduced government participation in tribal affairs with the Klamath, with other tribal groups in western Oregon and in California, with the Alabama-Coushatta of Texas, with the Chitamacha of Louisiana, and with the Prairie Island Band of Minnesota. The discussion of reduced government participation served as a prelude to total withdrawal of the United States from its trust relations with the Indian nations. The Interior Department reported additional meetings to discuss termination with the Osage of Oklahoma, the Menominee of Wisconsin, the Colville and the Spokane of Washington, and the Flathead of Montana.[18] But in the following months, the federal government focused more on terminating the Klamath Tribe, most likely because some tribal members wanted that. However, one Klamath member said that the tribe had persuaded a congressional committee to visit the reservation and that the committee found a substandard educational level and little evidence for self-government.[19] The Klamath were simply not ready for termination, although the government scheduled them as one of the first tribes to undergo trust withdrawal.

On January 15, 1954, the Klamath General Council supported the Crawford faction and Senator Arthur Watkins, the congressional leader of termination, and his joint subcommittee in their efforts to push on with the removal of the Klamath's trust status with the United States. To pressure the tribal voters, Watkins's subcommittee deliberately withheld a $2.6 million judgment from the Klamath, an old trick from the 1800s that had been used to force tribes to agree to land cession treaties by refusing to release annuities and supplies promised in earlier treaties.

Over the following months, the Klamath termination movement reached the secretary of the interior's office. On August 10, 1954, Assistant Interior Secretary Orme Lewis recommended termination of federal responsibility for the Klamath Tribe in Oregon. Lewis stated, "It is our belief that the Klamath Tribe and the individual members thereof have ... sufficient skill and ability to manage their own affairs without special Federal assistance."[20] Lewis observed that intermarriages with non-Indians and cooperative work and association with non-Indian neighbors in adult education, technical assistance programs, and public schools, especially since World War II, had prepared the Klamath for integration into the mainstream society. The termination policy was now in full force.

On the same day, Deputy Attorney General William Rogers wrote to Rowland Hughes, director of the Bureau of the Budget, that sixty small Indian bands, tribes, and groups living in the timberlands of western Oregon could also undergo termination; He recommended that President Eisenhower sign the termination legislation,[21] and

Senate Bills 2745 and 2746 were soon drafted to satisfy this request. The government deemed that these groups and the Klamath were self-sustaining since the Klamath generated an annual gross income of $2 million from their tribal timberlands; the fact that ten percent of the Klamath families required some form of welfare assistance was ignored. Two days later, Roger Jones, assistant director for legislative reference of the Budget Bureau, informed President Eisenhower that his office had studied the monetary matters of the tribes and now supported Senate Bills 2745 and 2746 to terminate the Klamath and other groups in Oregon. Such swift, paternalistic actions at the federal level evoked criticism from the antitermination faction, but it came too late.[22]

Releasing the Klamath Tribe from trust status would involve 1,624 allotments encompassing 247,515 acres. In the closing months of the year, a conciliatory Congress asked the Bureau of Indian Affairs to draft another bill to satisfy both the Wade and Jackson factions. In the final hours of the 1954 congressional session, the debate over the Klamath termination finally yielded the Klamath Termination Act (Public Law 587). But trouble lay ahead as the Klamath Tribe finalized its tribal membership in the following years and worked to meet the termination deadline. This preparation involved an estimated remaining 1,130 allotments with approximately 133,000 acres, encompassing a large expanse of forest.[23]

Outspoken conservationists claimed that the termination of trust limitations would allow lumber barons to seize Klamath properties and cut the timber for quick profits. Meanwhile, in another part of Indian Country, the Menominee in Wisconsin were in a similar situation. They were already experiencing mismanagement and were plagued by outsiders wanting their timberlands. Conservationists in both Oregon and Wisconsin believed that unmonitored cutting would permanently damage the lands and destroy the natural habitats of many animals. Previously, the Bureau of Indian Affairs had regulated timber harvesting in both regions, but the withdrawal of trust restrictions also meant completely removing this responsibility from the BIA. Harold B. Anthony, deputy director of the American Museum of Natural History, expressed considerable concern about the wildlife and recommended that the Klamath be involved in wildlife conservation efforts. Anthony believed that, if home environments were destroyed, the life patterns of the birds and other animals would be disrupted and their populations would be decreased. Aware of the political repercussions, he warned that the situation would provoke conservationists to lobby their representatives in Congress to protect the environment and wildlife.[24] Ultimately, after assessing the problem, the conservationists recommended a training program in forest management for the Klamath as a part of the preparation for termination.[25]

Like their ancestors, the twentieth-century Klamath would at last be free of government restrictions. They were invited to live in the white society's world of individualism and materialism. In preparation for this limitless freedom, the Klamath attempted to finalize their membership rolls for distribution of the tribal assets. The tribe considered its own people on the reservation as the true members and closed the tribal roll, although many persons traveled long distances to claim they were members in the tribe in anticipation of receiving substantial per capita payments. In the end, the tribe added 270 new members. Estimates of tribal assets ranged from $60 million to $100 million, creating rumors that each tribal member would receive an enormous sum, from $25,000 to $40,000.[26] Fearing possible chaos for individual Klamath, the government appointed three local private-management specialists—Thomas Watters, William Philips, and Eugene Favell—to supervise property appraisals and manage the tribe's business affairs.

The Bureau of Indian Affairs anticipated that, upon receiving their portions of tribal wealth, the Klamath would use local public services just like other Americans. But feeling socially and culturally alienated, the Klamath, especially the full-bloods, were reluctant to do so. Furthermore, mainstream public officials and businesspeople did not always accept the Klamath as their social equals. Religious groups who knew the Klamath and were sensitive to their dilemma immediately criticized the government for misleading the tribe in this regard. They believed that the Klamath lacked sufficient education and business experience in negotiating their timberlands with their shrewd white counterparts. They also understood that the sociocultural values of American society emphasized education and economic status, which were less important to traditional Klamath.

To avoid instantly thrusting the Klamath into the mainstream, the Bureau of Indian Affairs carefully implemented a federal procedure for termination. Again, the BIA drew criticism. The concern for protecting the Klamath aroused complaints from progressive, protermination tribal members who interpreted this as paternalism. Tribal elder Wade Crawford, a member of the Klamath Investigating Coordinating Committee, testified before the Senate Appropriations Committee that the tribe wanted more participation in supervising its own business affairs to prepare for the termination deadline of 1958.[27] Federal officials acknowledged the tribe's difficult position as they worked to direct the BIA management specialists who supervised tribal leases, timber-cutting planning, sales, and other business matters. Overseeing the complicated business affairs of the tribe required extensive time as the Klamath legislation proceeded to congressional committees. During a hearing before the House Interior Subcommittee of Indian Affairs, Senator Richard Neuberger of Oregon requested an amendment to the Klamath Termination Act to extend the 1958 deadline. A sensitive Neuberger argued that the Klamath needed more time to understand the law's provisions and to settle their individual business affairs connected with the tribe's timberlands and other natural resources.[28]

Growing apprehension over termination led to increased factionalism among the already divided Klamath Tribe as a new coalition emerged, composed of members of the Klamath Information and Education Office, which had been created by the State Department of Education as advised under the Klamath Termination Act. Now, the tribe was split into three factions: the protermination Crawford faction, the Wade antiterminationists, and the new coalition from the Klamath Information and Education Office. The newest faction, trying to remain apolitical, urged tribal members to investigate issues resulting from termination so that individual Klamath might decide intelligently to request withdrawal of the trust status. Most members of this group had remained apart from the Wade-Jackson troubles, and they began creating a new civic image for the Klamath Tribe.[29]

Internally, termination created confusion and an emotional maelstrom for the Klamath people. Composed of many full-bloods, the group remained cautious about severing relations with the federal government. Younger Klamath generally supported termination; they believed that it offered financial benefits and freedom from federal restraints. Older Klamath expressed ambivalence since they did not fully understand termination. Recognizing the Klamath's concerns, the BIA reassured the elders that they would have continued trust protection and access to government services, but the whole situation confused and frustrated the tribal members. Their unsettled emotional state was substantiated in a report issued by Stanford University Research Institute, which acknowledged that the Klamath were misinformed about the final termination date of 1958. Of 100 Klamath interviewed, only 14 believed that the tribe had requested trust withdrawal, and just 6 thought that they were more advanced than other tribes scheduled for termination. The report also disclosed that the tribal members did not understand the Klamath Termination Act. On behalf of the tribe, two of the three management specialists appointed by the BIA, Watters and Favell, visited the Bureau of Indian Affairs in Washington to ask for protective amendments to the act. They requested additional time for preparing the tribal members and some form of federal protection guarantee for the elders.[30]

The new BIA commissioner, Glenn L. Emmons, a banker from New Mexico, held a hearing with the Oregon and Washington tribes on September 17–18, 1956. To check on the progress of the tribes, Emmons also held several hearings throughout Indian Country. With only two years remaining before the termination deadline, he discovered that many Klamath believed termination was so unusual a move that it would not occur, especially when delays, disagreements, and the various views of diverse interest groups appeared to undermine the federal government's experiment to integrate the Klamath.

More important, the Klamath were not sufficiently educated for this move, although many embraced the materialism of the mainstream. The lack of substantial educational achievement appeared to be due to a typical disinterest in education.[31] The Klamath had not embraced the idea a good education was required to qualify for a well-paying job that would be needed to purchase necessities of life and other material items.

The future did not look promising for the Klamath or for all those affected by the termination policy. On October 2, 1956, Montana senator James E. Murray, chairperson of the Committee on Interior and Insular Affairs, wrote Colorado senator Eugene D. Milkin about the concerns of Oregon citizens. The local population anticipated that the Klamath Termination Act would endanger both the Klamath and the entire economy of the Klamath Basin. They feared that the removal of trust status over rich Klamath timberlands would unleash too much lumber on the open market, potentially causing timber prices to fall to a dangerously low level. As August 1958—the termination deadline— approached, their fears and those of all concerned parties intensified.

The timber crises even overshadowed other very real problems facing the Klamath, such as the social and cultural impacts of assimilation and the effects of prejudice and racism that they might encounter. Changes affecting the Klamath, the animal life, the natural environment, the local whites, nearby tribes, and the economics of the Klamath Basin threatened to have a ripple effect on the entire Pacific Northwest. Stalling for time in order to find a solution to these problems, Senator Neuberger introduced a bill in the Senate to delay the Klamath deadline for eighteen months. He received collegial support when Representative Albert Ulman cosponsored the bill in the House. The concern of the local citizens confirmed Neuberger's caution that if the Klamath's pine timber was sold recklessly, the entire southeastern Oregon economy might collapse.[32] Hearings for the bill were being held when another bill, H.R. 2471, was introduced, calling for a delay of termination. The minutes of the meetings between Commissioner of Indian Affairs Emmons and the old and new members of the Klamath Executive Committee substantiated the senator's fears about erratic timber cuttings. These minutes also reflected the Klamath's inadequate understanding of the legislation. Most important, only a small number of tribal members realized that the Klamath Termination Act would end tribal benefits and that no more per capita payments would follow after final termination.[33] Over the next several months, the best move seemed to be to delay the deadline. Consequently, the BIA asked Congress to amend the law to postpone the deadline to August 31, 1961.[34]

The whole issue surrounding the Klamath provoked criticism from many individuals. Concerned government officials, such as Senator Neuberger and others who knew the Klamath and their affairs, were constantly blamed by the news media for the tribe's situation—the termination of the richest tribe holding timberlands in America. Critics accused Neuberger of harboring ulterior motives for delaying the termination deadline. *The Oregonian*, a local newspaper, reported that the senator had denied a hearing for Klamath members who opposed a delay, although one meeting had actually been held specifically for them at Klamath Falls on October 18, 1956.[35] Speaking in his own defense, Neuberger faulted other federal officials, claiming the Klamath problem was "a legacy from the Republican 83rd Congress which hatched the hasty and (I think) unwise termination bill, with [Interior Secretary Douglas] McKay's consent."[36]

A small number of federal officials like Neuberger sincerely wanted to assist and protect Indian Americans, although the terminationists outnumbered them. A growing bloc of terminationist members of Congress and bureaucrats felt pressure from constituents who wanted the Indian lands. As the Klamath case became more controversial, the federal government moved cautiously to dispossess the Klamath from their forest areas. During late May, Secretary of the Interior Fred Seaton warned presidential assistant Sherman Adams that termination endangered the Klamath's huge forest reserve, "one of the country's most valuable ponderosa pine forests."[37] Seaton added that the Klamath Marsh, its water conservation, and the wildlife population of the Klamath Basin would be ecologically damaged. Simultaneously, he said, acquiring a fair price for the tribe posed a serious problem for the Klamath, with possible consequences affecting the image of the Bureau of Indian Affairs and harming the local Oregon economy.

Two days later, Sherman Adams wrote to Governor Elmo Smith of Oregon about federal concerns and the congressional amendment to the Klamath legislation. Considering the impact on the Klamath, the House of Representatives debated the extent to which the government should protect Klamath minors and others who might require future assistance to manage their assets. Both Congress and the Department of the Interior agreed to extend the deadline for termination to August 31, 1961.[38] Adams also expressed the hope that the government's concern would relieve the governor's worry about available Klamath timberlands.

At the same time, the delay hindered other tribal members who were ready for termination and wished to enter the free enterprise system. These business-oriented individuals categorically supported the termination policy of the Eisenhower administration, and they argued against tribal trust status. Their view added to the developing factionalism among the Klamath. The group of conservative full-bloods led by Boyd Jackson opposed the proterminationists, but most of the people were mixed-bloods who worked and/or lived in nearby white communities, and they supported the sale of tribal assets for per capita distribution.[39] The mainstream society had heavily influenced them, and many Klamath had attended public schools since 1927. They appeared competent to handle their own business affairs, but this proved to be a false assumption. When the Klamath Termination Act passed, for example, the academic performance of forty percent of the 225 Klamath students attending public schools in Klamath County was not satisfactory enough for promotion to the next grade. From 1934 to 1947, only 10 Klamath had graduated from high schools in Klamath County. Furthermore, an estimated two-thirds of the 270 able-bodied males between thirteen and the early twenties remained undereducated.[40]

The 1950s witnessed materialistic change among the Klamath, adding to the tribe's vulnerability. During December 1957, the Indian Education and Training Program produced a report entitled "Termination of Federal Supervision Over the Klamath Reservation" that addressed this issue. In appearance, the Klamath seemed no different from their non-Indian neighbors; they lived like non-Indians and spoke English very well. But as the report revealed, they experienced maladjustment because they were socially unaccepted by the local non-Indian community. Yet the prospect of leaving the quiet routine of reservation life for a new urban lifestyle intrigued those with adventurous spirits. Even small towns excited the Indian youths, luring them away from traditionalism and encouraging them to indulge in the mainstream culture. An alarmingly high juvenile delinquency rate existed on the Klamath Reservation, where idleness and easy money lured the youth away from school. Realizing this, management specialists employed by the government developed the Tribal Management Plan. Their efforts focused on urbanizing younger Klamath, particularly those from eighteen to thirty years of age, who were not set in their ways and could adjust to urban life.[41]

Daily contact with white society increased alienation from traditionalism, creating a dichotomy between those members who wanted to remain in the tribe and those who believed that termination held advantages. Such a dichotomy would not be resolved until the mainstream culture socially accepted the Klamath. The Klamath situation represented the classic case of tribal traditionalism versus modern life; and tribal identity hung in the balance.

Sensitive to the Klamath's problems, a resourceful Neuberger proposed a congressional amendment to the Klamath Termination Act calling for the United States to spend $100 million or more to buy the tribe's properties at a fair price. His proposed measure requested federal management of the properties during the business transition, involving the transfer of the traditionalists' shares to a tribal corporation or a trustee. Neuberger planned for the U.S. Forest Service to manage the timberlands and the Wildlife Department to supervise the marshlands. The Neuberger plan called for the government to play a protective role in regard to the interests of the tribe, wildlife, and non-Indians in the Klamath Basin.[42]

Aware of the increased bureaucracy created by the entire affair, Neuberger sponsored a three-day hearing in Oregon during October 1957 to listen to the various interest groups as he prepared his bill. Several witnesses (particularly those who favored private enterprise) voiced opposition to having federal agencies manage the land. The Western Forest Industries Association and the Weyerhaeuser Timber Company guaranteed the Klamath a higher price for their land. Eager for Klamath timber, the companies became a threat to non-Indians, too. Civic groups from Klamath Falls and from chapters of the Izaak Walton League and the Audubon Society sided with the Neuberger plan as well, for Klamath timberlands were estimated to cover 800,000 acres of prime ponderosa pine (which would yield approximately 4 billion board feet of lumber) and 15,689 acres of marsh and grazing land.[43]

The enormous amount of timber that could potentially enter the market motivated all interest groups as the new termination deadline approached. Local capitalists and the federal government were in competition for the Klamath timberlands. Under pressure, the Department of the Interior wanted to sell only timberlands belonging to the Klamath who chose termination after receiving their individual lands. Two stipulations were made. First, the buyers had to agree to manage the forest land on a sustained-yield basis. Second, if this condition was not met, the Klamath were to be paid the government-appraised value of the property, and the secretary of agriculture would incorporate the timberlands as national forests.

The distribution of lands, like allotment under the Dawes Act years earlier, presented further problems involving the Confederated Tribes of the Warm Springs Reservation, also located in Oregon. Unlike the Klamath, the Confederated Tribes wanted to keep their tribal lands in trust status. Relations between the tribes became complicated due to intermarriages, and the government had to determine the memberships of the two tribes in order to sort out ownership of the tribal lands since protermination Klamath desired absolute ownership of their individual properties.[44] In addition, the Modoc, who were originally a part of the Klamath Reservation, learned from the BIA area office at Portland that they would share in the disbursement of the land sale moneys. The Modoc interest derived from a treaty signed with the Klamath in 1864, ceding land to the United States.[45]

The developing complications involved in termination in the Klamath Basin radiated from the Pacific Northwest to Washington, D.C., and compelled the federal government to act. During January 1958, Secretary of the Interior Fred Seaton, whose department included the Bureau of Indian Affairs, proposed an amendment to the Klamath Termination Act. Seaton stressed that the Klamath forest lands had to be protected, and he warned of the threat posed by surplus timberlands coming on the market. He also emphasized the significance of the nesting and feeding grounds for the wildlife. An estimated 15,689 acres of marshlands would be obtained, preserving a migrating area for redhead, canvasback, and ruddy ducks.[46]

At this point, Neuberger's and Seaton's amendments were in competition, causing further confusion for the Klamath. In Senator Neuberger's view, the government had not resolved the Klamath problem. With time running out before the termination deadline, he wanted to submit his bill seeking a delay of that deadline. Undersecretary of the Interior Hatfield Chilson compared the two amendments in terms of the best interests of the Klamath Tribe. He found that the Interior's bill called for selling seventy percent of the Klamath's timberlands based on the number of terminated tribal members and that Neuberger's amendment stipulated selling all tribal lands. The Interior's measure authorized private individuals to purchase the tribal timberlands at the appraised value, allowing the government to save a good deal of money. The Neuberger bill allowed only the federal government to obtain the timberland, at a high cost to the taxpayers.[47] The concern for wildlife added to the termination problem. And then, another issue emerged regarding the actual value of the timber-land areas for their subsurface minerals.

While the undersecretary studied the amendments, Senator Neuberger asked if the Interior Department had consulted the Klamath or the management specialists hired by the government during the drafting of the Interior's bill. His suspicion was based on the fact that part of the bill setting a period for further study and planning had been eliminated. Neuberger claimed that it was replaced with a "crash sale" of tribal properties without the Klamath's knowledge. Further-more, a per capita payment of $250 that had been included in the bill raised his doubts.[48]

The Klamath also questioned the accuracy of the appraisal. Officials of the Klamath Federal Council and Klamath Executive Committee stated before the Senate Indian Subcommittee that the appraisals were underestimated at $118 million. Tribal officials figured their estimates at $209 million, contending that not all Klamath resources were appraised: Subsurface resources, pumice, titanium, diatomaceous earth, water, and power resources were left out.[49] The subsurface minerals only added to the problem of establishing an actual value for Klamath land.

Furthermore, the Interior's bill eliminated the purchaser's agreement to sustained-yield cutting. Robert Holmes, the newly elected governor of Oregon, joined the Klamath in opposing the Interior's bill. He warned that the state's economy would be deluged with Klamath timber and that the Indians would not receive a fair price.[50] Considering the opposition from the governor and the Klamath, authors of the Interior's bill ultimately reinstated the sustained-yield provision and increased the amount that the Klamath would receive for their timberlands. This offer satisfied Neuberger, who then dismissed his own bill.

In January 1959, the Department of the Interior finally announced that Klamath lands had been appraised at $90,791,123. After the sale of tribal assets, the government estimated that 1,659 terminated Klamath would receive $44,000 per capita. Furthermore, the Interior Department announced that a revolving fund would make loans available to Klamath possessing at least one-quarter Indian blood who agreed to withdraw from the tribe.[51] Undoubtedly, this provision persuaded many Klamath to support the withdrawal of trust relations with the United States.

In an effort to protect the business interests of the Klamath, the Department of the Interior announced on March 4 that the National Bank of Portland, Oregon, would assume the trusteeship of Klamath property. This action called for the bank to replace the Bureau of Indian Affairs as trustee of business matters for the 473 members remaining on the tribal roll. Deeds for approximately 140,000 acres of land and $737,608.61 in cash were turned over to the bank; but problems soon developed.[52] L. B. Staver, vice president of the National Bank and executive trust officer, explained that the bank had experienced difficulty in supervising Klamath affairs because of the complex details of tribal members' business and tribal contracts with the government and outside interests.[53] These problems jeopardized the entire economy of the Klamath Basin. Simultaneously, termination procedures delayed Klamath timber sales to area mills.[54] As more delays occurred, local mill owners worried that the Klamath's problems would not be resolved soon enough to prevent them from going bankrupt.

The Klamath Termination Act, Public Law 587, terminated federal supervision over the property of the Klamath Tribe, which also included the Modoc and the Yahooskin Band of Snake Indians. The law released all tribal property that contained rich timberlands, consisting of some 590,000 acres capable of producing 3.8 billion board feet of commercial lumber. Klamath landowners were undoubtedly prime targets for opportunists when the government dissolved the tribe's trust relationship.

The termination of the Klamath, the Menominee, and other tribes disturbed the Association on American Indians (AAIA), a national Indian support organization in New York that adamantly opposed all termination bills introduced in Congress. A growing number of critics also expressed opposition, claimed that the real goal of termination was the exploitation of Indian lands for their natural resources. In the following weeks, Interior Department officials announced that Klamath lands could not be sold before termination was complete. Necessary postponement of the sales prompted the Interior Department to propose legislation that would permit the BIA to make interest-free loans to the terminating Klamath. Department officials estimated that from 250 to 275 Klamath families would require financial assistance. Regarding tribal members of less than one-fourth Klamath blood, approximately 253 members, or fifteen percent of the tribe, would be allowed to file for these loans.[55] Congress finally established that each withdrawing member would receive $43,000 in one per capita payment. An estimated seventy-eight percent of the Klamath voted for cash settlements, and the government distributed approximately $68 million to the Klamath Tribe.

In the ensuing years, the termination of trust status caused confusion and financial mismanagement among the Klamath. When they decided on an individual basis to accept termination, originally set for

April 1958, 70 percent of the Klamath elected to withdraw. No less than 48.9 percent were defined as protected under provisions of the termination legislation, and an additional 13.6 percent who were deemed competent to manage their own affairs decided to remain under a group trust operated by the United States National Bank. Another 18.3 percent were absentee members to be subjected to federal supervision.[56]

Tribes that, like the Klamath, possessed a large amount of natural resources created complications. Such situations frequently overwhelmed the Bureau of Indian Affairs. Each tribe presented a unique situation, and the termination policy was not applicable to all tribes. Furthermore, the size of the population, amount of assets, types of properties, and various logistics caused more concern for the BIA.[57]

The unfortunate legacy of the termination policy inherited from the Eighty-third Congress—and from Dillon S. Myer, Arthur Watkins, and other staunch terminationists—plagued later humanitarians who tried to assist the Indian people, such as Commissioner of Indian Affairs Glenn Emmons. Other government officials, among them Senator Neuberger, remained sincere in their support of the terminated groups, but the controversy surrounding the termination of various Indian tribes tarnished their reputations. In retrospect, they appeared to be a part of the bloc of Western representatives who sought Indian lands and their natural resources.

During the Eisenhower years in the 1950s, thirty-five California rancherias (small reservations), the Oklahoma Choctaw, the Oregon Klamath, the Wisconsin Menominee, and the mixed-bloods of the Uintah-Ouray of Utah were scheduled for final termination in 1961. Throughout the entire termination period, which lasted into the 1960s, 109 cases of termination were initiated, affecting a minimum of 1,362,155 acres and 11,466 individuals.[58] This congressional movement and the BIA's support of it spelled the end of the special status that many tribes had held, based on old agreements between sovereign nations.

The termination of the Klamath brought only sadness to the Native people. In the Klamath Basin, the lumber companies became the real beneficiaries of the termination. Although federal officials expressed concern about the exploitation of the Klamath, the lumber interests in southwestern Oregon forced actions to resolve termination and thereby free Klamath timber. In the region, lumber companies, banks, and numerous merchants depended on the Klamath timber cuttings for their capitalistic livelihood. Although conservationists fought to prevent the lifting of restrictions on Klamath lands, they, too, were more concerned with the land itself than with the people who inhabited it. They argued that removal of trust restrictions would open up wilderness areas to lumber companies and that wildlife breeding and feeding grounds would be destroyed.[59]

On an individual basis, Klamath termination brought monetary windfalls from timber sales to tribal members—and the many repercussions that followed. All the Klamath receiving large per capita payments became fair game for local merchants, who sold them automobiles, televisions, and other goods at inflated prices. Unfamiliar with exploitative capitalism, many Klamath people were vulnerable to manipulation when dealing with unscrupulous merchants and opportunists. Numerous accounts reveal that unethical individuals and lumber companies tricked the Klamath out of their properties and their wealth. The Klamath experience was but another chapter in the old story of Indians being cheated—another tribe, another time but with the same results.

Termination impacted the Klamath Tribe in two critical ways. In the first place, daily cultural contact with white society after World II caused a sociocultural change from traditionalism to quasi-assimilation into the mainstream. Ironically, with the federal government's policy of dismantling tribes, many Klamath individualized themselves like whites due to cultural materialism and the decrease of traditional communal norms in their lives. They then experienced the worst effects of assimilation. Widespread drinking began on the former reservation, the family unit started to disintegrate, and loss of identity followed as members of the Klamath Tribe lost their perspective on life. Klamath youths cut their hair in ducktails and donned leather jackets like the young people in the mainstream, unknowingly forcing a generation gap as well as a cultural gap with the traditional elders. Undoubtedly, cultural contact with the mainstream altered the individual Klamath's outlook and personality.[60]

The Klamath as a tribe faced their greatest test in this post–World War II period. As they became a part of mainstream America, change occurred in two ways: under force, which made transformation slow or almost impossible, and voluntarily, which accelerated transformation. After experiencing the materialism of the mainstream, the Klamath Tribe accepted termination of their trust status as a tribe and severed legal ties with the United States.

On the verge of de-tribalization, the Klamath started a restoration process in the late 1960s, beginning with their legal status. Presumably, the fear of permanently losing their identity convinced the Klamath of the need for tribal restoration during the rise of a nationwide Indian pride movement called Red Power.

For the rest of the 1960s and the 1970s, influenced by Red Power activism, the Klamath Tribe struggled to recover from termination, and a retribalization effort ensued. As precedent, the terminated Menominee of Wisconsin were restored to federal tribal status in 1973. On August 27, 1986, Public Law 99-398 restored the federal recognition of the Klamath as a tribe, with their former trust status. The Klamath experience with termination and the exploitation of their timberlands is an example of a tribal struggle to hold on to natural resources. Despite the economic potential of their rich timberlands, the Klamath were not equipped to do well within a modern capitalistic society, especially since many tribal members were struggling to reconcile the conflicting values of the traditional community and of the American mainstream into which they hoped to assimilate.

Nonetheless, the Klamath as a group have done well in recovering from the sad episode. Other tribes have not been so fortunate. Some are still struggling to hold onto their natural resources in the face of white greed. In the Great Lakes region of Wisconsin, for instance, the Chippewa fought to retain their traditional fishing rights. This conflict over fishing also illustrated the importance of clans in connecting life and nature in the Chippewa culture.

NOTES

1. Leslie Spier, "Klamath Ethnography," *University of California Publications in American Archaeology and Ethnology* 30 (1930): 22–23.
2. Theodore Stern, *The Klamath Tribe: A People and Their Reservation* (Seattle and London: University of Washington Press, 1966), p. 19.
3. Theodore Stern, "The Klamath Indians and the Treaty of 1846," *Oregon Historical Quarterly* 57 (1956): 229–273.
4. Stern, *Klamath Tribe*, p. 55.
5. Ibid., p. 62.
6. Ibid., pp. 132 and 145.
7. Verne F. Ray, "The Klamath Indians and Their Forest Resources," Exhibit R–1, Docket No. 100-b–2, Indian Claims Commission, Federal Archives and Records Center, Seattle, Washington.
8. Stern, *Klamath Tribe*, pp. 250–251.
9. Verne F. Ray, "The Klamath Oppose Liquidation," *The American Indian* 4, no. 4 (1948): 16–20.
10. Stern, *Klamath Tribe*, p. 62.
11. Ibid., p. 250.
12. "Preliminary Planning for Termination of Federal Control Over the Klamath Tribe," report by Stanford Research Institute, Menlo Park, Calif., 1956, pp. 20–22.
13. Statement by William A. Brophy in a meeting with William Zimmerman and Boyd Jackson, May 6, 1946, Box 15, William Brophy Papers, Harry S.

Truman Presidential Library, Independence, Missouri.

14. U.S. Congress, House Committee on Public Lands, "Emancipation of Indians," Hearings Before the Subcommittee of the House Committee on Public Lands on J.R. 2958, H.R. 2165, and H.R. 1113, 80th Cong., 1st sess., 1947, 79, 80, 84, and 104–106.

15. Senator Wayne Morse of Oregon introduced Senate Bill 1222 in the Eightieth Congress, 1st sess., May 2, 1947, Box 21, William G. Stigler Papers, Carl Albert Congressional Center, University of Oklahoma, Norman.

16. U.S. Congress, House, Congressman Morse speaking for termination of the Klamath Indians, S. 1222, 80th Cong., 1st sess, May 2, 1947, *Congressional Record* 93: 4458.

17. Harry S. Truman to Julius A. Krug, March 29, 1948, Box 397, Official File, Harry S. Truman Papers, Harry S. Truman Presidential Library, Independence, Missouri.

18. "Reduced Federal Participation in Indian Affairs Reported," news release, Department of Interior, June 30, 1953, Box 43, White House File, Philleo Nash Papers, Harry S. Truman Presidential Library, Independence, Missouri.

19. "Concurrent Resolution 108 and Treaties," statement by Klamath member, ca. 1953, Box 368, Accession Number 68-A–2045, Record Group 75, Federal Archives and Records Center, Suitland, Maryland.

20. Orme Lewis to Rowland R. Hughes, August 10, 1954, Box 12, Bill File, Dwight D. Eisenhower Presidential Library, Abilene, Kansas.

21. William P. Rogers to Rowland R. Hughes, August 10, 1954, Box 12, Bill File, Dwight D. Eisenhower Presidential Library, Abilene, Kansas.

22. Roger W. Jones to Dwight D. Eisenhower, August 12, 1954, Box 12, Bill File, Dwight D. Eisenhower Presidential Library, Abilene, Kansas.

23. Stern, *Klamath Tribe*, p. 145.

24. Harold B. Anthony to John Collier, July 13, 1954, John Collier Papers, microfilm, series 3, Reel 33, Newberry Library, Chicago.

25. J. P. Kinney, "Will the Indian Make the Grade?" *American Forests* 60 (December 1954): 24–27, 52–53.

26. Harold E. Fey, "The Indian and the Law," *The Christian Century* 72 (March 9, 1955): 297–299.

27. Excerpts of testimony of Wade Crawford Before Senate Appropriations Committee, March 15, 1956, Box RN–12, Richard L. Neuberger Papers, Special Collections, University of Oregon Library, Eugene.

28. Statement by Senator Richard L. Neuberger of Oregon to House Interior Subcommittee on Indian Affairs, n.d., Richard L. Neuberger Papers, Special Collections, University of Oregon Library, Eugene.

29. Stern, *Klamath Tribe*, p. 250.

30. "Question Validity of Klamath Plan," *The Christian Century* 73 (July 25, 1956): 882–883, and Susan Hood, "Termination of the Klamath Tribe in Oregon," *Ethnohistory* 19 (Fall 1972): 379–392.

31. Hearings with Washington and Oregon Tribes, held by Commissioner of Indian Affairs Glenn L. Emmons, September 17–18, 1956, Box 3, Glenn L. Emmons Papers, Special Collections, Zimmerman Library, University of New Mexico, Albuquerque.

32. Senate Bill 469 was sponsored by Senators Richard L. Neuberger and Wayne Morse, H.R. 258 was introduced by Senator Albert Ullman, and H.R. 2471 was introduced by Congressman Miller, Statement by Senator Richard Neuberger, October 1956, Box RN–12, Richard L. Neuberger Papers, Special Collections, University of Oregon Library, Eugene.
33. Minutes of Meeting Between Commissioner of Indian Affairs and Old and New Members of Klamath Tribe Executive Committee, Portland, Oregon, October 29, 1956, Box 2, Klamath Agency Files, no acc. no., Record Group 75, Federal Archives and Records Center, Seattle, Washington.
34. "Postponement of Sales of Klamath Tribal Lands Recommended by Seaton," news release by the Department of Interior, January 7, 1957, Box RN–12, Richard L. Neuberger Papers, Special Collections, University of Oregon Library, Eugene.
35. Richard L. Neuberger to Editor of *The Oregonian*, Portland, Oregon, February 26, 1957, Richard L. Neuberger Papers, Special Collections, University of Oregon Library, Eugene.
36. Richard L. Neuberger to Al McCready, February 26, 1957, Box RN–12, Richard L. Neuberger Papers, Special Collections, University of Oregon Library, Eugene.
37. Fred A. Seaton to Sherman Adams, May 27, 1957, Box 618, Official File, White House Central Files, Dwight D. Eisenhower Library, Abilene, Kansas.
38. Sherman Adams to Elmo Smith, May 29, 1957, Box 618, Dwight D. Eisenhower Library, Abilene, Kansas.
39. Mrs. Wade Crawford, "An Indian Talks Back," *American Forests* 63 (July 1957): 4, 48–50.
40. Hood, "Termination of the Klamath," p. 382.
41. Data on Termination of Federal Supervision Over the Klamath Indian Reservation, compiled by Rex Putnam, December 31, 1956, Box 110, Bureau of Indian Affairs Correspondence, acc. no. 68-A–4937, Record Group 75, Federal Archives and Records Center, Suitland, Maryland.
42. William Dean, "Klamath Hearings in Oregon," *American Forests* 63 (November 1957): 12, 65–67.
43. Ibid.
44. C. E. Nash to Richard L. Neuberger, December 6, 1957, Box RN–12, Richard L. Neuberger Papers, Special Collections, University of Oregon, Eugene.
45. Report of Meeting Held With the Modoc Tribe of Indians, Miami, Oklahoma, February 6, 1958, Box 393333, Muskogee Area Office Correspondence, acc. no. 69-A–430, Record Group 75, Federal Archives and Records Center, Fort Worth, Texas.
46. Fred A Seaton to Dwight D. Eisenhower, January 13, 1958, Box 618, Official File, White House Central Files, Dwight D. Eisenhower Library, Abilene, Kansas; "Secretary Seaton Asks Congress to Protect Conservation Features of Klamath Indian Forests," news release by the Department of Interior, January 13, 1958, Box 12, Fred A. Seaton Papers, Dwight D. Eisenhower Library, Abilene, Kansas; and Senator Richard L. Neuberger Speaking on Administration Recommendations Regarding

Klamath Indian Reservation at Klamath Falls, Oregon, January 16, 1958, Box 16, Subject File, Fred A. Seaton Papers, Dwight D. Eisenhower Library, Abilene, Kansas.

47. Statement of Under Secretary of the Interior Hatfield Chilson on Senate Bill 3051 and Senate Bill 2047, February 3, 1958, Box 17, Fred A. Seaton Papers, Dwight D. Eisenhower Library, Abilene, Kansas; and Fred A Seaton, "Seaton Outlines Klamath Indian Proposal to Congress," *American Forests* 64 (February 1958): 12–13, 38–39.

48. Richard L. Neuberger, "Solving the Stubborn Klamath Dilemma," *American Forests* 64 (April 1958): 20–22, 40–42.

49. Combined Statement Before Senate Indian Subcommittee Considering S. 2047 and S. 3051 by Sheldon E. Kirk, Chairman of Klamath General Council; Jesse L. Bird, Sr., Vice-Chairman of Klamath General Council and Vice-Chairman of Klamath Executive Committee; Dibbon Cook, Secretary of Klamath General Council and Acting Secretary of Klamath Executive Committee; and Boyd Jackson, Treasurer of Klamath Tribe, February 4, 1958, Box RN–13, Richard L. Neuberger Papers, Special Collections, University of Oregon, Eugene.

50. Telegram, Robert Holmes to Richard Neuberger, July 15, 1958, Box RN–13, Richard L. Neuberger Papers, Special Collections, University of Oregon, Eugene.

51. "Klamath Indian Lands Reappraised," news release by the Department of Interior, January 14, 1959, Box 393333, Muskogee Area Office Correspondence, acc. no. 69-A–430, Record Group 75, Federal Archives and Records Center, Fort Worth, Texas, and Roger Ernst to Richard L. Neuberger, January 13, 1959, Box RN–13, Richard L. Neuberger Papers, Special Collections, University of Oregon, Eugene.

52. "Portland Bank Takes Over Trusteeship of Residual Klamath Indian Estate," news release by the Department of Interior, March 4, 1959, Box 393331, Muskogee Area Office Correspondence, acc. no. 69-A–430, Record Group 75, Federal Archives and Records Center, Fort Worth, Texas.

53. L. B. Staver to Fred A. Seaton, March 12, 1959, Box 27, Fred A. Seaton Papers, Dwight D. Eisenhower Presidential Library, Abilene, Kansas.

54. Richard L. Neuberger to Lawrence E. Slater, June 29, 1959, Box 7, Richard L. Neuberger Papers, Oregon Historical Society, Portland.

55. "Interior Department Proposes Bill Authorizing Special Loan Program Withdrawing Klamath Indians," news release by the Department of the Interior, and "Change in Regulations Will Permit Indian Bureau Loans to Withdrawing Klamath Members Regardless of Degree of Indian Blood," news release by the Department of Interior, July 16, 1959, Box 393331, Muskogee Area Office Correspondence, acc. no. 69-A–430, Record Group 75, Federal Archives and Records Center, Fort Worth, Texas.

56. Stern, *Klamath Tribe*, p. 159.

57. William Dean, "Klamath Hearings in Oregon," *American Forests* 63 (November 1957): 12, 65–67.

58. Report on United States Indian Population and Land, 1960, Box 149, Philleo Nash Papers, Harry S. Truman Presidential Library, Independence, Missouri, and Charles F. Wilinson and Eric R. Briggs, "The Evolution of

Termination Policy," *American Indian Law Review* 5 (Summer 1977): 151.
59. See Charles C. Brown, "Identification of Selected Problems of Indians Residing in Klamath County, Oregon—An Examination of Data Generated Since Termination of the Klamath Reservation," Ph.D. diss., University of Oregon, Eugene, 1973.
60. For insight into the Klamath individual, see James A. Clifton, "Explorations in Klamath Personality," Ph.D. diss., University of Oregon, Eugene, 1960.

5

CHIPPEWA FISHING AND HUNTING
RIGHTS IN THE GREAT LAKES

During the 1980s, a long-dormant issue concerning Indian fishing and hunting rights exploded in the state of Wisconsin. Battles in the courts, fistfights at lakes, and racial slurs yelled at Indian people plagued the state as racism caused hostilities pitting whites against Indians. Indian-white relations reached a new low, reminiscent of a frontier past when whites hated Indians and Indians fought back. This period of racial unrest became an ugly chapter in the history of Wisconsin, and the real issue of Chippewa fishing and hunting rights was lost in the turmoil. Furthermore, the historical importance of wildlife resources and their significance to the Chippewa became obscured as well.

This controversy began in 1974 when two brothers, Fred and Mike Tribble, who were enrolled members of the Lac Courte Oreilles (LCO) Chippewa (Ojibwa), were arrested by state game wardens Milton Dieckman and Larry Miller. The wardens of the Wisconsin Department of Natural Resources (DNR) charged the brothers with attempting to spearfish in an area beyond their reservation, as well as failing to have a license attached to the shanty they used while ice fishing.[1] Circuit Judge Alvin Kelsey found the Tribble brothers guilty of possessing a spear for taking fish on inland waters and for occupying a fish house without an attached name and address. The brothers were fishing on Chief Lake, outside of their LCO Reservation.[2] The story continued with a controversial court ruling and led to the *Voigt* decision.

The story is rooted in the origin of the Ojibwa and the ethnogenesis of their relationship with the Great Lakes environment. However, the purpose of the present account is to illustrate the significance of the clan among the Ojibwa and other woodland peoples who have clanship systems and how clan laws must be obeyed by all in order to achieve tranquillity and harmony in the community. When clan laws are disobeyed and the natural relationships with the environment are disrupted, human controversy and natural calamity will result. Like the other essential elements of native society—person or self, extended family, community, and nation—clan or society has a fundamental role in constituting the internal nature of Native Americans.

For most Indian people of the woodlands culture, plants and animals were an integral part of their infrastructure and ethnogenesis. By 1600, the Ojibwa (or Chippewa) world consisted of an estimated 30,000 individuals in the area that would become the United States and another 50,000 in Canada. Their homeland extended east to west from Lake Ontario to Lake Winnepeg and north to south from the Severs River Basin to Minnesota, Wisconsin, and Michigan.[3] This wide-ranging and large population has been divided into five major groups: the Southeastern Chippewa of Michigan's Lower Peninsula and nearby Ontario, the Chippewa of Lake Superior, the Southwestern Chippewa of interior Minnesota, the Northern Chippewa of the Laurentian uplands, and the Plains Chippewa of lower Canada.[4] The Chippewa of Wisconsin, like many other tribes of the woodlands east of the Mississippi River, developed a series of clans (twenty-four in all) based on human-animal alliances as a fundamental element of their society.[5] The Lac Courte Oreilles Chippewa of northern Wisconsin are a classic case of a Native people with great respect for and ties to the animal world, and they have fought long and hard to legally protect their fishing rights in the Great Lakes area. During the 1980s, the LCO Chippewa found themselves in a court battle to preserve both their hunting and fishing rights (especially the latter) against the non-Indian public of northern Wisconsin. Known as the *Voigt* decision, the Chippewa fishing rights case would become the second major landmark ruling in this regard after the *Boldt* case of 1974, which involved Indian fishing rights in the state of Washington. The roots of the LCO legal controversy dated back to the historical and traditional relationship of the Chippewa with the animals indigenous to the Wisconsin woodlands.

Providing twenty percent of the world's freshwater supply, the Great Lakes served as a bountiful environment for both animals and humans. Finding a flourishing environment of flora and fauna, the Chippewa easily adapted to the area in spite of the sometimes harsh winters, during which temperatures might dip to minus twenty degrees. Their dome-shaped bark lodges protected their families against the cold winds and snow.

Known as the Chippewa of Lake Superior, the people developed an economy based on hunting, trapping, fishing, and gathering.[6] Streams and fast-flowing rivers carried muskies and walleyes in large numbers, and the Chippewa developed fishing to supplement their hunting and their horticultural economy based on berries, wild grains, and herbs. They cultivated the "three sisters"—corn, pumpkins, and squash—plus peas and beans. They also tapped maple trees in late March, during "the Crusted Snow Supporting Man Moon," and early April, during "the Putting Away Snowshoes Moon," to make maple sugar. Women and children gathered blueberries, chokeberries, and Juneberries during the summers. From about mid-August, "the Blueberry Moon." to early September, "the Turning of the Leaves Moon," they collected wild rice. The Chippewa could fish all year round, but they primarily fished in late May, "the Flowering Moon," and again in autumn; in the winter, they ice fished. They set fishnets and used torches at night to lure muskies and walleyes to the surface of the water, where they then speared them.[7] The fish were so numerous that the Chippewa could take as much as they wanted, even during the fish breeding seasons. The spring runs of the spawning fish occurred at the right time to help the people, who were weakened from the winter; indeed, the fish offered immediate relief from hunger. The spawning fish in the fall included trout and whitefish, which needed cold water to start their breeding cycle that lasted from September through December. Smaller fish could be caught in nets or by trolling with a hook or line, but the larger species had to be speared. Traditionally, the harpoon head of the Chippewa spear was made of bone or antler.[8] Fish were taken by several methods: use of seines (the most common method); spearing at night spearing through ice using a decoy; traps; use of bait; use of fishhooks; and trolling. While spearfishing from a boat at night, a torch was used to attract the larger fish. The torch was made of a stake about four feet long that had a split end, around which strips of birch bark about six inches wide and eighteen inches long were twisted to serve as the torch end; the torch extended over the water with the other end fastened to the bottom of the canoe.[9]

The origin of the Chippewa dates back to a much earlier time when only one people—the Anishnabe—existed in the Great Lakes area. The people spoke one language. In Michigan, the Ojibwa, Ottawa, and Potawatomi—historically known as the Three Fires or Three Brothers—understand the same dialect today.[10] Other groups such as the Miami, Cree, and Huron populated the land around Lake Michigan. The area of Lake Superior also was home to the Menominee, Fox, or Mesquakie, and the other tribes lived near the Great Lakes of Erie and Ontario. Lake Huron was the native area of the Tobacco, Neutral, and Erie, as well as the Iroquois Nations of the Mohawk, Seneca, Cayuga, Onondaga, and Oneida. In all, about sixteen Indian nations called the Great Lakes their homeland.[11]

The oral tradition of the Great Lakes peoples speaks of a much earlier time when power and blessings emanated from Mackinac Island. The people did not live there but visited the island because of its supernatural aura. Other islands of the Great Lakes, such as Manitoulin Island, held similar importance, perhaps because they were considered extensions of the water where inexplicable things happened. The same sacred source was believed to change the weather and move the waters of the Great Lakes. Shrouded in mystery and empowered by the Creator, called Gitchimanitou, Mackinac Island was called the Great Turtle, likely deriving from the Algonkian tradition of respect for the turtle, who represented durability, continuity, and long life.

In those earlier times, people understood the animals and called them brothers and sisters, just as they did the plants. In the Great Lake environment, the plants and animals overpopulated the region. Fur-bearing animals, small and large, made this land their home, and fish of many species, including large ones like the muskie, coho, and sturgeon, swam in the rivers and lakes. The plant life included a plethora of grasses, flowers, herbs, and trees. Birch, oak, poplar, cedar, walnut, and several kinds of maple were in such abundance in the Great Lakes area that the forests blocked the sunlight in many spots. The people understood that they were a part of the environment and that they had much to learn about and from it.

The streams, rivers, lakes, meadows, and forests had special meaning for the people. Believing that all beings had roles and responsibilities; the people sought to understand their own roles in the context of the greater order.. The Anishnabe believed there was a circular order to the universe and life: All things came back to the beginning in a continuum, and all things were connected. The ethos for life among the Anishnabe held that any action of importance affected all others in the circular order, which encouraged them to be positive in their daily living.

The Anishnabe learned to live in accord with the nature of the Great Lakes environment, its seasons, and its climate The climate varies considerably with the four seasons in a constant cycle.[12] On the average, the sun shines only thirty percent of the time during the winter and forty percent during the summer in Michigan and most of the Great Lakes area. The rainfall averages from twenty-four to forty inches annually.[13] Learning to adjust to these conditions was essential for those living among the flora and fauna of the Great Lakes.

The kindred feeling among people and animals led to the development of spiritual relationships of human-animal alliances. These alliances or clans had an order based on the characteristics or strengths of the animals and plants. Although all beings, including plants and animals, were a part of the order of life, they differed according to their strengths and special qualities. The eagle and other fowl could fly and represented clans of "above," including thunder in this category. Animals and plants of "below," like the deer, marten, sturgeon, and bear, had different strengths. The people respected the plants and animals and attempted to copy their strengths and qualities. Stout and strong, members of the bear clan tried to be like the bear, which is also a medicine animal among some Native peoples. Symbolically, the plants and animals were also considered sources of knowledge because Gitchimanitou had empowered them.

During these early Anishnabe years, the people were few and the plants and animals were many. For example, in Michigan, the first French explorers of the late 1600s estimated that the Native population did not exceed 15,000 people[14] (although considering the span of all of the Chippewa in the United States and in Canada, the number was likely much greater).

Around campfires, the elders told stories to the young about how the plants and animals helped the people. Stories about good and bad and right and wrong were told as lessons in morality, and often the animals were the main characters in tales of wisdom and folly. The stories, myths, legends, and songs contained messages, parables, prophecy, and oral history. The oral tradition reminded the people about who they were, maintaining and reinforcing their identity as Anishnabe as a kind of mythos. Undoubtedly, the lakes affected the people and their thinking about life, and they became a vital part of the culture and ethos. The Chippewa, in particular, believed in a great water monster called Manitouk and the great Thunderbirds above. Other water monsters or great manitous were believed to frequent other parts of the lakes; in Lake Superior, for instance, oral tradition said that one such creature lived on the north shore near Thunder Cape and another resided below the waters at the mouth of Superior Bay, causing storms and unpredicted changes in the current that sometimes pulled fishermen under or caused them to wreck their canoes.[15] Life took on a different reality when the physical and metaphysical were combined. Some animals were believed to be half animal and half manitou, and according to the oral tradition, people physically interacted with animals in dreams, men married beavers, the wind impregnated women,[16] and the thunder beings fought the manitous "in a constant battle for balance in the world."[17]

Simultaneously, the Chippewa developed a system of religious belief centered on the Creator, or Gitchimanitou, who blessed the earth and the waters for producing animal and plant life. Reflecting their respect for the flora and fauna, the Chippewa organized themselves into as many as twenty-four clans in a series of five phratries. Under the Awause (Fish) phratry were the catfish, merman, sturgeon, pike, whitefish, and sucker clans. The Busineause (Crane) phratry included the crane and eagle clans. The Ahahwauk (Loon) phratry included the loon, goose, and cormorant clans, and the Noka (Bear) phratry included only the bear clan. The Monsone (Marten) phratry included the marten, moose, and reindeer clans.[18] Clan laws guided the people's lives and stressed respect for the brother animals. Unfortunately, this order of life became disturbed by the influx of white settlers, miners, and lumberjacks during the early 1800s.

Whites became interested in the Indian homelands of the western Great Lakes area of Michigan, Wisconsin, and Minnesota during the early decades of the nineteenth century. As settlers pushed westward from Michigan, Indian Commissioner Lewis Cass negotiated for the U.S. government the Treaty of Saginaw in Michigan Territory on September 24, 1819. This treaty ceded Chippewa lands, defined remaining tribal lands, and established "the right of the Indians to hunt upon the lands ceded" and "enjoy the privilege of making sugar upon the same land."[19] Another treaty negotiated with the Chippewa at Sault Sainte Marie the following summer called for an additional cession of land in Michigan, but "the Indians [retained] a perpetual right of fishing at the falls of St. Mary's, and also a place ... convenient to the fishing ground."[20] Weeks later, on July 6, 1820, Lewis Cass negotiated another treaty that included the Ottawa with the Chippewa and called for further land cessions; it was signed at L'Arbe Croche and at Michilimackinac.[21]

On August 5, 1826, Commissioners Cass and Thomas L. McKinney negotiated a treaty with Chippewa leaders at Fond du Lac in Wisconsin. This agreement called for a confirmation of the 1825 Treaty of Prairie du Chien, and it established the boundaries between the Chippewa and Menominee and Winnebago.[22] A year later, Cass negotiated another treaty with the Chippewa at Butte des Mortes on the Fox River in Michigan Territory. This treaty also included the Menominee and Winnebago and defined their lands in Wisconsin as well.[23] The objectives of these agreements became clear and confirmed by the passage of the Indian Removal Act of 1830 under President Andrew Jackson, the well-known Indian fighter and champion of western interests. On September 26, 1833, three government commissioners negotiated a removal treaty with the Chippewa, Ottawa, and

Potawatomi, requiring them to cede their lands in exchange for new territory located west of the Mississippi River.[24] A treaty made with the Chippewa groups of Black River and Swan Lake in 1836 called for additional tracts of Chippewa land in Michigan to be ceded to the government.[25] In 1837, the United States made three treaties with the Chippewa: one at Detroit on January 14 affecting the Michigan Indians, another on December 20 at Flint River in Michigan, and the third at the confluence of the Saint Peter and Mississippi Rivers involving the Wisconsin Chippewa."[26]

The last agreement, made on July 29, 1837, proved the most legally important treaty in terms of establishing Chippewa hunting and fishing rights in Wisconsin. Article 5 of this agreement guaranteed "the privilege of hunting, fishing, and gathering the wild rice, upon the lands, the rivers and the lakes included in the territory ceded."[27] This article proved to be the key provision for the *Voigt* decision rendered in the 1980s. Additional events impacted the Chippewa from the 1830s to the 1850s. For example, Michigan Territory and Wisconsin Territory obtained statehood, in 1837 and 1848, respectively. A treaty with the Chippewa on October 4, 1842, at La Pointe in Wisconsin called for the ceding of additional lands in northern Wisconsin and in western Michigan's Upper Peninsula. This agreement also reinforced the Chippewa legal right to hunt on ceded lands.[28]

In February 1850, President Zachary Taylor issued a presidential order for the Chippewa living on ceded lands in Wisconsin to prepare for removal, disregarding a request from Chippewa leaders who had traveled to Washington, D.C. to protest this move. One year earlier, the Chippewa leaders had asked to be given lands surrounding seven of their villages, plus sugar maple orchards and rice fields. Although Taylor's presidential order was rescinded by President Millard Fillmore, a treaty with the Chippewa on September 30, 1854, established permanent reservations for the Chippewa in Wisconsin, Michigan, and Minnesota.[29] In the following year, on February 22, 1855, the Michigan Chippewa agreed to a treaty on the final cession of lands to the United States in exchange for territory west of the Mississippi River.[30] In the end, the Chippewa ceded nearly all their lands in Michigan, Wisconsin, and Minnesota, but they retained a handful of reservations in each of the three states. They also retained their hunting, fishing, and gathering rights—rights that would not be challenged for more than 100 years. Ultimately, these treaties would serve as the basis for the Chippewa's later legal claims to privileged fishing on ceded lands, especially during the 1970s.

Four days after the arrests of Fred and Mike Tribble on March 8, 1974, the Lac Courte Oreilles Chippewa Tribe filed suit in the Western District Federal Court in Madison, Wisconsin. The LCO Tribe requested that the state of Wisconsin stop enforcing state laws against their tribal members, claiming that that had "reserved" treaty rights. In this regard, the tribe cited their treaties made in 1837 and 1842. Four years later, federal judge James Doyle ruled against the Lac Courte Oreilles Chippewa, concluding that they had relinquished their off-reservation rights when they accepted a permanent reservation according to the Treaty of 1854. Doyle further concluded that the 1850 presidential removal order had withdrawn the "rights" in question. The Lac Courte Oreilles appealed Doyle's decision in the U.S. Court of Appeals, Seventh Circuit, in Chicago.

After several months, the Federal Appeals Court in Chicago issued its ruling in both *Lac Courte Oreilles Band of Lake Superior Chippewa Indians et al. v. Voigt* and in *U.S. v. State of Wisconsin* on January 25, 1983. The Seventh Circuit Court agreed with the LCO Chippewa Tribe and returned the case to Judge Doyle's federal district court in Madison. In doing so, the appeals court held that (1) "treaties of 1837 and 1842 did not confer unlimited discretion on executive [authority] to terminate the Indians' usufructuary rights, but rather required that Indians be denied such privileges only if they were instrumental in causing disturbances with white settlers"; (2) "the doctrines of *res judicata* or *collateral estopel* did not preclude consideration of the question of the validity of the removal order of 1850"; (3) "the 1850 removal order exceeded the scope of the 1837 and 1842 treaties and was therefore invalid"; and (4) "the Indian band's usufructuary rights established by the 1837 and 1842 treaties were neither terminated nor released by the 1854 treaty."[31] In upholding the Chippewa treaties of 1837 and 1842, the appellate court reaffirmed the rights of six Chippewa bands to hunt, fish, trap, and gather wild rice on nonreservation lands in Wisconsin.[32]

The Seventh Circuit Court remanded the case to District Judge Doyle, with instructions "to enter judgment for the Chippewas to determine the scope of state regulation over the Chippewas' exercise of their usufructuary rights."[33] The official wording of the appellate court ruling of January 25, 1983, stated, "The Treaties of 1837, 1842, and 1854 are consistent in that each treaty includes both a cession of land and a reservation of usufructuary rights on the ceded land ... we conclude therefore that ... the usufructuary rights were neither terminated nor released."[34]

At the time of the *Voigt* decision, another case challenged Chippewa rights. In February 1983, the Supreme Court ruled on *Wisconsin v. Lemieux* after the state had appealed the initial findings twice. The events involved John and Peter Lemieux of the Chippewa, who were cited for violating a state law prohibiting possession or transportation of uncased or loaded firearms in vehicles. The Court ruled that the law actually infringed on Chippewa rights established in the Treaty of 1854, which guaranteed their hunting rights.[35]

During the four-year hiatus before Doyle's ruling in the *Voigt* decision, Indian-white relations appeared peaceful, but an undercurrent of racial unrest was growing stronger in northern Wisconsin, especially near the eleven reservations. Governor Anthony Earl, sensing some potential problems in northern Wisconsin, appointed Paul DeMain as his adviser on Indian affairs on the reservations. DeMain, who was very much aware of the situation regarding Chippewa relations with white residents, had been the editor of the *Lac Courte Oreilles Ojibwa Journal*, the LCO newspaper. DeMain assisted the Earl administration in drafting the state's first executive order defining the relationship between state and tribal agencies. In fact, under Public Law 280, passed by Congress in 1953, Wisconsin was one of six states declared to legally hold criminal and civil jurisdiction over their Indian residents.[36] Almost six months after Doyle's ruling in the *Voigt* case, the Earl administration produced its state Indian policy. "Basically, it recognizes the existence of tribal governments and it directs state agencies to deal with them on a government-to-government basis," said DeMain.[37] To improve Indian relations with the state, Governor Earl appointed thirty-eight Native Americans to various influential advisory committees, boards, and commissions affecting state affairs in general. But the real issue of Chippewa fishing rights remained unsettled for the next year and a half. In mid-September 1985, the Chippewa nations prepared to go to court over the issue of "what methods of harvesting fish, game and wild rice should be permitted."[38] Northern Wisconsin remained tense, and the heated issue of Chippewa fishing undoubtedly caused stress for Judge Doyle; the court proceedings had to be rescheduled to November 18 when the judge became ill. Finally, Doyle issued his thirty-seven-page decree. In it, he denied the motion to grant "extra" fishing rights to the Chippewa and declared that "gill-netting and spearing are unquestionably radical means of harvesting fish." Delegates from the Wisconsin Conservation Congress in attendance at the court applauded loudly, and Attorney General Bronson C. LaFollette, who represented Wisconsin in the case, commented that the ruling was "a welcome relief to the people of Wisconsin."[39] The attorney general was actually referring to the people of northern Wisconsin who had interests in fishing, such as cannery officials, sports enthusiasts, and individuals involved in tourism.

The Lakeland Chapter on Equal Rights complained when one of their members claimed that tourism in northern Wisconsin would suffer and bring economic woes to the region. Tourists in northern Wisconsin generated seventy cents of every dollar in the region's economy. As many as 1.2 million sports fishermen visited each year, and the many hunters who arrived annually did not understand the treaty rights guaranteed for the Chippewa. The people in the tourist business and Wisconsin hunters held rallies, carrying signs proclaiming, "I'm a native, too."[40]

The chief of the Department of Natural Resources Enforcement Division, George Meyer, was the department's main negotiator on the Indians' side. Meyer put Judge Doyle's decision into perspective, stating that "federal courts have not yet defined the scope of the treaty rights and the extent of the state's power to regulate those rights."[41]

The Chippewa and the state of Wisconsin clashed again when a proposed state safety law restricted hunting from a vehicle, a move that would affect handicapped individuals who normally were issued special permits allowing them to hunt in this manner. The proposed law would require that the driver and the vehicle had to be off the road and at least fifty feet from its center. The Chippewa interpreted the measure as anti-Indian. As tribal judge Thomas Maulson of the Lac de Flambeau Chippewa said, "The bill is ridiculous. It was targeted at the Indian people and not the handicapped. I feel the bill is racist."[42]

Indian-white relations remained strained in northern Wisconsin as the trial date approached. On December 9, 1985, the precise definition of Indian legal rights would be established by the court, affecting 12,000 Chippewa. A group of Indians gathered outside of the federal courthouse to protest and proclaim their rights. Kathryn Tierney, the counselor for the six Chippewa bands, remarked, "The guiding legal principle is that the Chippewa reserve the right to continue to live as they did when the treaties were signed."[43] However, the Indian protest had little effect; in fact, it only added to the growing anti-Indian sentiment as the media focused on the increasing hostility between the two sides.

As the 1985–86 spearfishing season began, anti-Indian feelings were voiced more loudly in northern Wisconsin. Rumors spread, charging that the Lac du Flambeau Chippewa had violated their agreement with the state of Wisconsin to limit their fishing. Furthermore, the anti-Indianists said that tribal judge Thomas Maulson should be asked to step down from his position because "he has participated in spearing" fish. The Chippewa replied that they "fish to eat, not to put trophies on walls."[44] On the morning of May 16, 1986, a forum of non-Indians gathered in Wausau, Wisconsin, to take a political position on hunting and fishing rights claimed by the Lac Court Oreilles Band of

Chippewa under the Treaty of 1854. The meeting rocked with angry opinions protesting the special treatment of Indians. One person later wrote an antagonistic, racist editorial in the *Milwaukee Journal*, claiming that the courts have "handed the American Indians rights far superior to those of all other American citizens" and adding that Indians were "laying false claims under the treaty [and] declaring themselves above the laws of this state in a very arrogant and obnoxious fashion. ... There is no way that Indians are entitled to more than you and I. ... The entire situation is truly a nightmare and people must speak out to protect the rights of the majority of the citizens of this land and end this silly discrimination in favor of a few. Indian treaties must be ended in favor of both Indians and non-Indians!"[45]

The early months of 1986 witnessed angry outbursts from both Indians and whites. Frequently, state and federal officials had to intervene and sometimes physically stop antagonists from assaulting each other. People feared that bloodshed would occur and someone would be killed before the fishing season was over. One anti-Indian organization calling itself "Equal Rights for Everyone" (ERFE) claimed the whole situation was a question of civil rights. The organization asserted that the Chippewa were "being treated better than whites of that region."[46] Before the whole racial affair ended, at least nine organizations would emerge as anti-Indian on the fishing rights issue. They included Equal Rights for Everyone, Wisconsin Alliance for Rights and Resources (WARR), Protect Americans' Rights and Resources (PARR), Stop Treaty Abuse Inc. (STA), Butternut Lake Concerned Citizens, Michigan United Conservation Club, Enough Is Enough, White Earth Equal Rights, and Total Equal Americans (TEA).

On behalf of Indians, the following six organizations formed to voice views in favor of Chippewa fishing and hunting rights: Orenda, Citizens for Treaty Rights, Wisconsin Greens, Wisconsin NOW, Wisconsin Equal Rights Council, and Wisconsin Indian Resource Council.

The racial problems in Wisconsin regarding Indian hunting and fishing rights (especially the latter) intensified further, with physical threats made and sometimes carried out. A member of the U.S. Civil Rights Commission commented that he was "appalled at the rampant racism he found in northern Wisconsin" and shocked at "the way many whites looked upon their Indian neighbors."[47] At a news conference sponsored by the commission, a member of the Wisconsin Advisory Committee remarked on the bigotry against Indians in the northern region: "There's no doubt in our mind that non-Indians are harboring racist animosity toward the Indians."[48]

The *Milwaukee Sentinel* published an editorial on May 12 contending that though the Chippewa held traditional hunting and fishing rights based on treaties signed in the 1800s, they did not use traditional fishing and hunting methods. "Now the Indian wants his special season with modern, high powered rifles and an outboard motor-powered aluminum boat, a blazing spotlight and a carbon steel spear."[49] Basically, the editorial argued that modern Indian fishing did not show a respect for nature and that since the Indians' hunting and fishing methods had changed, so too should their traditional rights.

Indian-white relations deteriorated as more of the nation learned about the racism in northern Wisconsin. The immediate issue causing the problem was the spearfishing, but roots of the poor relations lay deeper. Governor Anthony Earl established a white-Indian panel to study the fishing controversy. The commission consisted of members from each of the six Chippewa nations; representatives from among sports fishermen, local governments, and industry; and officials from the Department of Natural Resources. The governor charged the commission with the responsibility to "close the cultural gap between Wisconsin's white and Indian communities."[50]

The commission met in September 1986 to hear both sides. Francis W. Murphy, former chairperson of the State Conservation Congress, argued that "tourism could be improved and tensions in the north between whites and Indians could be less if the Chippewa Indians leased their treaty-guaranteed hunting and fishing rights to the state."[51] Murphy suggested that the state of Wisconsin could lease these rights from the Chippewa for an estimated $2.2 million annually.

The Chippewa position was weakened when members of the Bad River Band of Lake Superior were convicted for using nets to catch lake trout in a restricted off-reservation area. The court ruled in *State of Wisconsin v. Newago* that state regulation of fishing did not discriminate against Indians and was not preempted by tribal sovereignty or federal law. The Bad River Chippewa filed for a review of the case.[52]

In 1986, the newly elected governor, Tommy Thompson, met secretly with leaders of the six Chippewa nations on January 10 at his governor's mansion. For four hours, the leaders expressed their views. Thompson replied that he respected the treaties and stated that "Wisconsin can't abrogate the treaty." Using diplomacy to negotiate, the governor wanted an open line of communication to produce joint resolutions for the racial problems.[53]

On February 23, 1987, Judge Doyle complied with the federal appellate court in Chicago, ruling in favor of the Chippewa's off-reservation fishing rights and upholding the treaties.[54] Although Doyle was in agreement with the appellate court, the limit of the state of

Wisconsin's role in respecting the extent of Indian rights remained ambiguous. The attorney for the Lac du Flambeau Chippewa, James Janneta, did not believe that the Chippewa could exercise their full rights until a federal court issued an injunction against Wisconsin, preventing it from enforcing its fishing and hunting regulations on Native Americans.[55] In the end, although the Chippewa nations held full legal rights to hunt and fish on nonreservation lands, they chose not to exercise them. In a sincere attempt to improve racial relations, the Chippewa nations and the Department of Natural Resources of Wisconsin negotiated an agreement to limit the Indian fishing season and the number of fish caught. As an example, in 1986, the Chippewa were permitted ten percent of the total allowable catch for the state; the remaining ninety percent was reserved for sports fishermen.[56]

The negotiated agreement for 1987 permitted each Chippewa nation to spearfish for a period of fifteen days, which would end by May 2. In addition, Chippewa could spearfish until 3:00 A.M. (two hours later than the limit in 1986) and spearfish twenty percent of the total allowable catch of walleyes and muskies. Indian fishing was permitted on all lakes of 500 acres or more (in 1986, spearing was limited to the lakes of more than 1,000 acres). The Chippewa could not spearfish in spawning streams and fish refuges. Regarding fishing for walleyes, the Chippewa set limits for each lake for each night. Every bag of walleyes taken could contain one fish up to twenty-four inches and another of any size beyond that length. The remaining fish in the take had to be under twenty inches long. The harvest for muskie was limited to one fish of any size per night per person.[57]

All people involved in the *Voigt* decision received shocking news on March 20, 1987, when Judge Doyle announced his resignation from the remainder of the case due to ill health. The case was reassigned to Federal Judge Barbara Crabb, chief judge for Wisconsin's Western District of Federal Court. This action raised some concerns due to the complexity and long history of the issues involved in Chippewa fishing rights. Doyle had worked extensively on the Chippewa fishing rights cases since 1974.[58]

The negotiations between the Chippewa nations and the DNR did not help racial relations, nor did Doyle's illness. Meanwhile, an editorial in the *Milwaukee Journal* suggested that fishing and bear hunting in northern Wisconsin would be co-managed by the DNR and the Chippewa nations. The two sides had to be in agreement, according to James Schlender, chairman of the Great Lakes Indian Fish and Wildlife Commission; he was quoted as saying, "We need to meld together the impact of tribal harvest on the resources [of the DNR and tribes]." As an example of the Indians' respect for wildlife, the Chippewa applied for 223 bear-hunting tags in 1986 but killed only 16 bear during a specially designated season.[59] As the tribes and the DNR continued to talk, they agreed to extend the spearing season by five days and double the Indians' share of fish harvested from the northern lakes. Even with the additional regulations, however, the Chippewa would take only about twenty percent of the total allowable catch. Moreover, the Indians accepted numerous other restrictions and agreed not to sell their catch during the spearfishing season."[60]

This agreement was immediately called "bad news" by Larry Peterson, chairperson of PARR, an organization that opposed treaty rights and favored white hunters and sports fishing. PARR passed its own resolution, calling for a nonviolent response to the Chippewa fishing in 1987. In a meeting with Governor Thompson on March 7, PARR requested National Guard assistance, ostensibly to prevent any possible violence but primarily to be on its side against the Indians.[61] It was clear the sports hunters and fishermen wanted the support of the state of Wisconsin. On March 28 and 29, 1987, PARR held a meeting in Wausau to publicize the supposed neglect of the civil rights of white citizens in northern Wisconsin and to increase its own membership.

Hostilities between Indians and whites intensified with each fishing season. Those who opposed treaty rights, mainly hunters and sports fishermen, confronted Indian fishermen at the lakes. While the Indians spearfished on the lakes, the hostile whites slashed the tires of the Chippewa's vehicles and broke their windshields. Racial slurs and all kinds of derogatory terms were shouted at the Indians, and the Indians shouted back. Ultimately, the racism sparked by the spearfishing controversy became so intense that Indian and white children could not go to the same schools and their parents could not eat at the same restaurants.

Another attempt at negotiating between the state of Wisconsin and the Indians occurred when Attorney General Don Hathaway invited the tribal leaders of the six Chippewa nations and their lawyers to a meeting in April 1987. As their conversations progressed, a long-term settlement became the goal. That settlement would include "new state payments to Indians or economic development programs for their benefit [in an] attempt to end expensive lawsuits."[62] By the end of the month, the state officials and the Chippewa leaders reached twenty-three interim agreements. Further discussion led to a final settlement to end all of the legal and racial controversy.

Clearly, racism and spearfishing were intertwined, even though Governor Thompson tried to deny this tandem. A growing sentiment against the Indians resulted in outright ridicule when "Treaty Beer" was introduced during the summer, with sales used to support the effort against Indian treaty rights. Production of the offensive beverage came to halt due to boycotts. Nonetheless, 700,000 cans of beer had been brewed by Hiberna Brewery, Ltd.

In June and July, the Chippewa nations agreed to meet again with state officials, and as summer came to an end, the two groups met for two and a half hours. They agreed to continue negotiations, for both sides remained interested in reaching a final solution. However, the tribes would not compromise their treaties and insisted upon their legal importance.[63]

On August 21, Judge Barbara Crabb of the U.S. District Court of Wisconsin set the legal standards for determining "the permissible bounds of state regulation" regarding Chippewa off-reservation fishing. Even though her order backed Indian rights, it also supported the conservation practices of Wisconsin in the interest of public health and safety.[64] This federal action by the judge encouraged the antitreaty activists to criticize Indian rights harshly, although they cloaked their views in words about conservation and public safety. During October, a non-Indian group at Rhinelander, Citizens for Treaty Rights, began promoting biased racial relations in its own way. Members of the group wanted a peaceful settlement and reacted to Indian protests. Bumper stickers and posters appeared with slogans such as "Send Rambeau to Flambeau," "Spear an Indian," and "Spear a Squaw." Within a few weeks, the group's size increased from six to fifty members. They planned to launch a letter-writing campaign to legislators, to circulate petitions in support of treaties, and to make presentations on treaties in schools, churches, and communities to promote their views on limiting Indian fishing rights.[65]

The racial harassment intensified again as a final interpretation of the Chippewa's fishing and hunting rights was expected. To deter the white racism against the Indians of Wisconsin, the American Civil Liberties Union filed a suit on the behalf of the Chippewa.[66]

In defining Chippewa hunting and fishing rights in the *Voigt* decision, Judge Crabb defined the final scope of the Chippewa hunting, fishing, and gathering rights in all of Wisconsin. The Chippewa were given the right: "(1) to harvest and sell hunting, fishing, and gathering products, (2) to exercise these rights on private land if necessary to produce a modest living, and (3) to harvest a quantity sufficient to produce a modest living."[67] Furthermore, Judge Crabb placed additional limits on the amount of game and forest products (excluding commercial timber) that the Chippewa could take. The state and the LCO Tribe had until May 1991 to appeal the Crabb ruling, but neither group did so, and on May 20, 1991, the LCO announced the tribes' acceptance of the court ruling by releasing a statement: "The ... Lake

Superior Chippewa ... have preserved [their hunting, fishing, and gathering] rights for generations to come [and they] have this day foregone their right to further appeal. ... They do this as a gesture of peace and friendship towards the people of Wisconsin, in a spirit they hope may be reciprocated on the part of the general citizenry and officials of this state.[68]

Today, the Chippewa possess treaty rights supported by the doctrine of sovereign immunity. Because the nineteenth-century treaties were signed between two sovereign nations, the agreements must be recognized, and their provisions must be carried out in good faith. Unfortunately, although the treaties were intended to end confrontations between Indians and whites many years ago, they have, in practice, caused racial tensions in the twentieth century. Perhaps only time will heal the wounds of racial hostilities in northern Wisconsin, but the true violence was against nature's wildlife. The Chippewa animal clans were desecrated with the impurity of human greed and disrespect. *Ahocozzi*, the Chippewa word for "out of balance," properly describes the situation they faced.[69] However, the hostilities and disharmony have also provoked a revitalization of tradition among the Chippewa in Wisconsin. Of about 30,000 Indians there today, a quarter are under sixteen years of age, and the youth are identifying with their clans again. The beat of the drum is loud, calling the Chippewa to the roundhouses in the communities to renew their relations with the animals' world and the earth, for they are the Anishnabe.

NOTES

1. "Background of the Voigt Decision," *Masinaigan: A Chronicle of the Lake Superior Ojibway*, March 1987.
2. Ibid.
3. Theresa S. Smith, *The Island of the Anishnaabeg: Thunders and Water Monsters in the Ojibwe Life-World* (Moscow: University of Idaho Press, 1995), p. 4.
4. Edmund J. Danziger Jr., *The Chippewas of Lake Superior* (Norman: University of Oklahoma Press, 1979), p. 8.
5. Donald L. Fixico, "The Persistence of Identity in Indian Communities of the Western Great Lakes," *Ethnicity and Public Policy*, special edition entitled "American Indians: Social Justice and Public Policy" 9 (1991): 109–148.
6. Danziger, *Chippewas of Lake Superior*, pp. 8–12.
7. Ibid., p. 12.
8. Carol Mason, *Introduction to Wisconsin Indians: Prehistory to Statehood* (Salen, Wis.: Sheffield Publishing, 1988), pp. 102–103.
9. Francis Densmore, *Chippewa Customs*, reprint ed. (Saint Paul: Minnesota

Historical Society Press, 1979), pp. 124–127.

10. The Three Fires alliance or Three Brothers was also called the Lakes Confederacy; see Donald L. Fixico, "The Alliance of the Three Fires in Trade and War, 1630–1812," *Michigan Historical Review* 20, no. 2 (Fall 1994): 1–25.

11. Helen Tanner, *Historical Atlas of the Great Lakes* (Norman: University of Oklahoma Press, 1987).

12. The climate and temperature vary widely in the Great Lakes area. For example, the record high in Michigan is 112 degrees Fahrenheit (1936), and the record low is 51 degrees below zero Fahrenheit in 1934, according to Willis F. Dunbar, *Michigan: A History of the Wolverine State*, 4th printing (Grand Rapids, Mich.: William B. Eerdmans Publishing, 1968), p. 27.

13. Ibid.

14. Ibid., p. 35.

15. "Lake Superior Water Gods [Chippewa]" in Terry Hardin, ed., *Legends and Lore of the American Indians* (New York: Barnes and Noble, 1993), p. 134.

16. "A Gust of Wind [Ojibwa]" told by David Red Bird, in Richard Erodes and Alfonso Ortiz, eds., *American Indian Myths and Legends* (New York: Pantheon Books, 1984), pp. 150–151.

17. This exact quote in this regard is: "In the Ojibwe mythos birds speak to us, men marry beavers, women are impregnated by the wind, and the Thunders battle water monsters in a constant struggle for balance in the world," in Smith, *The Island of the Anishnaabeg*, p. 23.

18. Robert E. Ritzenthaler, "Southwestern Chippewa," in Bruce Trigger, ed., *Handbook of North American Indians: Northeast*, vol. 15 (Washington, D.C.: Smithsonian Institution, 1978), p. 753.

19. "Treaty With the Chippewa, 1819," September 19, 1819, at Saginaw, Michigan Territory, in Charles J. Kappler, comp. and ed., *Indian Treaties, 1778–1883*, 3rd printing (New York: Interland Publishing, 1975), pp. 185–186.

20. "Treaty With the Chippewa, 1820," June 16, 1820, at Saint Mary's, Michigan Territory, in Charles J. Kappler, comp. and ed., *Indian Treaties 1778–1883*, 3rd printing (New York: Interland Publishing, 1975), pp. 187–188.

21. "Treaty With the Ottawa and Chippewa, 1820," July 6, 1820, at L'Arbre Croche and Michilimackinac, Michigan Territory, in Charles J. Kappler, comp. and ed., *Indian Treaties 1778–1883*, 3rd printing (New York: Interland Publishing, 1975), pp. 188–189.

22. "Treaty With the Chippewa, 1826," August 5, 1826, at Fort du Lac of Lake Superior, Wisconsin, in Charles J. Kappler, comp. and ed., *Indian Treaties 1778–1883*, 3rd printing (New York: Interland Publishing, 1975), pp. 268–273.

23. "Treaty With the Chippewa, etc., 1827," August 11, 1827, at Butte des Morts on Fox River in Michigan Territory, in Charles J. Kappler, comp. and ed., *Indian Treaties 1778–1883*, 3rd printing (New York: Interland Publishing, 1975), pp. 281–283.

24. "Treaty With Chippewa, etc., 1833," September 26, 1833, at Chicago, in Charles J. Kappler, comp. and ed., *Indian Treaties 1778–1883*, 3rd printing (New York: Interland Publishing, 1975), pp. 402–415.

25. "Treaty With the Chippewa, 1836," May 9, 1836, at Washington, in Charles J. Kappler, comp. and ed., *Indian Treaties 1778–1883*, 3rd printing (New York: Interland Publishing, 1975), pp. 461–462.
26. "Treaty With the Chippewa, 1837," January 14, 1837, at Detroit; "Treaty With the Chippewa, 1837," December 20, 1837, at Flint River, Michigan Territory; and "Treaty With the Chippewa, 1837," July 29, 1837, at Saint Peter and Mississippi Rivers, Wisconsin, in Charles J. Kappler, comp. and ed., *Indian Treaties 1778–1883*, 3rd printing (New York: Interland Publishing, 1975), pp. 482–486, 501–502, and 491–492.
27. "Treaty With the Chippewa, 1837," July 29, 1837, at Saint Peter and Mississippi Rivers, Wisconsin, in Charles J. Kappler, comp. and ed., *Indian Treaties 1778–1883*, 3rd printing (New York: Interland Publishing, 1975), pp. 491–492.
28. "Treaty With the Chippewa, 1842," October 4, 1842, at LaPointe, Wisconsin, in Charles J. Kappler, comp. and ed., *Indian Treaties 1778–1883*, 3rd printing (New York: Interland Publishing, 1975), pp. 542–545.
29. "Treaty With the Chippewa, 1854," September 30, 1854, at La Pointe, Wisconsin, in Charles J. Kappler, comp. and ed., *Indian Treaties 1778–1883*, 3rd printing (New York: Interland Publishing, 1975), pp. 648–652.
30. "Treaty With the Chippewa, 1855," February 22, 1855, at Washington, D.C., in Charles J. Kappler, comp. and ed., *Indian Treaties 1778–1883*, 3rd printing (New York: Interland Publishing, 1975), pp. 685–690.
31. *Lac Courte Oreilles Band of Lake Superior Chippewa Indians et al. v. Voigt* and *U.S. v. State of Wisconsin*, Nos. 78–2398 and 79–1014, U.S. Court of Appeals, Seventh Circuit, January 25, 1983, *Federal Reporter*, Vol. 700 F.2d; *Cases Argued and Determined in the United States Courts of Appeals in the United States Courts of Appeals and Temporary Emergency Court of Appeals* (Saint Paul, Minn.: West Publishing, 1983), pp. 341–365.
32. Donald L. Fixico, "Chippewa Fishing and Hunting Rights and the Voigt Decision," in Donald L. Fixico, ed., *An Anthology of Western Great Lakes Indian History* (Milwaukee: University of Wisconsin–American Indian Studies Program, 1987), p. 488.
33. *Lac Courte Oreilles Band of Lake Superior Chippewa Indians et al. v. Voigt* and *U.S. v. State of Wisconsin*.
34. Ibid.
35. *State of Wisconsin v. John and Peter Lemieux*, February 15, 1983, Supreme Court of Wisconsin, Wis. 327 N.W.2d 669.
36. "Criminal and Civil Jurisdiction Act," P.L. 280, August 15, 1953, *U.S. Statutes at Large*, 67:588–590.
37. "Earl Aide Bridges Gaps for Indians, State," *Milwaukee Journal*, July 1, 1984.
38. "Chippewas Argue for Treaty Rights," *Milwaukee Sentinel*, September 25, 1984.
39. "Doyle Says Indians Must Comply With State Fishing Regulations," *Milwaukee Sentinel*, June 2, 1984.
40. "Treaty Rights, Tourist Dollars Back on Trial," *Milwaukee Journal*, December 9, 1985.
41. "Doyle Says Indians Must Comply With State Fishing Regulations."

42. "Few Indians Out on Last Days of Hunting From Vehicles," *Milwaukee Sentinel*, September 30, 1985.
43. "Treaty Rights, Tourist Dollars Back on Trial."
44. "Indian Leader Offers Solution," *Milwaukee Journal*, December 9, 1985.
45. "Old Tribal Traditions Threaten State's Future," *Milwaukee Journal*, December 9, 1985.
46. "Are Chippewas Victims of Racism and Greed?" *Milwaukee Sentinel*, May 27, 1986.
47. Ibid.
48. "Racism Cited in Fishing Dispute," *Milwaukee Sentinel*, April 11, 1986.
49. "Indians Should Return to Primitive Fishing," *Milwaukee Sentinel*, May 12, 1986.
50. "Earl Plans to Set Up White-Indian Panel," *Milwaukee Sentinel*, May 31, 1986.
51. "Conservationist Urges Lease of Fishing Rights," *Milwaukee Journal*, September 21, 1986.
52. *State of Wisconsin v. Thomas Newwago, John H. Pero Jr., and John Lemieux*, October 28, 1986, Court of Appeals of Wisconsin, 397 N.W.2d 107 (Wis. App. 1986).
53. "Governor Meets Voigt Tribes," *Lac Courte Oreilles Journal, A Chronicle of the Lake Superior Ojibway*, February 1987, and "Chairmen Define Key Issues With Gov. Thompson," *Masinaigan: A Chronicle of the Lake Superior Ojibway*, February 1987.
54. "Treaty Rights Ruling in Effect Now," *Milwaukee Sentinel*, February 24, 1987.
55. Ibid.
56. "Treaty Ruling May Restrict Sport Fishermen," *Milwaukee Sentinel*, February 21, 1987.
57. "Cold Weather Delays Indian Spearfishing," *Milwaukee Sentinel*, April 1, 1987.
58. "Ill Judge Withdraws From Chippewa Suit," *Milwaukee Sentinel*, March 21, 1987.
59. "Chippewas Seek More Input With DNR to Manage Resources," *Milwaukee Journal*, March 22, 1987.
60. Ibid.
61. "Spearing Accord Called 'Bad News,' " *Milwaukee Sentinel*, March 16, 1987.
62. "Hanaway Invites Indians to Treaty Talks," *Milwaukee Journal*, April 29, 1987.
63. "Of Course Racism Plays Role in Treaty Rights," *Milwaukee Journal*, August 16, 1987; "Chippewas Are Willing to Listen," *Milwaukee Journal*, August 21, 1987; and "Long Trial Ahead for Indian Treaty Talks," *Milwaukee Journal*, August 23, 1987.
64. "Court Decision Favorable to Tribes," *Masinaigan: A Chronicle of the Lake Superior Ojibway*, September 1987.
65. "Pro-Treaty Group Says Stickers Incite Violence," *Milwaukee Journal*, October 13, 1987.
66. Donald A. Grinde Jr., "Northeast," in Duane Champagn, ed., *The Native*

North American Almanac: A Reference Work on Native North America and Canada (Detroit, Mich.: Gale Publishing, 1994), p. 251.

67. Ibid., pp. 250–251; Ronald Satz, *Chippewa Treaty Rights: The Reserved Rights of Wisconsin's Chippewa Indians in Historical Perspective* (Madison: Wisconsin Academy of Sciences, Arts and Letters, 1991), p. 100.

68. Ibid.

69. Richard L. Kenyon, "If We Give Up Our Ways, We Die," *Wisconsin: The Milwaukee Magazine*, July 23, 1989.

6

CONTROVERSY AND SPIRITUALITY
IN THE BLACK HILLS

The Black Hills rest on an extraordinary site of natural beauty with two monuments—Mount Rushmore and the Crazy Horse Mountain—commemorating the long and troubled history between Indians and whites in this area. Indian and white interests differed, and their attitudes clashed. Their cultures were opposites, reflecting diverse ideologies and life values. This sacred area of the Lakota was sought by the whites for its mineral resources, primarily gold, and the Indians desired it as a religious site, for it represents the heart of the Lakota people. Towering and majestic, this mystifying area is where East meets West. Eastern and western trees both grow in the Black Hills, and there, in the middle of the continent, cold and warm winds from the North and the South carry seeds and pollens to the area. And from the East came the white people who would confront the Lakota in a struggle for the Black Hills that has lasted for over 100 years.

Of the Lakota people, the Oglala and Brule led the westward migration after generations of war with the Chippewa in the Lake Superior area. War with the Chippewa, lasting for approximately a century, left the Lakota people exhausted and their ranks of warriors depleted. The Brule found the White River area in southwest South Dakota to be a favorable site for relocation, and they established new homes there while the Oglala continued moving westward. Reaching the Badlands, the Oglala decided to settle there and made the Black Hills their new homeland.[1]

6. Buffalo in the Black Hills. Courtesy of Sharon O'Brien.

A land of beauty, the Black Hills held a special meaning for the Oglala, and it was a location where the people could thrive. Buffalo fed on native grass amidst the stands of Scotch pines, black and white spruce, burr oak, elm, white birch, and ash trees. The people gathered wild plums, cherries, and various kinds of berries to supplement the game they hunted. The grizzly bear, panther, mountain lion, mountain sheep, elk, antelope, deer, and wolf also made their homes in the Black Hills, which the Creator had blessed with abundance.

In the Black Hills, the Lakota found special meaning to their past about the purpose of life. They established a respectful bond with the environment, and certain sites became places for prayer and vision quests (requests for mental images of the future). The spirit of the people was embodied in the Black Hills—which held their identity, answered their questions, and offered glimpses into life beyond the earthly world. This spirituality permeated the Black Hills and the people and created a close connection between them; indeed, it was almost as though they were one.

The spirit of the people is the final element that bonds an Indian community together, although all of the elements described in the preceding chapters—person or self, extended family, community, clan, and nation—must be present in order for the spiritual energy to hold the people and community as one. This spiritual element also attaches the people to their natural environment in an intangible but intimate relationship that permeates the people in an abstract way and unifies Native identity.

The Black Hills have also been the site of much conflict and anguish. They were the final stronghold of the Lakota whose war leaders—such as Crazy Horse, Red Cloud, and Sitting Bull—led their people's efforts to save the land. However, American settlers pushing westward wanted the additional property, and the Treaty of Fort Laramie negotiated between the Lakota and the United States established a peace between the two sides in 1868.[2] Under this agreement, the Lakota refused to surrender the Black Hills to the United States, but this failed to quash the settlers' demand for the Black Hills—the homeland of the Lakota.

The Lakota were in awe of the Black Hills and called them *Paha Sapa* when they first saw them, referring to the color of the pine trees seen from a distance. By the 1820s, the Lakota people began arriving in greater numbers in the Lake Superior region. Legend says the Indians set up camp in the lower hills and at times heard strange sounds coming from the higher hills. The mysterious sounds seemed to be telling them something or perhaps warning them. The wisest people were sent to investigate. In this way, the Lakota knew white strangers would arrive.

Rumors of gold in the Black Hills began as early as the Lewis and Clark Expedition in 1804. Some say that the first gold mine was opened in 1834 but that Indians killed the isolated miners who worked the area. The rumors about gold continued, and anyone who tried to prove them false had to deal with the Lakota. In the following decades, the American Civil War sparked hostilities between the Lakota and federal troops, forcing a peace commission, led by General Alfred Sully, to arrange a meeting with the Indians after the war. Cautious (with good reason), Lakota elders recalled that the soldiers had attacked them during the summer of 1865, and they wondered if this meeting was actually a trick.

In response to persistent efforts by whites hoping to settle in the area, a meeting was held at Fort Laramie in 1868, leading to the Treaty of Fort Laramie. Lakota leaders met with federal and military officials, and the Indians were pressured to surrender land and allow the Bozeman Trail to be open to traveling settlers. In exchange, the United States recognized a large reserved area that became known as the Great Dakota Reservation. Undaunted, white settlers wanted the Black Hills for themselves and pressured government officials into negotiations with the Indians. Although the federal government had promised to protect the Lakota's interests and land in the treaty, President Ulysses S. Grant violated the agreement when he ordered that troops be withdrawn from the Black Hills. A local historian wrote: "The people of Dakota dislike to have to see so large and important [a] portion of their Territory set apart for an Indian reservation, but if it must be so for awhile, they will cheerfully submit to it and make the most of it."[3]

During the spring of 1872, the frontier rumors about a group of settlers who had caught gold fever and planned to invade the Black Hills reached Washington. Rumors circulated during the next several months, forcing the government to establish a commission to investigate the prospect of an Indian war. After the failure of a first commission, Felix Brunot was appointed chairman of the Board of Indian Commissioners and charged with assessing the situation. One general argued the army's position, which called for reducing the Lakota's land, and he stressed that reports indicated that, with only one Indian for every twenty square miles, they Lakota had little chance of stopping the settlers and prospectors. General William T. Sherman endorsed this position in a letter to the War Department. The ultimate outcome was predictable: Trouble engulfed the Black Hills. As Bishop William Hare put it, "No power on earth could shut out our white people from that country if it really contained valuable deposits of gold."[4]

In January 1873, the Legislative Assembly of Dakota Territory requested two items from Congress: first, authorization for a scientific exploration of the territory; and second, notification in reference to the Black Hills serving as a retreat for hostile Indians. In a biased opinion, Congress decided that the Indians were not using the Black Hills except as a hideout for their hostile warriors and argued that they should be confined to another part of the territory. The Dakota settlers wanted the Black Hills opened to settlement, and Congress agreed.[5]

Obligations from the Treaty of Fort Laramie forced the U.S. military to be responsible for keeping settlers out of the area, but the rumors of gold made those obligations irrelevant. In Sioux City, Iowa, Charles Collins and T. H. Russell organized the first settler expedition to the Black Hills on October 6, 1873 Tom Gordon served as the captain of the party and directed its arrival near Sturgis on December 6. The party included Annie D. Tallent, her husband, and their nine-year-old son. After completing the 350-mile trek, she became the first white woman in the Black Hills.[6]

On July 2, 1874, Lieutenant Colonel George Armstrong Custer left Fort Abraham Lincoln near present-day Bismarck in North Dakota, leading ten companies of cavalry and two companies of infantry, amounting to more than 1,000 soldiers. Custer's force proceeded toward the southwest and reached the Belle Fourche, the "beautiful fork" of the Belle Fourche River and Redwater Creek, near the Black

Hills in South Dakota. This trip lasted sixteen days, bringing the troops to the heartland of the Black Hills. Scientists on the expedition were impressed with the geologic and botanic specimens that they collected in the area. In August, Custer sent two dispatches to Bismarck in which he casually mentioned a possibility of gold in the Black Hills. On August 27, 1874, a newspaper correspondent, hungry for news, wrote a graphic account in the *Inter-Ocean* about the expedition's findings and described the possibility of locating gold, and *Harper's Weekly* devoted a full page to the subject in its issue of September 12. Some of the men under Custer's command illegally drew up papers for an enterprise to be known as Custer Mining Company, and gold fever spread throughout the nation. Having just suffered through the panic of 1873, people sought ways to recover from their financial losses and believed the Black Hills might hold the answers.

On June 18, 1875, the United States established a commission to meet with the Lakota for negotiations. The secretary of the interior appointed Senator William B. Allison of Iowa to negotiate for the Black Hills on the government's behalf. On September 20, a large council of Indian and white officials gathered at the White River, approximately eight miles from the Red Cloud Agency. The commission met with frustration when mixed-bloods convinced the Lakota leaders to demand an outrageous sum of $30 to $50 million for the Black Hills. Plotting to force the Lakota into an agreement, Congress passed a law on August 15, 1876, declaring that no funds would be appropriated for the Lakota's subsistence unless they surrendered their claim to the Black Hills.[7] Having failed to reach an accord with the Lakota through his first commission, Interior Secretary Zachariah Chandler appointed a second commission, which signed a treaty with the Indians on September 26, 1876. Congress ratified the agreement, under which the Indians would be paid a fair price for their land, and several months later, on February 28, 1877, the president signed it.[8]

While the army attempted to persuade gold rushers from storming the Black Hills, the northern Plains Indians gathered in one last great council. This included seven of the Teton Sioux tribes—the Brule, Oglala, Miniconjou, Hunkpapa, Blackfeet, Two-Kettle, and San Arc— in addition to the Lower Brule, Santee, Yankton, and two non-Sioux tribes, the Arapaho and Northern Cheyenne. Perhaps as many as 20,000 Indians gathered, but they were unable to agree on anything.

The military tried its own solution a few months later. Washington had issued an order that all Sioux who were not camped at their agencies by January 31, 1876, would be considered hostile. But a severe winter prevented the message from reaching all of the tribes in time.[9] Fearing an outbreak of war, Washington sent George

Manypenny to lead a commission to meet with the Lakota leaders. The Manypenny Commission succeeded in getting an agreement that ten percent of the adult Lakota would be required to sign a treaty for the Lakota releasing their rights over the Black Hills—despite the fact that the 1868 Treaty of Fort Laramie had stipulated that signatures from three-fourths of the adult male Lakota were required for such an agreement. Consequently, when Congress made the agreement of the Manypenny Commission law on February 28, 1877, it created a federal law that violated the Fort Laramie treaty.[10]

Increasing tension and frustration set the stage for a Sioux war with the United States, and in 1876—America's centennial—continued westward pressure forced troops of the U.S. military, under George Armstrong Custer, into a major confrontation. This was the suicidal battle leading to the death of "Yellow Hair" and the destruction of the famed Seventh Cavalry.

The desire for the Lakota's Black Hills only intensified when further rumors about the gold that lay hidden there circulated through the country in the remaining years of the 1870s. The rumors became reality during that decade when mining actually developed in the Black Hills. Mining operations included the Father de Smet Gold Mine, Homestake Gold Mine, Carbonate Silver Mine, Galena Silver Mine, and the Black Hills Placer Mining Company. One expert estimated the mines yielded $3.5 million in 1878, $4.5 million in 1879, and approximately $6 million in 1880.[11]

In 1880, the Great Sioux Reservation was bordered on the east by the Missouri River, on the south by the Nebraska line, on the north by the Cannonball River and the present line between North and South Dakota, and on the west by the eastern foothills of the Black Hills. The Teton Lakota's seven bands shared the reservation, and six agencies served them, including Red Cloud and Spotted Tail, which had been closed in Nebraska during the autumn of 1877 and moved northward. Red Cloud became Pine Ridge, and Spotted Tail became the Rosebud Agency. Other agencies included Standing Rock, Cheyenne River, Lower Brule, and Crow Creek.[12]

During the ensuing years, the U.S. seizure of the Black Hills renewed the struggle between the Lakota and the whites for ownership of the area. Complicating the problem by the 1880s, railroad companies wanted to lay tracks across the Sioux Reservation. The Chicago and Northwestern Railroad Company had constructed tracks as far as Pierre, South Dakota. The Chicago, Milwaukee, and St. Paul Railroad had pushed to Chamberlain.[13] Lakota concerns increased when the railroads brought more whites to the territory, crossing Sioux land to reach the Black Hills. Whites claimed that the Black Hills no longer "legally" belonged to the Sioux—citing the U.S. claim that the Sioux had violated the Treaty of 1877 and therefore lost the area.

The Lakota world approached its end. Defeated and placed on the reservations, the Lakota existed without a cause. Elaine Goodale, a schoolteacher, observed pitiful conditions when she traveled from the Black Hills to the Missouri and north to the Cannonball River to inspect the Indian schools and the people. She wrote, "The pitiful little gardens curled up and died in the persistent hot winds. Even young men displayed gaunt limbs and lackluster faces. Old folks lost their hold on life, and heart-broken mothers mourned the last of a series of dead babies."[14]

In the depths of their despair, the Lakota were awakened when a ceremonial movement of spirituality called the Ghost Dance reached them from the west. Promising a renewed earth for the Lakota and other western Indian groups, the new religion inspired the people even as white settlers, ranchers, and everyone else feared an Indian uprising. Unfortunately, the Native revival ultimately brought destruction, for on December 29, 1890, the U.S. Army's Ninth Cavalry massacred Big Foot and his Miniconjou Ghost Dancers at Wounded Knee. Almost 350 Lakota lost their lives in this confrontation. For their role in the atrocity, the U.S. government decorated its soldiers with medals for "defeating" the Lakota.[15]

The Lakota would never forget the massacre at Wounded Knee. In the following generations, they struggled to regain their lives as prospecting opportunists flooded the Black Hills. Towns literally emerged overnight, the most famous among them Deadwood, and a host of outlaw celebrities followed, such as Wild Bill Hickok, Calamity Jane, Deadwood Dick, Alabama Jane, and Wild Horse Kate. Central City became another boomtown, and others included Galena, Spearfish Creek, Whitewood, Crook City, Sturgis, and Rapid City. The Homestake Mine became the most well-known gold mine in the Western Hemisphere, and exhausted prospectors also found significant amounts of silver, lead, coal, iron, quartz, nickel, and copper.[16] The Black Hills was a popular site for more and larger mining operations with each decade. Finally, the Lakota took action to secure the return of their homeland.

In 1920, the Lakota filed a claim in the Federal Court of Claims requesting the return of the Black Hills, but no official action was taken until 1942, when a decision was finally rendered. An act on June 3, 1920, which ruled that the Court of Claims would judge all claims against the United States "under any treaties, agreement, or laws of Congress for the misappropriation of any funds or lands of said tribe or band or bands thereof," failed to help the Lakota. The act did not allow the Court of Claims to question the 1877 statute as to whether it authorized just compensation to the Lakota.[17]

An appeal was filed, but in 1943, the Supreme Court refused to review the Court of Claims's decision. The Lakota case fell into limbo until three years later. In 1946, Congress enacted the Indian Claims Commission Act, leading to the filing of a Sioux claim in 1950. For four years, the Sioux waited patiently. Then, in 1954, the Indian Claims Commission ruled that the Sioux had failed to prove their case, but this did not daunt the Indian effort. Another four years later, the Sioux initiated action again, and the Court of Claims ordered the Indian Claims Commission to reopen the tribe's case on the grounds that the Sioux had been inadequately represented by counsel. This error seemed rectified when new attorneys took the Sioux case.

In 1961, the Court of Claims denied a petition by the United States for mandamus to the Indian Claims Commission, and the Sioux won a small victory. One year later, however, the state of South Dakota purchased the Black Hills for the development of a state park. The state decreed the Black Hills "closed to all," which disturbed the Lakota who worshiped there annually in the month of May for life renewals. During the following years, the government created projects under the Department of Game, Fish, and Park. State plans encouraged tourism to the Black Hills, which conflicted with the interests of the Lakota and the Cheyenne (who were related to the Lakota) and threatened their religious ceremonials.

In 1968, the Indian Claims Commission ruled on three important points concerning the Sioux claim case. It asked (1) what land rights the United States acquired in 1877, (2) what consideration had been given in exchange, and (3) if no consideration had been given, what if any payment had been made by the United States.[18] In 1974, the Indian Claims Commission rendered a preliminary opinion that in 1877, Congress used eminent domain power to seize the land rather than acting in its role as a trustee for the Sioux, and that the United States thus owed compensation to the Indians for the Black Hills.[19] In the following year, on an appeal by the United States, the Court of Claims ruled that the Indian Claims Commission was barred under the legal doctrine of *res judicata* for not arguing successfully a claim based on the Fifth Amendment. After the Supreme Court denied the Sioux petition to review the Court of Claims decision,[20] the case then was returned to the Indian Claims Commission, which established $3,484 as the value of rations issued to the Sioux under the act in 1877, but it refused to set this amount off against the $17.5 million assessment of the worth of the Black Hills in 1877.

As a part of the continued effort to regain the Black Hills, Matthew King and other Indians established Camp Yellow Thunder in the area. The camp became a spiritual and educational camp where Indian people could return to the earth, learn about their tribal ways and philosophy, and identify with *Paha Sapa*. Politically, the camp leaders also defied the seizing of the Black Hills and challenged the government's seizure as a violation of the rights guaranteed them in the First Amendment and the American Indian Religious Freedom Act passed in 1978.[21]

Members at the camp learned about the sacredness of the Black Hills to the Lakota. They learned that a sacred hoop surrounded the Black Hills for protection and that Harney Peak—the tallest point in the area, standing at an altitude of 7,242 feet—represented the center of the universe for the Lakota. This was where Black Elk, the famed holyman of the Oglala, went to pray. Other important sites included Red Lodge Canyon, where pictoglyphs illustrated the seven rites of the sacred pipe—a guide for life for the Lakota. Rock writing described Lakota life and its history, the meaning of existence for these people.

In addition, state regulations seriously hindered the Lakota's opportunity to hold worship ceremonials in the Black Hills. The construction of access roads and parking spaces marred the land and insulted the Lakota. In their eyes, the white people's construction diminished the butte as a ceremonial ground, and the viewing platforms that had been built for tourists to watch sacred rituals of the Lakota aroused their anger. With continued construction, the Lakota encountered difficulty in getting to their sacred area to camp on the traditional grounds, and new regulations even required them to obtain permits before conducting religious ceremonies!

In an effort to regain the sacred Black Hills, the religious leaders of the Lakota and Cheyenne filed a lawsuit, *Fools Crow v. Gullet*, in Rapid City, South Dakota.[22] The leaders of the two groups wanted a halt to additional construction of tourist facilities at Bear Butte, known as Mato-Paha, which resembles a huge bear and stands approximately 1,200 feet tall. Mato-Paha is one of the sacred sanctuaries in the Black Hills.

On June 13, 1979, the Court of Claims affirmed the Indian Claims Commission's 1974 ruling that would award the Sioux $17.5 million plus five percent simple interest computed annually from 1877, amounting to some $122.5 million. In the following year, the U.S. Supreme Court upheld the Court of Claims decision in *United States v. Sioux Nation of Indians*.[23] The decision in 1980 acknowledged that Congress had taken the Black Hills in 1877 when rumors of gold caused a rush of miners to the region and that Congress had acted illegally. In addition, the Court acknowledged that Bear Butte was the most sacred ceremonial site for the Lakota and Cheyenne in the Black Hills, although it stated that the Indians' religious freedom was not violated under the First Amendment of the U.S. Constitution. In ruling that the tribes did not possess a property interest in Bear Butte, the Court said its decision was based on a distinction between the tribes' religious belief and their religious practice. The Court ruled that the two tribes were not forced from their religious beliefs, nor were they prevented from practicing their religion in spite of the loss of Bear Butte. The Court ruled in favor of the overall interest of the public, stressing that the Department of Tourism was not in violation and that efforts to inform people of the "traditional Indian religious experiences" and provide tourist facilities were in the public's interests. The roads enabled the public to visit the site, the ruling said, and the viewing platforms assured the Indians of privacy by containing the tourists.[24]

In 1981, the Oglala Sioux filed a claim against the United States and North Dakota, as well as a number of towns, counties, and individuals, asking for possession of the Black Hills and total damages of $11 billion. On September 22, 1981, the case was dismissed. In an appeal, the U.S. Court of Appeals for the Eighth Circuit affirmed the district court's decision that the Indian Claims Commission Act was an exclusive remedy and did not allow courts to hear claims for the land. An attempt by the Oglala to appeal the case to the Supreme Court failed in 1982.[25] Three years later, the Court of Claims rendered a final judgment in the Indian Claims Commission docket, involving the Black Hills claim filed by lawyers representing the Lakota for monetary damage to the Sioux, but tribal members refused the compensation that was offered to them because they wanted the Black Hills instead.[26]

The controversy entered another phase when large deposits of coal in the Black Hills attracted energy companies as early as the 1970s; by the 1980s, numerous companies were in the area. With the legal battle for the Black Hills still unresolved, the energy companies wanted to extract the wealth of fossil fuels as quickly as possible. Unfortunately, environmental concerns did not deter them, and the number of energy corporations mining in the Black Hills grew considerably. Indeed, no less than twenty-six multinational corporations have obtained state leases to explore for fossil fuels over one million acres in the area. These corporations are Union Carbide, Gulf, Exxon, Wyoming Minerals (owned by Westinghouse), Mobil, Endicott Copper, Nokota Company, John Mansfield, Cyprus Exploration, International Nickel, Power Resources, Mineral Exploration, Century Mining, Kerr-McGee, American Copper, Chevron, Natrona Service, Energy Transportation System, Peter Kewitt, Rio Agum, M & M Iron Company,

Pittsburgh Pacific, Colorado Fuel and Iron, United Nuclear Homestake, Western Geophysical, and Shell. Ironically, in response to the intrusion of the energy companies in the Black Hills, Indian and white residents joined together to form the Black Hills Alliance in 1979 in order to protect their homes and the environment. With a membership of approximately 300, the alliance discussed ideas and methods of acquiring additional information about energy sources in the Black Hills to help their cause; at the same time, they also were concerned that the spread of any new information might only intensify the greed for the Black Hills, which encompass an estimated 1.3 million acres.[27] The intense coal mining that began in the 1970s represented the second major phase of mining in the Black Hills, as the Homestake Mining Company had strip-mined in the western portion since the late 1800s.

Seeming to have lost the legal battle, the Lakota insisted on being heavily compensated. The U.S. Supreme Court had ruled in 1980 that the federal government had to pay the Lakota Nation $17 million plus interest that accrued over the years, amounting to a total of $106 million. However, the Lakota refused to accept the money, proclaiming that the Black Hills were not for sale. Then, in June 1986, the Lakota filed an appeal in the U.S. Supreme Court, asking for the return of Bear Butte and the Black Hills.. Unfortunately for them, the Court refused to hear their case. Over the following weeks, the South Dakota Democratic Convention discussed the Black Hills controversy and tried to resolve the situation. The convention adopted a platform stating that the "people of South Dakota can [no] longer ignore the Black Hills claim" and urging a study of the issue.[28]

The Oglala Sioux Tribe won an important court decision involving the Docket 74 case, referred to as the 1886 Fort Laramie Treaty Land Claim, on December 5, 1986—100 years after the infamous original agreement. The U.S. Court of Appeals for the Federal Circuit decreed in favor of the Oglala Tribe and reversed a 1985 decision of the U.S. Claims Court, which had implemented an offer from the federal government to settle the Docket 74 case with the tribes of the Sioux Nation for an estimated $40 million. The tribe had previously rejected the offer and asked for the Black Hills returned. The claims court ruled that the Sioux Nation had ceded all its lands outside of the Great Sioux Reservation (western South Dakota), including fourteen million acres east of the Missouri River in North and South Dakota and thirty-four million acres southwest of the Missouri River in North Dakota, South Dakota, Wyoming, Nebraska, Colorado, and Kansas. The Oglala argued that the award should be reversed because the Sioux did not cede any land in the 1868 treaty. The tribe said the land was seized in the 1877 act, along with the Black Hills, thus entitling the Sioux tribes to interest on the award if they should accept compensation.[29]

Attempting to find a resolution to the Black Hills controversy, Senator Bill Bradley of New Jersey introduced a bill in Congress during early 1987. On March 10, Senator Daniel Inouye of Hawaii cosponsored the bill known as S.R. 705, and Bradley reintroduced it. In the House of Representatives, James Howard of New Jersey cosponsored the Bradley bill (H.R. 1506) with Congressmen Morris Udall of Arizona and George Miller of California. The bill involved returning 1.3 million acres of federal land, including the Black Hills, to the Sioux.[30]

Throughout Indian Country and in Washington, D.C., the Black Hills controversy aroused attention, and it was the focus of the meeting of the Aberdeen area tribal chairmen's association at Pierre, South Dakota in August 1987. During the meeting, a mild shock occurred when, in the middle of August, Los Angeles millionaire Philip Stevens, who claimed to be the great-grandson of Oglala leader Standing Bear, offered a plan to the chairmen and then asked to be appointed their "chief negotiator." Stevens claimed, "I guarantee that by the [national] election [of 1988], I will get you the Black Hills and $3 billion."[31] The tribal chairmen made no immediate response but announced that they would take this proposition back to their tribal councils. Surprisingly, the Rosebud Sioux Tribal Council adopted a resolution rejecting Stevens's proposition.[32]

Stevens's hard-line proposal was not easily dismissed. During the first week in October 1987, Gerald M. Clifford of the Black Hills Steering Committee went to Washington, D.C., with Philip Stevens and Mario Gonzales, counsel for the Oglala Sioux Tribe, to meet with staff members in the Senate, House, and Senator Bradley's office to discuss the possibility of the Stevens plan.[33]

A couple of weeks later, on October 20, the Oglala Sioux Tribal Council adopted a resolution supporting Stevens and his plan. Furthermore, the council directed the Steering Committee in Washington to support Stevens. This course of action caused some difficulty with delegates of the Steering Committee, and they did not meet again to discuss the Stevens proposition. Clifford was suspicious of Stevens's promise and doubted his claim of being the great-grandson of Standing Bear. About the same time, U.S. Senator Tom Daschle of South Dakota organized the Open Hills Association to oppose the Bradley bill and any land return of the Black Hills.[34] Factions with diverse opinions began emerging, representing certain Lakota tribes and elements within the tribes.

In November, the Standing Rock Sioux Tribal Council held a forum to disseminate information on the Black Hills controversy. Taking no action, the Standing Rock Sioux maintained their previous position of support for the Bradley bill and the Black Hills Steering Committee. During the same month, the Rosebud Sioux Tribal Council adopted a resolution requesting Bradley to reintroduce the Sioux Nation Black Hills bill.[35] Disunited, the Lakota tribes saw no answer in the near future, except for the return of the Black Hills.

On December 9, 1987, the *Lakota Times* took a poll among the Sioux people to learn of their opinions on the Black Hills controversy. A surprising nineteen percent of the respondents wanted to accept the $1.3 million in compensation for the Black Hills. Calculated on a per capita basis, this would give the Sioux $2,800 each.[36]

On December 23, a forum was held in South Dakota to discuss the effects of the Bradley bill. Gerald Clifford, coordinator of the Black Hills Steering Committee, which supported the measure, described the bill as a reconciliation between the Sioux and non-Indians. He argued that racial tension clouded the Black Hills issue in South Dakota and stated that he hoped to bring a settlement and put an end to the racial tension between Indians and whites, a tension that had been brewing for more than 100 years. The Bradley bill had not been resolved when the congressional session ended; it would have to be considered the following year.[37]

In February 1988, Senator Bradley sent a letter to the Black Hills Steering Committee, stating in part that "I will not amend my bill, S. 705, to include additional millions or billions."[38] The Bradley effort lost some of its support in Congress and among the Sioux on March 23 when Representative James Howard, a backer of the bill, died. Then, on May 16, the Oglala Sioux Tribal Council officially withdrew from the Black Hills Steering Committee, stating that "the Steering Committee has not supported the Oglala Sioux Tribe's position in Resolution 87–143 [support for Stevens and compensation] and has in fact opposed the Oglala Sioux Tribe in this regard" and that the Oglala Sioux Tribe "should pursue its goals in the Black Hills claim independently or with any Sioux tribe that wishes to join it." The council said that it would work with the Grey Eagle Society (a group of Sioux elders who opposed the Bradley bill) and the Black Hills Sioux Nation Treaty Council.[39]

In January 1989, the Lower Brule and Crow Creek Tribal Councils reaffirmed their resolutions to support both the Steering Committee and the Bradley bill and requested that the legislation be reintroduced.[40] Dubious of the contents of the Bradley bill, the eight bands of the Sioux asked a law firm in Washington, D.C., to represent them. They requested that the firm research the court case in light of pos-

sible malpractice by the three claims attorney involved in the closing
of the case two week earlier. They were referring to Arthur Lazarus,
William Sonosky, and William Howard Payne.[41]

March 20 to March 22, 1989, the Sioux tribes held a meeting, but
only two tribal chairmen attended—Pine Ridge leader Paul Iron Cloud
and Rosebud chairman Alex Lunderman. In spite of the lack of leaders present, many Sioux turned out for the meeting—mainly the elderly and grassroots Lakota people of Rapid City and the nearby reservations who opposed compensation for the Black Hills and wanted
their return. "Money is like snow; it melts away," said Chairman Iron
Cloud about the compensation. Furthermore, Chairman Lunderman
claimed that the federal government was using the Black Hills controversy to "keep us fighting against each other."[42] The only consensus that resulted from the meeting was that everyone there agreed
not to agree.

And so, the Black Hills controversy remains unsettled. Once again,
the lust for gold, the most powerful symbol of wealth for non-Indians,
had torn Native Americans—in this case, the Lakota—from their lands.
Centuries earlier, the Spaniards' search for an El Dorado had disrupted the Pueblo people in the Southwest and other groups in Mexico
and South American. Later, Americans chased the Cherokee out of
Georgia with rumors of gold in the 1830s. And the neighboring tribes
of Ishi, the last Yahi, were exterminated during the California gold
rush in the 1840s.

The strong demand for fossil fuels in contemporary times has in-
jected new life into the controversy surrounding the Black Hills of
the Lakota. The conflict involves the driving forces of two very different cultures, two incongruent sets of values, and two divergent per-
spectives on the same geographic area. Both factions want this land—
one as a source of valuable natural resources and the other as a spiritual center, a link to the understanding of life. Today, the Lakota and
the Cheyenne continue to fight for control of the Black Hills—their
Mother Earth—just as their predecessors did 100 years ago. The reason why they continue this fight is simple: In the souls of the Lakota,
they *are* the Black Hills, a part of the earth. It is a desecration that
the future of the sacred hills will likely be settled in the courts, in an
arbitration pitting economic interest against cultural interest.

The ancient words of a Lakota holyman, Black Elk, described the
hills and all of creation, explaining the interrelationship of all parts of
the Creator's world: "All things are the works of the Great Spirit. We
should know that He is within all things: the trees, the grasses, the
rivers, the mountains, and all the four-legged animals, and the winged
peoples; and even more important, we should understand that He is

also above all things and peoples. When we do understand all this deeply in our hearts, then we will fear, and love, and know the great Spirit, and then we will be and act and live as He intends."[43] Acknowledging the humble role of human beings and that the Great Spirit of life is within all of us, we share this spirituality with all things. The respected elder of the Lakota did not want us to forget this.

The multiple issues raised in the legal battle for the Black Hills have obscured the true meaning of this sacred area to the Lakota, the original caretakers. To them, the Black Hills represent the heart of their identity. These hills are filled with the abstract spirituality of life, and it is this spirituality that shapes the Lakota's identity and tells them how they should live. To the white settlers, ranchers, miners, and energy companies, by contrast, the Black Hills and their rich minerals have represented a source of capitalistic gain. The recent work of energy companies in the Black Hills, seeking to extract the abundant fossil fuels, is but one example of the mining operations found throughout Indian Country today, and the unseen consequences of this enterprise are vast. But the special connection between human spirituality and the environment cannot be broken as long as the Lakota people remember who they are.

NOTES

1. Ernest L. Schusky, *The Forgotten Sioux: An Ethnohistory of the Lower Brule Reservation* (Chicago: Nelson-Hall, 1975), p. 33.
2. "Treaty of Fort Laramie, 1868," in Charles J. Kappler, comp. and ed., *Indian Treaties, 1778–1883*, 3rd printing (New York: Interland Publishing, 1975), pp. 998–1007.
3. Schusky, *Forgotten Sioux*, p. 63, originally quoted in James S. Foster, *Outlines of History of the Territory of Dakota* (Yankton, S.D.: M'Intyre and Foster, 1870), p. 39.
4. Schusky, *Forgotten Sioux*, pp. 86–89.
5. John R. Milton, *South Dakota: A Bicentennial History* (New York: W. W. Norton, 1977), p. 26.
6. Ibid., p. 24.
7. *Act of August 15, 1876*, ch. 289, 19 *U.S. Statutes at Large*, 176, 192.
8. Report of the Commission Appointed to Treat With the Sioux Indians for the Relinquishment of the Black Hills," Commissioner of Indian Affairs Annual Report, 1876, serial 1680, 686–702, and Reverend Peter Rosen, *Pa-Ha-Sa-Pah or The Black Hills of South Dakota* (St. Louis: Nixon-Jones Printing, 1895), pp. 341–344.
9. Milton, *South Dakota*, p. 26.
10. *Act of February 28, 1877*, ch. 71, 19 Stat. 254.
11. Milton, *South Dakota*, p. 24, and Rosen, *Pa-Ha-Sa-Pah*, p. 352.

12. Robert M. Utley, *The Last Days of the Sioux Nation* (New Haven and London: Yale University Press, 1963), p. 20.

13. Francis Paul Prucha, *The Great Father, The United States Government and the American Indians,* vol. 2 (Lincoln and London: University of Nebraska Press, 1984), p. 633.

14. Utley, *Last Days of Sioux Nation,* p. 77, originally quoted in Elaine Goodale Eastman, "The Ghost Dance War and Wounded Knee Massacre of 1890–91," *Nebraska History* 26 (1945): 29. Brigadier General L. W. Colby, who commanded the Nebraska National Guard, wrote, "The drought and consequent failure of crops were everywhere general throughout the western states and territories and especially in the Dakotas, Wyoming and Nebraska," quoted in L. W. Colby, "The Sioux Indian War of 1890–91," *Transactions and Reports of the Nebraska State Historical Society* 3 (1892): 144–190.

15. W. F. Kelley, who was present at the Wounded Knee massacre, described the event in "The Indian Troubles and the Battle of Wounded Knee," *Transactions and Reports of the Nebraska State Historical Society* 4 (1892): 30–50.

16. The famous Homestake Gold Mine is described in detail in Roderick Peattie, ed., *The Black Hills* (New York: Vanguard Press, 1952), pp. 280–310; gold in the area is the focus in Watson Parker, *Gold in the Black Hills* (Lincoln and London: University of Nebraska Press, 1982), which was originally published in 1966 by University of Oklahoma Press. Outlaw celebrities of the Black Hills are discussed in Robert J. Casey, *The Black Hills and Their Incredible Characters* (Indianapolis and New York: Bobbs-Merrill, 1949).

17. *Sioux Tribe v. United States,* 97 Ct. Cl.613 (1942).

18. *United States v. Sioux Nation,* 448 U.S. 371, 385.

19. *Sioux Nation v. United States,* 33 Indian Claims Commission 151 (1974).

20. "*U.S. v. Washington,*" U.S. Court of Appeals, Ninth Circuit, 1975, 520 F.2d 676, certiorari denied, 423, U.S. 1016 (1975).

21. *American Indian Religious Freedom Act.* P.L. 95–341, May 15, 1978. *U.S. Statutes at Large,* 92:469.

22. *Fools Crow v. Gullet,* 541 F.Supp. 785 (D.S.D. 1982).

23. *United States v. Sioux Nation of Indians,* 448 U.S. 371 (1980).

24. In an unrelated but important event, 2,000 Indian activists held a protest on October 5, 1979, against the development of uranium mining in the Black Hills. See Sharon O'Brien, "Chronology," in Duane Champagne, ed., *The Native North American Almanac: A Reference Work on Native North Americans in the United States and Canada* (Detroit: Gale Research, 1994), p. 81.

25. J. Gregory Merrion and Robert L. Bayless et al, and Amoco Production Company and Marathon Oil Company v. Jicarilla Apache Indian Tribe," January 25, 1982, 455 U.S. 907 (1982).

26. *Sioux Tribe v. United States,* 7 Cl. Ct. (1985).

27. "The Black Hills Alliance," *Akwesasne Notes* 2, no. 2 (May 1979).

28. "Tribal Factions Agree to Disagree Over Black Hills Issue," *Lakota Times,* March 28, 1989, p. 11.

29. "Ost Wins Major Victory in Land Claims," *Lakota Times*, December 17, 1986, p. 1. Full coverage of the Black Hills claim is given in Edward Lazarus, *Black Hills White Justice: The Sioux Nation Versus the United States, 1775 to the Present* (New York: Harper Collins, 1991).

30. "Mickelson Lists Objections to Bradley's Hills Bill Measure," *Lakota Times*, May 13, 1987.

31. "Tribal Factions Agree to Disagree."

32. Ibid.

33. Ibid.

34. Ibid.

35. Ibid.

36. "The Hills Are Not for Sale, Says Reader," *Lakota Times*, December 30, 1987.

37. "Intent of Bradley Bill Sparks Debate," *Lakota Times*, December 30, 1987.

38. "Tribal Factions Agree to Disagree."

39. Ibid.

40. Ibid.

41. "Oldest Land Claim May Not Be Over Yet," *Lakota Times*, August 19, 1987.

42. "Tribal Factions Agree to Disagree."

43. Joseph E. Brown, ed., *The Sacred Pipe: Black Elk's Account of the Seven Rites of the Oglala Sioux* (Norman: University of Oklahoma Press, 1953), p. xx.

PART TWO

DEFENSE STRATEGIES FOR TRIBAL
NATURAL RESOURCES

7

THE DEMAND FOR NATURAL
RESOURCES ON RESERVATIONS

More than 100 ago, Indian tribal leaders were forced to negotiate with white Americans and the U.S. government for possession of Indian lands. Today's tribal leaders face a similar
situation, due to the growing energy crisis and increased demands for
natural resources. Depletion of America's mineral reserves has caused
energy companies to look toward reservation lands to replenish needed
oil, coal, gas, and uranium supplies. Even water has become a precious resource for transporting coal in slurry pipelines. In almost every Western state, Indian and white interests are competing for this
priceless commodity.[1] And as a result of the increasing demand for
natural resources, relations between tribal reservation leaders and
white Americans have intensified.

Today, more than half of the nation's coalfields are west of the
Mississippi River.[2] One-third of the Western fields exist on lands of
twenty-two tribes,[3] and large portions of most of these tribes' reservations will be disrupted during mining operations. The Northern
Cheyenne, whose 440,000-acre reservation stands over a rich coal vein
in southeastern Montana, will have approximately fifty-six percent of
their land mined.[4] The Crow Reservation, adjacent to the Cheyenne,
will suffer similar disturbances, reducing the land available for the
Crow's own use. In Montana and North Dakota, coalfields are estimated to contain fifteen times the energy reserves of the Alaska North
Slope oil and gas fields. The Jicarilla Apache Reservation, in New
Mexico, contains 154 million barrels of oil and 2 trillion cubic feet of
gas. Overall, geologists report that twenty-five to forty percent of

America's uranium, one-third of its coal, and approximately five percent of its oil and gas are on Indian reservations in the West.[5]

Large-scale mining on reservation lands has occurred since the late nineteenth century. In the late 1800s and early decades of the twentieth century, for example, coal was mined on Choctaw and Chickasaw lands in southeastern Oklahoma. Water was vied for on the Fort Belknap Reservation in Montana in the early 1900s, and non-Indians aggressively pursued Pueblo irrigated lands in the 1920s. Oil was pumped from wells on the lands of the Osage, Creek, and Seminole in Oklahoma during the 1920s and 1930s. In the 1950s, tons of coal was mined on the Crow and Northern Cheyenne Reservations in Montana.[6] In the 1960s, Peabody Coal Company and Shell Oil operated coal mines on the Crow Reservation, and the latter made a record bid of $1.1 million for prospecting rights on 83,000 acres of Crow land.[7] In the late 1960s, the Department of the Interior encouraged the Navajo and Hopi Tribes to provide water and to forgo taxing non-Indians on their reservations so that a power plant using coal could be built at Page, Arizona. The Bureau of Indian Affairs convinced tribal leaders that nuclear power would replace the need for Indian coal in the area. But in the next few years, the coal industry raced to its highest profits ever, and the Navajo and Hopi were locked into contracts for many years.[8]

Mining operations on Indian lands can be monetarily beneficial; consequently, tribes bestowed with large mineral deposits on their reservations receive large royalty payments. Such revenue enables the tribes to promote various programs and to improve their economies. The Western tribes faced a grave dilemma, however. Should they allow mining development of their reservations? In 1977, Peter MacDonald, chairperson of the Navajo Nation, noted in a speech before the Western attorneys general in Seattle that "the history of Indian resource development reaches far into our past. Before the white man came to our lands, Indians developed their resources for their own needs. Our people used only what they needed, and they were very careful not to destroy the land. The railroads, trucks and powerlines transport this material [resources] off the reservation to provide Americans with a better life." "At the same time, most Indians still live in poverty, without such 'luxuries' as water and electricity, which most Americans regard as the barest necessities of life.' "[9]

The Indians' reaction to the demand for their energy resources is twofold: reluctance to allow the mining operations to continue, on one hand, and a progressive attitude toward increased mining to help develop tribal programs, on the other. Among the Western tribes, factions for and against mining have developed among the Native peoples.

Conservative traditionalists oppose mining. Progressives, especially tribal leaders, favor mining, but they are in the minority. Nevertheless, tribal leaders control their tribes' affairs, and they sometimes negotiate with energy companies without their peoples' consent.

Generally, the conservative blocs consist of the tribal elders. They see their traditional cultures threatened, leading them to believe that after the mining companies are gone, their lands will never be the same. David Strange Owl, one of thirty-six Northern Cheyenne on a fact-finding mission, visited the mining operations on the Navajo Reservation in the spring of 1977. He confessed, "Before, I didn't know much about coal." Observing the mining operations aroused in him feelings of repugnance: "What I've seen between the Navajo and Hopi is a sad thing, to see the strip-mining, on their reservations ... because it's going to hurt a lot of lives of [our] reservation—our lives, our culture."[10] Possessing a deep attachment to the land, traditionalists view themselves as a part of that land. According to Native tradition, the earth is mother to all, and no harm should come to her; in fact, the "Mother Earth" concept is one of the few universal concepts among American Indians. Those who still hold to this concept say that tribal members who want to exploit the land are no longer Indians.[11]

By 2025, more than 250,000 acres of Plains soil will be torn up by huge, steam-powered shovel machines called draglines that are as tall as a 16-story building, weigh 27 million pounds, and are able to move 220 cubic yards (325 tons) of "overburden"—earth—in a single pass. In the path of the draglines are croplands, wildlife refuges, and former residential areas. On the average, the steam shovels rip down through 100 to 150 feet of soil just to reach the coal veins.[12]

Many traditionalists bitterly oppose energy companies wanting to exploit their lands. They do not understand or care about the growing energy crisis. As one young Hopi Indian put it, "Don't tell me about an energy crisis. I don't even have electricity in my village."[13]

Mining operations are lending credence to the traditionalists' fears. As their machines scar mother earth and jeopardize the relationship between nature and mankind, the companies bring more non-Indians onto the reservation. Soon, the non-Indians may outnumber the Native people on their own lands. If current mining operations continue on the Northern Cheyenne Reservation, for instance, twenty non-Indians will be brought in for every Cheyenne living there.[14] Many Indians charge that tribal leaders are abusing not only their land but also their people and their culture by cooperating with energy companies.

Conversely, tribal leaders believe that they can improve the welfare of their people by generating revenues and funding programs from mining arrangements. They deem that now is the time to take advantage of the energy companies. And with the increasing demand for natural resources, there is no doubt that revenue received from mining companies will mean further changes in Indian lifestyles. For some Native people, social changes are already taking place. Residents of reservations who work at off-reservation jobs, for instance, are familiar with the mainstream society.[15]

The progressive Indian nations have elected to improve their situation socially, politically, and economically. Peter MacDonald asserted that his people have chosen to change: "We are an emerging nation. Like other underdeveloped countries with rich but exhaustible supplies of fuel and minerals, we realize we must use our natural resources to create jobs for our people and put us on the road to economic self-sufficiency. Otherwise, we will not have anything left when our resources are gone. That's why we are demanding more from the people who want to exploit our wealth."[16]

Speaking on behalf of the 4,500 members of the Crow tribe whose reservation possesses some fourteen to eighteen billion tons of coal, former chairperson Patrick Stands Over Bull said, "I'm for coal development, but I'm for control."[17] Stands Over Bull asserted that his tribe needed time to develop plans for land use and to pass zoning regulations and tax laws.

Navajo and Crow tribal members hesitate to allow mining companies onto their lands. In fact, many do not trust their own leaders, some of whom, they allege, have put tribal moneys into their own pockets. Moreover, lack of knowledge about mining techniques, operations, and legalities has made tribal members suspicious of their leaders. How to estimate the resources on their lands and how to judge their value are problems beyond the expertise of most reservation residents. Instances of mismanagement have upset them, and even though tribal members themselves do not understand the intricacies of mining, they blame their officials for any mishaps or miscalculations, especially for long-term leases that force the tribes to "give away" reservation minerals to mining companies.

Tribal leaders have been forced to rely upon non-Indian lawyers and non-Indian advisers who are experts in energy development areas and the legalities of leasing contracts. This dependency has been reduced in recent years as the number of trained Indian lawyers has grown, but lawyers still demand large fees for their services. Past relations with attorneys and non-Indian experts have caused tribal members to be distrustful of everyone.

Even without the support of their tribespeople, Indian leaders are confident that they can supervise mining operations and develop their own tribal mining companies. But the lack of training and, especially, of capital has hindered and sometimes discouraged them. Addressing the Indians' lack of mining knowledge, the late John Woodenlegs, a Northern Cheyenne, said, "Coal has been under the Cheyenne reservation a long time, and it can stay there until we known the best thing to do."[18]

Tribal leaders protest that the royalty payments from leases are too low and that tribes are locked into poorly negotiated leases for long periods of time. Because the secretary of the interior is empowered by law to approve leases, the energy companies can control Indian lands by entering into agreements with the Interior Department. Supposedly, the tribes will benefit from such agreements, but Indians criticize the government for failing to advise tribes correctly and for not protecting them from being victimized. Tribes endowed with energy resources are also angered by the lack of proper supervision by the Bureau of Indian Affairs in protecting Indian interests and by the bureau's urging of tribes to accept inadequate leases.[19]

The Northern Cheyenne have alleged that from 1969 to 1971, the U.S. government misadvised them repeatedly. During this period, Peabody, Amax, and Chevron were given exploration and mining leases for over half of the reservation's 450,000 acres. The tribe did not realize how unfair the ill-advised agreements were until 1972, when Consolidation Coal Company offered the tribe $35 an acre, a royalty rate of $.25 per ton of coal, and a $1.5 million community health center. After further investigation, the Cheyenne Tribal Council charged the federal government with thirty-six violations of leasing procedures.[20]

The tribe petitioned Rogers Morton, then secretary of the interior, to cancel all of their leases with energy companies. Instead, the secretary suspended the leases until a "mutual agreement" was worked out between the companies and the tribe. But the Northern Cheyenne demanded cancellation. "We don't negotiate with the companies until they tear those leases up in front of us and burn them," said Tribal chairman Allen Rowland. "And we can start over on our terms, not theirs."[21]

Government and industry officials have responded that, although some mistakes have been made, most leases were negotiated fairly. In 1974, Secretary Morton told Northern Cheyenne leaders that they would have to abide by lease agreements with Peabody, Consolidation, and other companies. Later that same year, however, Northern Cheyenne leases were suspended, and leasing was conducted by negotiation or competitive bidding.[22]

The Crow have charged the secretary of the interior with violating the National Environmental Policy Act and have said that, as a result, their coal leases do not comply with federal regulations. Since the government represents the tribes, through the BIA and the secretary of the interior, there are conflicting attitudes within the federal government, and the tribes are caught in between. The Omnibus Tribal Leasing Act of 1938 authorized the Department of the Interior to approve leases between the tribes and the mining companies.[23] "The government is the trustee of the Indians and the coordinator of national energy policy. That is a conflict of interests," stated Thomas J. Lynaugh, an attorney for the Crow Tribe.[24] Hopi chairperson Abbott Sekaquaptewa summed up the situation when he commented, "The energy situation has put us in a much better posture. We are going to make our decisions on whether to develop our resources, when it will be done, and how."[25]

Indian leaders are currently taking a more active role in the negotiations for their natural resources. In some instances, tribal officials are suing against long-term leases that underpay their tribes, especially because the American dollar has shrunk since these leases were originally signed. The Crow Indians are trying to regain control of some 30,000 acres in southeastern Montana leased to Shell Oil Company and 14,000 acres held by Amax Coal Company. In addition, Peabody Coal Company controls 86,122 acres of Crow land, and Gulf Oil Company holds 73,293.[26] If the Crow are successful in obtaining a favorable decision from the courts, new leases will benefit their tribal economy tremendously.

Another possible alternative for the Crow is to establish joint ownership by forming a new company with an energy firm. Instead of accepting the traditional royalty payments, Crow tribal leaders are asking for a percentage of the production results in raw material or profit. On April 4, 1983, Secretary of the Interior James Watt approved a coal-mining agreement between the Crow and Shell Oil Company to mine an estimated 210 million tons of coal from the reservation's Youngs Creek area. The tribe negotiated $12 million in preproduction and royalty payments. The agreement also provided the tribe with a fifty percent participation in a profit-sharing plan to be implemented after twenty years of mining operations.[27] A decline in coal prices forced Shell to negotiate with the Crow, but negotiations broke off in December 1985. In 1988, the Crow and Shell renewed agreements, and a total of sixty-seven contracts had been made between tribes and energy companies for coal, gas, oil, and uranium.[28]

As early as 1971, the tribes, the Bureau of Indian Affairs, and mining companies began to work on agreements for training and employing Native Americans in the mining industry. The Northern Cheyenne in a community action program proposed a joint venture to the

Indian Bureau through which they would work with Peabody Coal Company to produce "trained and well qualified" Indians to enter the construction and mining businesses.[29]

The Indian Mineral Development Act of 1982 allows tribes to enter into joint agreements to establish companies for developing oil, gas, and other mineral resources. The measure was passed during a lame-duck session of Congress with the expectation that President Ronald Reagan would sign the bill into law. Tribes endowed with energy resources—the so-called energy tribes—could now venture into business enterprises to develop their resources.[30] A contract between the Assiniboine, the Sioux, and the U.S. Energy Corporation was the first approved joint company under the new legislation. Assistant Secretary of the Interior Ken Smith stated that the contract "accords perfectly with [the] President's recently issued Indian policy which calls for the development of reservation economies and the strengthening of tribal governments." Under this particular agreement, the company will bear the entire cost of drilling and operating the first well; afterward, the company and the tribes will share the net proceeds from production.[31]

In another case, the Blackfeet formed a joint ownership with Damson Oil Corporation, a small energy firm. Once the company strikes gas on the Blackfeet Reservation, the tribe will receive 58 percent of the profits after paying operational expenses.[32] The Blackfeet also entered into another agreement, forming a joint company with Blocker Drilling Ltd. Distribution of the drilling company's profits will be based upon the tribe's fifty-one percent ownership and Blocker's forty-nine percent, with the understanding that 90 percent of the company's net cash flow will first be used for purchasing equipment for the company to operate. The agreement also includes an on-the-job training program for tribal members in both roughneck work and management.[33] The joint company worked out as promised, although the Blackfeet hoped for more control of the management.

The Chippewa-Cree Indians and other Native groups are exploring the joint venture idea, yet some tribes want to form their own energy companies in the future. "Up to now, we've always been satisfied in exchange for mineral rights," said Navajo leader Peter MacDonald. "That is no longer enough. We want a share of the income instead of the royalties. Eventually, we plan to go it alone in development of our natural resources."[34]

The Jicarilla Apache of New Mexico began drilling their own oil and gas wells, using their tribal funds. The Assiniboine and Sioux Tribes of the Fort Peck Reservation in Montana did the same in developing their own oil and gas wells.[35]

In an effort to protect reservation resources, leaders of twenty-five Western Indian tribes united in 1975 to form the Council of Energy Resource Tribes.[36] CERT is controlled by an executive board consisting of eight tribal chairpersons and a ninth chairperson who serves as the executive director. With one-third of all coal in the West located on Indian lands, CERT takes an aggressive business approach toward energy firms to bargain in the best interests of the tribes. It sought advice in the late 1970s from several members of the Organization of Petroleum Exporting Countries (OPEC) over the U.S. government's disapproval. To halt further OPEC assistance, the federal government awarded CERT grants totaling $1,997,000 from the Department of Energy (DOE), the BIA, and the Department of Health, Education, and Welfare. Initially, CERT opened offices in Denver, Colorado, and Washington, D.C., but it closed the doors of the Washington office when its 1982 budget of $6 million was cut to $3.1 million in 1983.[37] The council educates tribes in evaluating their energy sources, in the technology of mining natural resources, and in the development of human resources; it also provides management studies and computer services.[38] To prevent further exploitation of Indian lands, CERT has established a broad Indian policy "so that energy companies won't be able to pick us off one by one," according to Charles Lohah, the acting secretary for CERT.[39]

It should be added that despite its success, the organization has hardly been immune from criticism. In recent years, CERT has been severely criticized by Indians who charge that it is too "pro-development" regarding reservation resources. CERT has also been accused of holding "glittery, black-tie galas for federal officials and energy company brass."[40]

Today, coal is considered a key natural resource to meet the recurring energy crises, and mining companies are eager to develop reservation minerals. The nation's energy resources east of the Mississippi have been severely depleted, and mining firms look to the West for new fields of coal and other natural resources. Economic reasons have also forced companies westward because strip mining is more economical than shaft mining in the East. Vast reserves of coal in beds up 100 feet thick lie just below the surface, and over half of the 225 billion tons of coal in the West is available by strip mining. In the West, draglines can strip-mine 100 tons of coal per man-day of labor, more than eight times the rate from the deep Appalachian shaft mines. Health and safety conditions are also more favorable in Western strip mining, allowing coal to be mined at $3 to $5 per ton, as compared with $9 to $14 in the East.[41]

The list of corporations on Indian lands in the West is long. In the

Black Hills of South Dakota alone, 26 multinational corporations have obtained state prospecting leases for over one million acres.[42] Other examples include several energy companies working in the Four Corners area on the Navajo and Hopi Reservations, mining for coal and uranium. In Oklahoma, the Sac and Fox, Osage, Creek, Choctaw, Chickasaw, and other tribes have leases with energy companies extracting oil, gas, or coal.

Until recent years, energy firms have had easy access to Western coalfields. The Department of the Interior could persuade tribal officials to lease lands to companies, thereby easing the exploitation of Indian lands. As a result, the Utah International Mining Company has been operating the largest strip-mining project in the world in the Four Corners region on Navajo land.[43] In response to growing pressure to renegotiate with the Crow Tribe, Westmoreland Resources renegotiated its mining leases with the Crow in November 1973. The Crow Tribe formed the Crow Mineral Committee, which was elected by the tribal council and entrusted to negotiate directly with Westmoreland officials.[44] As of 1975, of the entire Crow Reservation of 2,226,000 acres, Westmoreland leased 30,876 acres, Shell Oil leased 30,248 acres, Peabody Coal leased 86,122 acres, and Gulf Minerals Resources leased 73,292 acres. A 1975 survey prepared by Rural Research Associates of Missoula and Edgar, Montana, estimated that the Crow Reservation contained four to five and a half billion tons of strippable coal, plus six to twelve billion tons of coal that would be more costly to mine.[45]

Today, as Native American officials who conduct negotiations with energy company officials, tribal leaders are developing a new image for themselves. Unlike their forebears, today's tribal leaders understand the complexities of handling land negotiations. Company and government officials have noticed the transition from the old tribal leadership; the new leaders are adamant in their demands and cognizant of white ways of dealing for land.

Reservation leaders have become more successful in negotiations, and the future looks brighter for Plains and Southwest tribes. With the increased knowledge and understanding of white ways, tribal leaders are also initiating and developing new programs to help their people. In this context, it is appropriate to cite the advice of the Sioux leader Sitting Bull. When the mighty Sioux Nation was in decline, mostly because of white influence, Sitting Bull warned: "Take the best of the white man's road, pick it up and take it with you. That which is bad, leave it alone, cast it away. Take the best of the old Indian ways— always keep them. They have been proven for thousands of years. Do not let them die."[46]

The younger tribal leaders of the Western reservations are making tremendous strides in improving the tribes' status. Beginning at the level of Third World nations, Indian groups are progressing rapidly toward parity with white American society. With competent leadership and additional aid from the Bureau of Indian Affairs, energy tribes have been able to develop successful industries. Federal funds have been appropriated to finance such tribal ventures as Yatay Industries, Sandia Indian Industries, Apache Indian Industries, and Ute Fabricating, Ltd.[47] Other tribal industries include Northern Pueblo Enterprises, Navajo Indian Wood Products, Zuni Enterprises, and White Eagle Industries. These business ventures are the result of careful planning, and they exemplify the entrepreneurial quality of modern Indian achievement.

Partly because such new tribal programs are highly visible, a resurgence of Indian nationalism is developing among Western tribal nations. Damson Oil president Barrie M. Damson has contended that this Native nationalism will grow and that energy companies need to recognize this.[48]

As Indian Americans entered the 1980s, some problems remained unresolved. A 72-page report from the Minerals Management Service of the Department of the Interior stated that $119.2 million in royalties had reportedly been paid to Indians in 1980. The next year, some $161.4 million in royalties went to Indians.[49] Unfortunately, in one known case, the royalty checks never reached the people. In Wyoming, seventy allottees from the Wind River Reservation have filed a lawsuit against Amoco Production Company for not paying royalties on 1.3 million barrels of crude oil taken from the Lander Oil Field between 1971 and 1982. The allottees, who have coalesced into the Wind River Allottees Association, petitioned their case to a federal court because they felt that the government would not act soon enough on their behalf. The group seeks either a return of the oil or payment at the current value, an estimated $41 million, plus compensation for punitive damages.[50]

An area of new importance opened after a court decision of 1982 in which the U.S. Supreme Court ruled that the Jicarilla Apaches could charge energy companies a severance tax for mining on their land. Two other tribes, the Shoshone and the Arapaho of Wyoming, are attempting to impose a four percent severance tax on oil and gas, pending approval by the secretary of the interior. With state governments also taxing the mining companies, the energy firms now face double taxation. Although the state taxes are generally higher, the energy companies are challenging the right of the tribes to tax them.[51] The 1982 ruling has opened up a new source for tribal income, but it is one that reservation leaders will have to fight to keep.

Many tribal leaders and reservation peoples, however, face serious problems. Some Americans assume that Indians are getting rich from royalty payments, though actually only fifteen percent of the Indian population has natural resources on tribal lands. In 1982, the BIA reported that royalties on reservations totaled more than $396 million, but if the royalties were distributed to the entire Indian population of 1.3 million (according to the 1980 census), the per capita payment would be only $290 for each person. For their oil, tribes received on the average $2 a barrel in royalties at a time when OPEC nations were demanding and receiving $40 a barrel. Four of the largest energy resource deposits are on the Blackfeet, Crow, Fort Peck, and Wind River Reservations in Montana and Wyoming. In 1980, more than 1,200 wells on the four Plains reservations produced 6.1 million barrels of oil. As for coal, in early 1981, when American coal was being sold to foreign buyers for $70 a ton, the Navajo were receiving only $.15 a ton from Utah International Mining Company and less than $.38 a ton from Pittsburgh and Midway Coal Company. These two companies negotiated leases with the Navajos in 1953, 1964, and 1966.[52]

In negotiations with the energy companies, tribal leaders were historically at a disadvantage, but conditions have changed in the 1990s. Their governments once could not pay for equipment to evaluate their natural resources, but with the assistance of CERT and their own resources, tribes now have a very good idea of the natural resources on their lands. During the late 1970s, the requisite trained personnel and exploratory data were in short supply, forcing tribes to give up a major share of their potential wealth by leasing their lands or entering into joint ventures with energy companies. This has also changed in the 1990s.

Nonetheless, despite these improvements, Indian affairs continue to have a low priority in Washington, and the entire budget appropriated for Indian affairs would buy just one aircraft carrier. Even worse, the BIA is a frequent hindrance to tribal leaders because it also lacks the expertise that the mining firms possess in the highly competitive business of energy development. For example, on January 25, 1982, ruling in favor of the Jicarilla Apaches, the Supreme Court maintained that Indian tribes "have the inherent power" to impose severance taxes. Nevertheless, a few months later, the BIA wrote regulations for the severance taxation, and in doing so, it invited the opinions of representatives from the oil and gas industry. Indian criticism forced the BIA to withdraw its regulations, and guidelines were substituted. The bureau's actions prompted additional criticism from U.S. Representative Sidney Yates, who chaired the House appropriations sub-committee that handles Indian affairs. Yates chided, "Tell me why an oil and gas industry association should be allowed to formulate guidelines by which the tribes will be able to tax members of that industry."[53]

Today's tribal leaders, unlike their ancestors, have had to adopt a hurried "get-tough" attitude in a businesslike, modern, "ruthless" way. Such behavior is foreign to the traditional nature of Indian leadership, and it is an obstacle that tribal representatives must overcome if their people are to survive. Although the leaders can probably use more expertise in running their reservation governments like corporations, they know how to hire such expertise. In a very short time, they have become educated in the high-finance business world, and they are experienced in dealing with the bureaucracy of the federal government.[54] Contemporary Indian leaders are sophisticated and forceful in order to protect their people and their reservations—lands that were deemed worthless in the nineteenth century.

The energy crises and the industrial demand for natural resources on Indian lands imply serious repercussions for the tribes' future. The anticipated outcomes are both positive and negative and will have tremendous impact on Indian leaders, tribal members, and reservation lands. The mining operations, the gasification plants to convert coal into gas, and the facilities necessary to produce electricity are extensive and cover large areas of land; as a result, reservation supplies of nonreplaceable natural resources are being severely depleted. In addition, land formations that have religious significance to the people are permanently damaged. Even with reclamation attempts to restore the land to its original state, it will never be the same to the traditional Indian.

Perhaps the fears of the tribal elders who oppose the mining of their mother earth are justified. While tribal leaders are trying to improve their tribes' economies through new programs, schools, and jobs, perhaps a greater harm will come to their people. Aside from the exploitation of their lands, the trend to adopt white ways may also mean that much of the tribal cultures will be forgotten.

Can Indians live with one foot in the traditional world and the other in the white world? Many are doing it now, but how much of their tribal heritage do they remember, and how successfully have they assimilated into white American society? Currently, more Indians than ever are receiving the same education as whites and are moving rapidly into the mainstream society. Indians who live on reservations are becoming more aware of the functions of white society as they travel to and from their reservations. Once living in poverty, many Native people have now raised their economic level and have become successful American citizens according to white standards. Perhaps it is premature to judge whether the Indian has opted for social change at the cost of losing Native identity. Certainly, the next generation will provide better answers.

As the twentieth century ends, America's need for natural resources to heat family homes, operate automobiles, and run industries continues to grow. As a result, coal mining in Wyoming has become a $1.2 billion industry, and the Kerr-McGee operation in the Powder River Basin is now the fourth largest coal mine in the country. By 1996, Wyoming was the nation's largest producer of low-sulfur coal, mining 279 million tons a year; West Virginia and Kentucky followed at 170 and 149 million tons, respectively. With typical houses depended upon coal for heating, the annual demand is seven tons. Clearly, the demand for natural resources has not abated.[55]

At the present time, the growing demand for natural resources on Indian lands has acted as a catalyst in forcing Indians, especially tribal leaders, to choose a new lifestyle for their peoples. They are confronted with the dilemma of making a social transition from the traditional world to the white society's lifestyle. It is ironic that today's Indian leaders are negotiating with white Americans and the federal government for tribal lands just as their ancestors did more than one hundred years ago.

NOTES

1. Dennis William, Gerald C. Lubenow, and William J. Cook, "Where Coal Is Not a Problem," *Newsweek*, March 20, 1978, p. 35. See also William H. Veeder, "Water Rights in the Coal Fields of the Yellowstone River Basin," *Law and Contemporary Problems* 40 (1976): 77–96.
2. Richard Boeth, Jeff B. Copeland, Mary Hager, and Phyllis Malamund, "A Paleface Uprising," *Newsweek*, April 10, 1978, p. 40.
3. "Indians Want a Bigger Share of Their Wealth," *Business Week*, May 3, 1976, p. 101; "A Crow Indian Threat to Western Strip Mines," *Business Week*, October 13, 1975, p. 37.
4. Melinda Beck, Jeff B. Copeland, and Merril Shiels, "Resources: The Rich Indians," *Newsweek*, March 20, 1978, p. 61.
5. "A Crow Indian Threat"; "The Black Hills Alliance," *Akwesasne Notes* 2, no. 2 (May 1979).
6. Joseph Campbell, U.S. Comptroller General, to Secretary of Interior, November 26, 1957, and Alfred Hitchcock, Coal Dealer of Crow Agency, Montana, to Senator Mike Mansfield, July 23, 1958, Lee Metcalf Papers, Folder 227–3, Box 227, Montana Historical Society Archives, Helena, Montana.

7. "Record Coal Lease Bid Received on Crow Indian Reservation," news release, Department of the Interior, April 30, 1968, Lee Metcalf Papers, Folder 223–1, Box 223, Montana Historical Society Archives, Helena, Montana.
8. Marjane Ambler, "Indian Energies Devoted to Self-Sufficiency," *National Forum* 71, no. 2 (Spring 1991): 22.
9. "Energy and Land Use Questions on Indian Lands," *Wassaja* 5, no. 6 (September 1977), originally stated in "A Major Statement to the Annual Meeting of Western Attorney Generals," Seattle, Washington, August 9, 1977, by former Navajo chairperson Peter MacDonald.
10. "Killing the Earth, Air, Water," *Akwesasne Notes* 9, no. 1 (Spring 1977).
11. Clyde Kluckhohn and Dorthea Leighton, *The Navajo* (Cambridge, Mass.: Harvard University Press, 1958), pp. 227–228; Philip Reno, "The Navajos: High, Dry and Penniless," *Nation*, March 29, 1975, p. 359.
12. Michael Garity, "The Pending Energy Wars, America's Final Act of Genocide," *Akwesasne Notes* 11, no. 5 (December 1979).
13. Fred Harris and LaDonna Harris, "Indians, Coal, and the Big Sky," *The Progressive* (December 1974): 25.
14. "Indians Want a Bigger Share of Their Wealth," p. 102.
15. Imre Sutton, *Indian Land Tenure: Bibliographical Essays and a Guide to the Literature* (New York and Paris: Clearwater Publishing, 1975), p. 201.
16. "American Indians Bargain 'Arab Style' to Cash in on Resources," *U.S. News and World Report*, June 3, 1974, p. 53.
17. "A Crow Indian Threat."
18. David R. Zimmerman, "Can Indians and Environmentalists Find Common Ground?" *The Progressive* (December 1976): 28.
19. "An 'OPEC' Right in America's Back Yard," *U.S. News and World Report*, August 2, 1976, p. 29; Zimmerman, "Can Indians and Environmentalists Find Common Ground?"
20. "The Black Hills Alliance."
21. "The Northern Cheyenne ... 'Defending the Last Retreat' ..." *Akwesasne Notes* 10, no. 1 (Spring 1978).
22. "An 'OPEC' Right in America's Back Yard"; Harris and Harris, "Indians, Coal, and the Big Sky," p. 23; "Tribes Being Plundered," *Wassaja* 6, no. 11 (December 1978).
23. *Omnibus Tribal Leasing Act of 1938*, May 3, 25, USCS–39a et seq., *U.S. Statutes at Large* 52:347.
24. "A Crow Threat."
25. "Indians Want a Bigger Share of Their Wealth," p. 100.
26. "A Crow Indian Threat."
27. "Watt Approves Coal Mining Agreement," *Lakota Times*, April 14, 1983.
28. Marjane Ambler, *Breaking the Iron Bonds: Indian Control of Energy Development* (Lawrence: University Press of Kansas, 1990), pp. 85 and 243.
29. Kenneth R. LaFever, Director of Community Action Program, to Senator Lee Metcalf, September 15, 1971, Lee Metcalf Papers, Folder 220–4, Box 220, Montana Historical Society Archives, Helena, Montana.

30. "Indian Mineral Development Act," *Lakota Times*, January 6, 1983. The act is Public Law 97–382, December 22, 1982, 96 *U.S. Statutes at Large* 1938.
31. "Ft. Peck Sioux Sign Agreement on Oil & Gas," *Lakota Times*, April 22, 1983.
32. "Indians Want a Bigger Share of Their Wealth," p. 100.
33. "Blackfeet Tribe Forms New Company," *Akwesasne Notes* 2, no. 9 (November 23, 1983). An insightful study of Blackfeet social interaction among mixed-bloods and full-bloods, tribal values, and new tribespeople's status from mining royalties is in Malcolm McFree, *Modern Blackfeet: Montanans on a Reservation* (New York: Holt, Rinehart and Winston, 1972).
34. "American Indians Bargain 'Arab Style' to Cash in on Resources."
35. Ambler, "Indian Energies Devoted."
36. "Indians Want a Bigger Share of Their Wealth," p. 101.
37. Beck, Copeland, and Shiels, "Resources," p. 63; Marjane Ambler, "Controversial Speech Draws Ire at CERT Convention," *Lakota Times*, November 9, 1983.
38. See Note 31. CERT sponsors the Tribal Resource Institute in Business, Engineering, and Science (TRIBES), a college scholarship program to educate Indian youths who will likely help their tribes; see "Rosebud Chairman Elected to CERT Executive Board," *Lakota Times*, December 9, 1982; "$2 Million for Tribes' CERT," *Wassaja* 6, nos. 9–10 (October–November 1978).
39. "Indians Want a Bigger Share of Their Wealth," p. 101.
40. John A. Farrell, "Empty Promises, Misplaced Trust," New Indian War Series, *Denver Post*, November 20, 1983.
41. Thomas Brom, "The Southwest: America's New Appalachia," *Ramparts* (November 1974): 17–18.
42. "The Black Hills Alliance."
43. The Four Corners Power Plant, located on the shore of Lake Powell, occupies 1,021 acres, plus 765 more for storing fly ash. The stacks tower to a height of 800 feet, dispersing more than 600 tons of sulfur dioxide, nitrogen oxides, and ash from about 23,000 tons of coal into the atmosphere each day. An estimated 40,000 acre-feet of water will be consumed annually to flow through the cooling towers at a rate of 270,000 gallons per minute for the transmission lines to carry away its output; see Brom, "The Southwest: America's New Appalachia," p. 18.
44. Pemberton Hutchinson of Westmoreland Resources to Senator Lee Metcalf, July 10, 1974, Lee Metcalf Papers, Folder 227–7, Box 227, Montana Historical Society Archives, Helena, Montana.
45. "Crow Tribal Coal Survey 1975," prepared by Rural Research Associates, Missoula and Edgar, Montana, April 6, 1975, Lee Metcalf Papers, Folder 227–7, Box 227, Montana Historical Society Archives, Helena, Montana.
46. Harris and Harris, "Indians, Coal, and the Big Sky," p. 22.
47. "An 'OPEC' Right in America's Own Back Yard," p. 30.
48. "Indians Want a Bigger Share of Their Wealth," p. 102; "An American 'Nation' Is Gaining Unity, Respect—and Results," *U.S. News and World*

Report, February 25, 1974, pp. 60–61.

49. "Indians Received $161.4 Million in Minerals Royalties in 1981," *Lakota Times*, November 18, 1982.

50. Marjane Ambler, "The Forgotten People," *Lakota Times*, November 2, 1983.

51. Marjane Ambler, "Victories for Tribes in Tax Cases," *Lakota Times*, September 14, 1983. The tribes may be able to use inherent sovereign powers to continue taxing non-Indian leaseholders of mining rights on reservations. See Jim Noble Jr., "Tribal Power to Tax Non-Indian Mineral Leases," *National Resource Journal* 19 (October 1979): 969–995. Two articles that cover the legal extent of tribal taxation of non-Indians are Carol E. Goldberg, "A Dynamic View of Tribal Jurisdiction to Tax Non-Indians," *Law and Contemporary Problems* 40 (1976): 166–189, and Quentin M. Jones, "Mineral Resources: Tribal Development of Reservation Oil and Gas Resources Through the Use of a Nontaxation-Based Tribal Joint Development Program," *American Indian Law Review* 9, no. 1 (1983): 161–194. On state taxes conflicting with tribal taxes, see Sharon E. Classen, "Taxation: State Transaction Privilege Tax: An Interference With Tribal Self-Government," *American Indian Law Review* 7, no. 2 (1979): 317–333.

52. Farrell, "Empty Promises, Misplaced Trust."

53. Ibid. The right of the tribes to impose a severance tax is based on the combined cases of *J. Gregory Merrion and Robert L. Bayless et al. v. Jicarilla Apache Indian Tribe, Amoco Production Company v. Jicarilla Apache Indian Tribe*, and *Marathon Oil Company v. Jicarilla Apache Indian Tribe*, January 25, 1982, 455 U.S. 130, 71 L.Ed.2d21, 102 S.C. 894 in *U.S. Supreme Court Reports*, Lawyers' Edition, vol. 71.

54. Daniel H. Israel, "The Reemergence of Tribal Nationalism and Its Impact on Reservation Development," *University of Colorado Law Review* 47 (Summer 1976): 617–652; Pattie Palmer McGee, "Indian Lands: Coal Development—Environment/Economic Dilemma for the Modern Indian," *American Indian Law Review* 4, no. 2 (1976): 279–288.

55. E. N. Smith, "Low-Sulfur Coal Puts Wyoming at Top of Heap," *South Bend Tribune*, August 18, 1997.

8

THE COUNCIL OF ENERGY RESOURCE TRIBES

The long history of the exploitation of Indian tribes for their natural resources provoked great concern among Native Americans and ultimately led tribes with natural resources on their lands to organize. In the 1970s, after more than seventy-five years of losing their resources to whites, the tribes formed the Council for Energy Resource Tribes to protect those commodities. In the years ahead, CERT would face many obstacles and challenges as it attempted to deal with a market that was hungry for fossil fuels.

As the industrialization of America during the late 1880s created a new demand for fossil fuels, tribes with natural resources on their lands—the energy tribes—remained vulnerable to both federal policies and white opportunists. A federal policy allotted tribal lands with full ownership to individual Indians, and without protective legislation, these people became prime targets of capitalistic exploitation until the early 1930s. At last, reform legislation during Franklin Roosevelt's administration shaped a different Indian policy designed to help, not exploit, Indians. With John Collier in charge of Indian affairs, Congress passed an omnibus Indian mineral leasing act in 1938, calling for the secretary of the interior to negotiate natural resources on behalf of the tribes. The tribes struggled against the paternalism of the law. The law gave full authority to the interior secretary to sign leases for the tribes, and the unforeseen success of the free enterprise system in lobbying for further exploitation meant that Indian lands would again be invaded for timber, water, minerals, and other natural resources. During the following decades, Indian people received small royalty payments while more and more mining companies grew rich and worked aggressively to deplete tribal natural resources as fast as possible.

Sporadic problems in Indian Country during the early 1970s forced action on the Indians' part. In Montana, the Northern Cheyenne learned that the Bureau of Indian Affairs, with approval from the Interior Department, had authorized companies to draft leases for the tribes to sign allowing one-third of the lands to be strip-mined for a return of $.17½ per ton. Moreover, facing the prospect that the number of non-Indians working on the reservation would exceed the Cheyenne population, the Indians rightly feared they could lose control of the situation simply by being outnumbered.

Nearby, members of the Crow Tribe hesitated but ultimately agreed to allow companies to mine approximately 250,000 acres of their land. Their caution was justified. The tribe learned from an article in *Fortune* magazine that one of the presidents of the coal companies involved in the negotiations stood to make a handsome profit from their coal. The fact that he was expected to make a 100 percent return on his investment in Indian mineral properties understandably incited the Crow.

Meanwhile, in the Southwest, the Jicarilla Apache in New Mexico had requested a federal investigation of the accounting practices of companies obtaining natural gas from them. When the federal government refused to do the auditing, the Jicarilla sued both the federal government and the companies. The companies offered millions of dollars to settle out of court, but the government would not allow the tribe to accept any such settlement unless it first agreed to not charge the government with being at fault.[1]

Frustrated and hostile to the white society's desire for their natural resources, twenty-six tribes of the northern plains arranged a meeting in 1974 to form the Native American Natural Resources Development Federation (NANRDF). Venting their anger and discussing their common problems, they agreed to take action together. The new Indian organization authored the Declaration of Indian Rights to the Natural Resources in the northern great plains states, which stressed the importance of protecting minerals, water, and agriculture via collecting data and sharing their expertise.[2]

Tribal leaders from the Southwest began to realize the importance of meeting with NANRDF leaders to raise their common concerns and to respond effectively, in a collective manner, to the growing pressure exerted by companies anxious to mine their lands. During the weeks of organization, the tribal leaders included Northern Cheyenne Allen Rowland, Navajo tribal chairman Peter MacDonald,

Blackfeet leader Earl Old Person, Laguna Pueblo governor Roland Johnson, Fort Peck tribal chairman Norman Hollow, and Jicarilla Apache vice president Dale Vigil.[3] All of these men were veteran leaders, experienced in attempting to spare their reservations from the energy companies. The cooperative efforts of the northern Plains tribal groups and those of the Southwest that possessed mineral resources unified the tribal groups west of the Mississippi River.

As the tribal leaders corresponded with each other, LaDonna Harris, a Comanche from Oklahoma and founder of Americans for Indian Opportunity (AIO), arranged for three interns from Dartmouth College to examine federal records before the first meeting of the energy tribes. After the Arab oil embargo of 1973, the United States strove to form a national program of energy conservation, emphasizing the importance of developing the country's own natural resources. Very concerned at the implications of this policy for Native Americans, Harris charged into Frank Zarb's office at the Federal Energy Administration on September 18, 1975, demanding that Indians not be left out the national energy policy. Using the information gathered by the Dartmouth interns and adding to it for the sake of making an impression, she convinced Zarb that the tribes possessed one-third of the nation's low-sulfur coal, one-half of its uranium, and huge amounts of oil and gas. With Zarb under her immediate influence, Harris then requested funding for organizational purposes, explaining that tribal lands needed to be environmentally protected. At the same time, she underscored the point that careful mining of energy resources could help the country.[4]

With support from national Indian organizations such as Americans for Indian Opportunity and the Native American Rights Fund (NARF), the tribes with mineral resources began to gather to discuss their common problems and their difficult relations with the federal government. The United States had signed treaties with the tribes during the 1700s and 1800s, guaranteeing them protection that later included exemption from the activities of the U.S. Army Corps of Engineers, the Bureau of Mines, national forest developments, and conservation programs. Uncertain about the federal government's ability to protect their interests and eager to assume more control over their own destinies, twenty-five Indian tribes whose reservations possessed vast amounts of natural resources gathered to form the Council of Energy Resource Tribes in 1975.[5] Government officials and public interest groups also helped tribal leaders establish CERT. In need of strong leadership, the CERT tribes selected Peter MacDonald as the first chairman. Edward Gabriel, formerly of the Federal Energy Administration, became the executive director, working out of CERT's second office in Washington, D.C.[6]

The rise of CERT caused the decline of NANRDF. CERT obtained increasing federal attention, and when NANRDF lost its federal funding, it ceased to exist. NANRDF's principal founder, Thomas Frederick, a Mandan-Hidatsa, resented the government's favoritism toward CERT, and his negative feelings threatened the immediate future of CERT, especially when he became the assistant secretary of the interior in charge of Indian affairs in 1980.[7] Frederick's appointment shifted the power struggle to Washington, starting a rift between the BIA and CERT. The BIA felt threatened by CERT due to its direct influence with the tribes and its funding from the federal government. Furthermore, the old Indian distrust of the Bureau of Indian Affairs, stemming from the nineteenth century, exacerbated CERT criticism of the BIA.

Since the turn of the twentieth century, tribes blessed (or cursed) with an abundance of coal, oil, uranium, and gas lying under their reservations had been increasingly pressured by energy companies. In addition, the federal government authorized long-term leases with energy companies. As the United States felt the impact of the oil embargo in the 1970s, the tribes with natural resources in Indian Country awaited strong-arm tactics from the government and the energy companies working together. The scarcity of developed fossil fuels soon brought long lines at gasoline stations and rationing in many states.

An unstable economy and especially the Watergate scandal and subsequent cover-up during Nixon's administration allowed the Democrats to elect the next president of the United States in 1976. The election of Jimmy Carter, a Southern Democrat, during America's bicentennial year led to a federal concern for conservation and the development of the Department of Energy. With the country's growing consciousness of conservation and environmental concerns, partially spurred by America's dependence on oil from the OPEC countries, the Carter administration passed four important laws: the Energy Conservation and Production Act (1976), the Surface Mining Control and Reclamation Act (1977), the Natural Gas Policy Act (1978), and the National Energy Conservation Policy Act (1978).

When CERT opened its offices in 1977, the Bureau of Indian Affairs decided to established a minerals technical assistance center in Denver. Due to limited federal spending and changes in the Carter administration, the federal government only filled five positions and left twelve unfilled.[8] A frugal Carter administration left the tribes to handle their own affairs under the policy of self-determination installed via legislation, the Indian Self-Determination and Education Assistance Act in 1975. Struggling to organize, CERT faced additional pressure when an oil embargo again produced long lines and rationing at gasoline stations during 1979, the second gasoline shortage in five years.

The energy tribes had specifically formed CERT as a defensive coalition to protect their holdings of natural resources, especially their fossil fuels (as opposed to timberlands and wildlife). CERT established a nine-member executive board, consisting of eight tribal chairpersons plus the board chair. In addition to the executive director, the officers included a vice-chair, a secretary, and a treasurer. Over the four years after its founding, CERT reached its bureaucratic height. It employed sixty-five people on its staff in 1980—twenty-three in Washington and forty-two in the Denver suburb office. In the following year, CERT's budget climbed to $3.9 million, with seventy-four percent coming from the federal government and twenty-six percent from the tribes. About half of this amount was used to pay salaries, and CERT rented lavish offices for $181,000 a year.[9]

The primary objective of CERT involved advising the tribes on protecting their natural resources, a goal that the organization accomplished in multiple ways. The sixty-five staff members of mostly non-Indian descent came from various backgrounds. In general, the staff was recruited from environmental organizations, state and federal governments, industry, and academia. One CERT engineer had previously worked for Western Coal, Pittsburgh and Midway (Gulf), and Peabody Coal. A CERT economist had worked for Mobil Oil and Stearns and Rogers (a construction company).[10] Other staff members had also worked for various companies that had mined natural resources on reservation lands.

In operation for over two decades, CERT now evaluates the amount of natural resources the tribes hold and advises them in the latest mining technology. In other areas, the council helps to develop jobs in mining operations by assisting tribes in training their members for various mining labor and management positions. With an eye on the future, CERT emphasizes the need for American Indian students to major in engineering and areas such as geology to help the tribes in future dealings with energy companies and the federal government.[11]

The Council of Energy Resource Tribes operates under the policy of strength in numbers so that individual tribes will not be victimized. One CERT official stressed that though the energy companies could manipulate and pressure isolated tribes and thus take advantage of them, they would have a much tougher time controlling tribes that are working together; by sharing information and talents, those tribes become a stronger force for protecting tribal natural resources.[12]

Originally, CERT established its base of operation in Englewood, Colorado, a suburb of Denver and the geographic center of Indian Country for western tribes. The operational organization of CERT initially consisted of an executive director assisted by a communications coordinator, a special legal counsel, an office of policy analysis, and a staff in Washington, D.C. The home operation in Englewood was then known as the Technical Assistance Center of CERT and had specific departments in assessment and development, environmental analysis, planning and management services, and education and resource development. To keep the energy tribes, the rest of Indian Country, and supporters of Indian interests informed, CERT published a biweekly newsletter called *The CERT Report*. The council believed that circulating information was essential for networking with the member tribes and updating them about CERT operations. Accumulated information resulted in an annual report known as the *Tribal Energy Directory*. To be sure, CERT's efforts to organize were challenged by other energy interests. But the council knew that with economic development slowly progressing on reservations, the natural resources on Indian lands held the future for tribal communities.

In the energy-minded years of the late 1970s, a group of governors from seven western states formed the Western Governors' Policy Office (WESTPO) to monitor natural resources in their states. Because the future of natural resources of course concerned non-Indians as well, especially those living west of the Mississippi, a group of people advocating private concerns in this arena organized the Western Regional Council (WRC) starting in 1978.[13] By 1982, the WRC had grown to include forty-seven major energy, mining, and petroleum companies in the West; its main office was located in Salt Lake City. Within a few years, the American West had become a new battleground, controlled by those who lived there and sought to protect their natural resources. They opposed all comers with power, greed, and the desire to seize huge amounts of coal, oil, uranium, and water.

In the early years of the 1980s, all three organizations—the WESTPO, WCR, and CERT—met together periodically to discuss their particular interests in natural resources. Continual meetings resulted in consent for general cooperation. After one week-long meeting, the groups issued a press release stating: "The time has come for the elected heads of states and tribes to join hands in responding to the federal energy programs which apparently assumed the consent and cooperation of the West. ... We must work together on the solution."[14] Realizing the growing stress on natural resources, CERT planned strategically for advantages in the best interests of tribes to protect and develop their natural resources wisely.

As an example, CERT opened a second office in Washington, D.C., to be near enough to Capitol Hill to meet with federal officials on a daily basis and to lobby on behalf of the tribes. The expense of maintaining two offices seemed warranted, but it also strained the budget of an already expensive operation. In 1983, CERT ran into difficult times and experienced a deficit. In August of that year, escalating expenses forced CERT to close its Washington office and lay off its staff there with only two days' notice; it also released nine staff members in Denver. David Lester, the chairperson of CERT, said that a deficit of $1.2 million in overhead and indirect costs had forced this action. Doubts about CERT's activities also emerged in 1983 following a lavish, black-tie fund-raising affair at the Kennedy Center in Washington, "The Night of the First Americans." CERT raised $300,000, but its books later indicated that it ultimately lost $250,000 for that one evening.[15] From this point on, CERT operated more carefully, as a mature organization facing difficult situations in advising all of its tribes on their natural resources. Simultaneously, CERT critics watched the organization very closely, particularly when the energy-conscious years ended. Increasing operational expenses have since forced CERT to relocate its main office. (Presently, CERT is located on Logan Street in Denver.)

CERT has learned to survive. For instance, during the years of the Carter administration, it gained international attention when it asserted its influence by threatening to work with the OPEC countries against the interest of the United States. This possibility pressured the United States into granting CERT moneys from various federal agencies, such as the Department of Energy, the Bureau of Indian Affairs, and the Department of Health, Education, and Welfare.[16] In October 1979, CERT chairman Peter MacDonald asked the federal government for one-half of one percent of the amount that President Carter put into his energy security budget, a sum of $60 million. This amount seemed to be a less than appropriate sum since approximately one-third of the coal in the West was on Indian lands and other tribal natural resources were in large supply. In 1979, the Department of Energy announced that CERT would receive $24 million, decreasing CERT's request by 60 percent for the first year and providing no extended funding in the following years. The DOE also specified how CERT was to use the money: $10 million for loan guarantees, $7 million for a minimal inventory program, $4 million dollars for developing managerial skills, and the remaining $3 million for the general operations. The DOE did not stipulate that $24 million was already allocated to Indian affairs in various ways in accounting, auditing, and regulating tribal natural resources and included this amount in the funding assistance to CERT.[17]

To help tribes in general, the federal government supported the Administration for Native Americans (ANA), a new program designed to strengthen tribal governments. Receiving funding from ANA, CERT worked with Indian officials on the Fort Berthold Reservation to develop a new governing structure. CERT's Office of Planning and Management Services had developed the model for this structure and helped to install it.[18] The first stage of the mission to protect tribal resources involved making the tribal governments more efficient with better organization. They would have to supply the leadership.

Organization and cooperation proved essential to the later success of CERT. As in the early part of the mid-1970s, CERT had filed approximately 100 reports on various ideas and projects during the Carter years. Only five of the reports focused on environmental studies; the rest concentrated on uranium potential, resource inventories, coal mining, power plants, synthetic fuels, and nuclear power plants. The thrust of CERT's efforts focused on extracting nonreplaceable natural resources with advanced technology.[19] In 1978, Caleb Shields, a Sioux of the Fort Peck Tribal Council said, "In three years, CERT has established a better track record than the whole history of the BIA."[20]

The early years of CERT's efforts earned immediate respect from energy companies, which recognized the sophistication of the tribe-controlled organization. Similar respect came from Congress and the Bureau of Indian Affairs, and the court systems began to hear cases involving tribal resources in the ensuing years. In 1977, Congress had passed a landmark bill composed jointly by CERT, the tribes who owed coal resources, and the federal Office of Surface Mining. The measure called for the tribes to have an opportunity to assume full regulatory authority over coal on their lands.[21]

After the election of Republican president Ronald Reagan, the tribes were forced to be increasingly on their own. In January 1980, the Reagan administration decontrolled oil prices, thereby stimulating increased domestic oil production and placing greater pressure on the oil-holding tribes and CERT. In addition, the Natural Gas Policy Act of 1978 implemented a decontrol of gas prices through 1985, and the administration wanted to accelerate the domestic leasing of coalfields. The government also continued to investigate the possibility of developing synthetic fuels, but the Reagan administration wanted private companies to take over more of this responsibility.

Greater pressure confronted the Interior Department when oil thefts in Indian Country began to be discovered. (There was no accurate estimate of how much tribal oil had been lost, particularly in Oklahoma and on the Wind River Reservation in Wyoming.) Continued theft forced the federal government to create the Commission on Fiscal Accountability of the Nation's Energy Resources (CFANER), and the commission's first hearing was scheduled for July 27, 1981. At additional hearings in Washington, D.C., New York City, and Denver during August, September, October, and November, testimony from both the states and the tribes was gathered.[22]

The Reagan years of deregulation in the airline industry and a laissez-faire economy gave new life to free enterprise capitalism in America. Huge profits were made, jeopardizing the future economy for immediate prosperity. In the end, the tribes had to brace themselves for exploitation much like that experienced in the late 1800s and the Roaring Twenties when Republicans held office. Such circumstances challenged CERT, which successfully lobbied for the passage of two measures, the Indian Tribal Government Tax Status Act and the Indian Mineral Development Act, both in 1982. These two victories allowed the CERT tribes more control over their economics and added to their movement for increased self-rule.

In the 1980s, CERT achieved important objectives for energy tribes in a flurry of action against the powerful energy companies and the influence of the Reagan administration. With CERT's help, the Jicarilla Apache Tribe became the first tribe to obtain total ownership of producing oil and gas wells in Indian Country. Wanting to control the production of their own natural resources, the Jicarilla developed their own oil and gas administration.[23] In addition, they negotiated oil and gas agreements with several companies, giving the tribe a fifty percent interest in operations and allowing the tribe to buy out some of their partners on agreeable terms.

Also in 1980 and with CERT's help, the Navajo Nation moved in the same direction as the Jicarilla Apache. The Navajo Tribe successfully negotiated an agreement for uranium development, calling for forty-nine percent tribal ownership in the mining.[24] Striving for self-determination and control of their own resources, the Navajo established the Navajo Energy Department Authority. This effort became independent as a nonprofit body. As a part of the Navajo tribal government, the department began competing with private developers in extending project proposals for energy development, with production and conservation as its primary concerns. In the same year, the Northern Cheyenne Tribe allowed a search for oil and gas on its reservation; the Cheyenne were now more confident because they had the assistance and protection of CERT.[25] Also on the northern plains, the Blackfeet agreed to oil and gas negotiations that benefited the developer, with the understanding that the tribe would gain eventual ownership. In other joint ventures, the Assiniboine and Sioux tribes of the Fort Peck Reservation entered into similar arrangements to own major interest in mineral productions. The Ute Mountain Ute Tribe in southwestern Colorado arranged for a geophysical exploration and development with a European company but kept the right to develop much of the lands to be explored.[26]

Paradoxically, CERT's need for funding led it away from the tribes because most of the monetary assistance came from the federal government. Moreover, the expenses involved in keeping CERT in operation has led to a growing need for funding and dependency on the federal government. The Administration for Native Americans, along with other governmental organizations, contributed funding to the council, and public and private donations have helped CERT financially.[27] But CERT's closer relationship with the federal government during the 1980s created apprehension among the tribes. As an example, in 1981, CERT took a step toward playing a liaison role between the energy tribes and the United States government when it began accepting funding for energy research development and management from the Office of Indian Affairs within the Department of Energy.[28]

Since the early 1980s, the Council of Energy Resource Tribes has been successful in representing the energy tribes and protecting their natural resources, but this has not decreased the criticism leveled against the intertribal organization. During the early 1980s, Indian people charged that CERT advocated too much development and mining of tribal natural resources. One scientist who worked for CERT claimed that the organization distorted facts for political purposes. He said that the figures on six tribal resources were "grossly exaggerated" and misrepresented their true potential to CERT member tribes.[29] Furthermore, Indian critics charged CERT officials with hosting too many expensive social events for government and energy company officials.[30]

The Hopi, one of the tribes with the largest resources, has been an inactive member of CERT. Former Hopi chairman Abbott Sekaquaptewa stated the cautious position of his people. He did not want his tribe entrapped in CERT's development program, and the Hopi feared that some tribal leaders on the organization's board of directors were using CERT to pressure the federal government to favor their particular tribes.[31]

CERT became embroiled in tribal politics, an unfortunate development that has added to the problem of tribal factionalism. In one case during a tribal election year for the Navajo, candidate Peterson Zah criticized Peter MacDonald for becoming too involved as the chairman of CERT and neglecting Navajo problems when the Navajo Tribe reached an annual indebtedness of $25 million. Criticism also came from Washington, alleging that the Navajo Agricultural Products Industries had created a deficit of $14 million; in addition, the federal government demanded the return of $7.3 million for misappropriating Comprehensive Employment and Training Act (CETA) grants. Furthermore, the tribe had leased its oil and gas reserves at low revenue rates to multinational corporations.[32] The Navajo election resulted in Zah defeating MacDonald for the tribal leadership position in a close election. It also marked the start of many problems for the former chairman, who was indicted by the Navajo Tribe for receiving bribes from corporations.

With the Four Corners area having the largest strip-mining operation in the world, the Navajo are continuously placed in a vulnerable position. Their history is replete with examples of their ongoing exploitation. A lease signed with Utah International dated July 26, 1957, for example, called for paying the Navajos between $.15 and $.20 per ton of coal, even though Arizona Public Service paid Utah International $6 per ton for the same coal.[33] The biggest threat, however, has been posed by Peabody, the largest coal-mining company in the United States, which also held one-third of all Indian mining leases in 1989.

The stability of CERT has been weakened by the suspicion that it is mismanaged and that it has given poor advice to tribes. Furthermore, four tribes have withdrawn from CERT. The Cheyenne River Sioux of South Dakota withdrew because they were convinced that CERT would force their tribe to mine its uranium. The Colville Confederated Tribes of Washington withdrew due to disagreement with CERT's aggressive public relations, and the Shoshone and Arapaho Tribes of the Wind River Reservation in Wyoming became skeptical that CERT had any special expertise to offer them. The Assiniboine-Sioux Tribes of the Fort Peck Reservation considered withdrawing from CERT after an article appeared in a national Indian newspaper claiming that the organization was not totally accountable to the tribes. CERT only met with the tribal board of directors twice a year, and critics claimed that the directors were not sufficiently involved with CERT business to direct the organization.[34]

Wisely, CERT operated with as many qualified Indian employees as possible. In effect, the involvement of Indian personnel in CERT validated the organization's sincerity in helping the tribes. In 1981, forty percent of the CERT staff was Indian, and more Indian experts were recruited to be in charge of CERT. At the end of the following year, projections called for this figure to increase to 70 percent, and

Ed Gabriel, the executive director, assumed that the tribes would be managing their own resources completely without CERT by 1987. When this goal was met, then the technical offices in Denver would be closed.[35]

Aware of its precarious position, CERT operated carefully to avoid arousing tribal criticism. In 1982, it agreed with the Bureau of Indian Affairs to draft a series of regulations concerning tribal severance taxation on mineral deposits, and it would work with major oil and gas trade companies. In *Merrion v. Jicarilla Apache Tribe*,[36] the Supreme Court had decreed that tribes could tax companies, and many tribes feared that CERT might succumb to the pressures of the oil and gas companies and thus work against them.[37] The Jicarilla Apache have been one of the most aggressive energy tribes in protecting and gaining control of their natural resources. As early as 1977, the Jicarilla levied a severance tax on energy companies, forcing the companies to appeal to the Supreme Court. CERT, other tribes in Indian Country, and Indian organizations supported the Apache's move, resulting in victory for the Jicarilla Apache—an important precedent for all the energy tribes.[38]

The *Merrion* case empowered the tribes with the legal right to tax non-Indians doing business on their reservations, thus supporting tribal sovereignty. However, this victory for the tribes received a setback when the ruling was interpreted by Justice Thurgood Marshall, who stated that he respected the "inherent" right of the tribes to tax but then limited this power by forbidding CERT tribes from forming their own OPEC business relations. He wrote: "The tribes' authority to tax non-members is subject to constraints not imposed on other governmental entities: the federal government can take away this power, and the tribes must obtain the approval of the Secretary [of the Interior] before any tax on non-members can take effect. These additional constraints minimize potential concern that Indian tribes will exercise the power to tax in an unfair or unprincipled manner, and ensure that any exercise of the tribal power to tax will be consistent with national policies."[39]

The federal government's next step favored the energy tribes and CERT by granting the tribes the right to tax outsiders. Tribal taxing power represents strong leverage in a high-stakes competition for natural resources, and the tribes need to expand their powers to increase their negotiating position.[40] What types of taxation and to what degree taxes should be levied against the energy tribes are questions demanding quick but careful responses from tribal leaders and CERT.

In one sense, CERT has become the replacement for the Bureau of Indian Affairs, which increasingly failed to properly advise the tribes and to represent their interests during negotiations with mining companies. CERT's geologists, mining engineers, and economists are vital to the Indians' future if tribal natural resources are to be safeguarded and developed carefully. To its credit, CERT has done several things very well over its history. It represented the tribes and lobbied hard against the Carter administration when energy development and disposal of toxic wastes first became a threat to the environment, the tribes, and the American public. CERT also opposed the Carter administration's Energy Mobilization Board (EMB) proposal, which could have resulted in federal jurisdiction over all energy projects on and near tribal lands. Moreover, the staff of CERT successfully defended the tribes' interests on issues surrounding nuclear-waste transportation and disposal near tribal lands.[41]

Yakima Tribal councilman Russell Jim testified against the threat of radioactive waste being deposited near reservations before the Senate committee studying nuclear waste. He stated: "By placing hazardous radioactive wastes near our reservation, they may well undermine our treaty rights by threatening a destruction which the implications of the treaty show to be illegal. Our lands may be contaminated irretrievably by action on nearby non-Indian land or from faulty transportation of radioactive waste. I believe that any of you gentlemen will realize that for Native Americans, 'evacuation' from their land is meaningless."[42]

In sum, after more than two decades in business, CERT has achieved phenomenal success in spite of some problems and criticism. Tribal natural resources have remained integral to domestic life in the United States, and CERT tribes have helped to influence the conservation of natural resources. The 1980s witnessed CERT's efforts to influence the production of additional conservation legislation. Such legislation included the Federal Oil and Gas Royalty Management Act (1982), Nuclear Waste Policy Act (1982); Clean Water Act amendments (1986), Safe Drinking Water Act amendments (1986), Water Resources Development Act (1986), and Comprehensive Environmental Response Compensation, and Liability Act (reauthorized and amended in 1986).[43]

Overall, CERT helped considerably in providing expertise to the tribes in the 1980s. For example, in May 1982, with CERT's advice, the Blackfeet Tribe of Montana received over $2.5 million in bonus payments from a sealed bid auction of 18,351 tribal mineral acres. The sale called for a five-year primary term to extend for no longer than forty-five years of production, with a twenty percent royalty before payout increasing to twenty-five percent after payout.[44]

During the summer of 1982, CERT offered tribes tax seminars in Montana, North Dakota, and Wyoming, aimed at developing agreements with energy companies and compliance with regulations. Another concern became Indian water rights as more cases involving this precious resource reached the courts. In July 1982, *The CERT Report* stated that forty-eight Indian water suits crowded the dockets in ten western states.[45]

CERT also helped the tribes renegotiate old leases throughout the 1980s. In September 1986, the Crow Tribe in Montana renegotiated its deal with one of the coal companies, which had leased dozens of square miles for surface mining for a royalty rate of $.17½ per ton for coal that brought more than $10 per ton on the market. The Northern Cheyenne arranged for a new agreement with the companies that had leased almost one-third of their reservation for strip mining. In the Southwest, the Navajo renegotiated a lease with two coal companies, raising the tribe's royalty rate from only pennies per ton to twelve and one-half percent of the value of the potential coal, for a possible revenue of $400 to $500 million while the mining was in operation. Other CERT efforts protected tribal rights-of-way and improved prices. One pipeline right-of-way that originally called for a one-time payment of $20,000 was changed to provide $1 million for the first-year payment and an additional $92 million over the life of the easement. Other renegotiations resulted in a pipeline right-of-way first appraised by the government and the company for $2,000 being reestablished at $286,000; another such right-of-way, originally set at $60,000, being resettled for $1,760,000; and yet another, a pipeline right-of-way originally set at $191,000, being reestablished at $1.5 million. The price for a road to be used for hauling coal, originally set at $3,200 for its grazing value, was renegotiated at $815,000, plus continued tolls based on volumes transported, with minimum payment provisions that will return $15 million to the tribe over the life of the easement.[46]

In an innovative area, CERT developed the comprehensive Indian Education Program in 1979 to develop and promote programs for Indian education. CERT held summer institutes stressing college preparation for promising students interested in energy resource management fields. The first institutes were held in 1980 at the University of Arizona, Arizona State University, University of Idaho, and Montana State University. During the following two years, institutes were held at the University of Oklahoma, Washington State University, and Colorado College. (The latter has started the Tribal Resource Institute in Business, Engineering, and Science [TRIBES].) As a result of CERT's efforts, more than 350 students have benefited from the organization, and CERT has also provided scholarships to a number of promising scholars and worked with the American Indian Science and Engineering Society (AISES) to maximize scholarships for Indian students.[47]

At the end of the 1980s, CERT's membership had increased to forty-three energy tribes; David Lester, a tribal official from the Muscogee Creeks in Oklahoma, served as the executive director. By 1994, the CERT membership had grown to forty-nine tribes.[48] Previously, Lester had served as director of the Administration for Native Americans, where he designed a grant program that arranged long-term funding for the energy tribes to develop programs. By developing such programs, Lester hoped that tribes would become self-sufficient and function through the collection of taxes or fees.[49]

The Council of Energy Resources Tribes faces ongoing challenges in its role as an arbiter between the energy tribes and the energy companies. As Americans use fossil fuels heavily every day throughout this large country, the nation will increasingly look more closely at Indian natural resources. The catalyst of public need will place even greater pressure on the U.S. government, on the tribes, and on CERT to respond to the developing energy crisis, which has, albeit sporadically, become more serious since the mid-1980s. Ironically, CERT has received criticism much like that endured by the Bureau of Indian Affairs throughout most of its history.

NOTES

1. "Indians Want a Bigger Share of Their Wealth," *Business Week*, May 3, 1976, p. 101.
2. Marjane Ambler, *Breaking the Iron Bonds: Indian Control of Energy Development* (Lawrence: University Press of Kansas, 1990), p. 92.
3. Ibid.
4. Ibid., p. 94.
5. "Indians Want a Bigger Share of Their Wealth."
6. Winona La Duke, "The Council of Energy Resource Tribes," in Joseph G. Jorgensen, ed., *Native Americans and Energy Development, vol. 2* (Boston: Anthropology Resource Center & Seventh Generation Fund, 1984), p. 59.
7. Ambler, *Breaking the Iron Bonds*, p. 94.
8. Marjane Ambler, "Uncertainty in CERT," in Joseph G. Jorgensen, ed., *Native Americans and Energy Development vol. 2* (Boston: Anthropology Resource Center & Seventh Generation Fund, 1984), p. 74.
9. Ambler, *Breaking the Iron Bonds*, pp. 106, 107, and 110.
10. La Duke, "Council of Energy Resource Tribes," p. 62.
11. "Indians Want a Bigger Share of Their Wealth." CERT sponsors Tribal Resource Institute in Business, Engineering, and Science (TRIBES), a college scholarship program to educate Indian youths who will likely help

their tribes; "Rosebud Chairman Elected to CERT Executive Board," *Lakota Times*, December 9, 1982; "$2 Million for Tribes' CERT," *Wassaja* 6, nos. 9–10 (October-November, 1978).

12. "Indians Want a Bigger Share of Their Wealth."

13. La Duke, "Council of Energy Resource Tribes," p. 58.

14. Ibid., p. 61.

15. Ambler, *Breaking the Iron Bonds*, pp. 108–109.

16. Melinda Beck, Jeff B. Copeland, and Merril Shiels, "Resources: The Rich Indians," *Newsweek*, March 20, 1978, p. 63; Marjane Ambler, "Controversial Speech Draws Ire at CERT Convention," *Lakota Times*, November 9, 1983.

17. La Duke, "Council of Energy Resources Tribes," p. 59.

18. Theodore W. Taylor, *American Indian Policy* (Mt. Airy, Md.: Lomond Publications, 1983), p. 148.

19. La Duke, "Council of Energy Resource Tribes," pp. 62–63.

20. Ambler, "Uncertainty in CERT," p. 74.

21. Marjane Ambler, "The Three Affiliated Tribes—Mandan, Hidatsa, Arikara—Seek to Control Their Energy Resources," in Joseph G. Jorgensen, ed., *Native Americans and Energy Development vol. 2* (Boston: Anthropology Resource Center & Seventh Generation Fund, 1984), p. 195.

22. "Oil Theft Commission Sets Fall Hearings," *The CERT Report* 3, no. 10 (August 10, 1981): 3.

23. Taylor, *American Indian Policy*, p. 147.

24. "Joint Venture," in *First Decade*, a CERT newsletter, 1985, p. 8.

25. "Negotiation," in ibid., p. 9.

26. "Joint Venture," p. 7.

27. Taylor, *American Indian Policy*, p. 86.

28. Ibid., p. 97.

29. Ambler, "Uncertainty in CERT," p. 75.

30. John A. Farrell, "Empty Promises, Misplaced Trust," New Indian War Series, *Denver Post*, November 20, 1983.

31. Ambler, "Uncertainty in CERT," p. 76.

32. Ibid.

33. Philip Reno, *Mother Earth, Father Sky, and Economic Development: Navajo Resources and Their Use* (Albuquerque: University of New Mexico Press, 1981), p. 133.

34. Ambler, "Uncertainty in CERT," pp. 71 and 76.

35. Ibid., p. 73.

36. *J. Gregory Merrion and Robert l. Bayless et al. and Amoco Production Company and Marathon Oil Company v. Jicarilla Apache Indian Tribe*, January 25, 1982, 455 U.S. 130, 71 L.Ed.2d21, 102 S.C. 894, in *U.S. Supreme Court Reports*, Lawyers' Edition, vol. 71.

37. Ibid.

38. Taylor, *American Indian Policy*, p. 148.

39. Rob Williams, "Redefining the Tribe ... ," *Indian Truth*, no. 262, (April 1985): 9.

40. Reno, *Mother Earth*, p. 130.

41. La Duke, "Council of Energy Resource Tribes," p. 67.

42. Ibid.

43. "CERT Accomplishments," in *First Decade*, a CERT newsletter, 1985, p. 6.

44. "Blackfeet Auction Nets $2.5 Million," *The CERT Report* 4, no. 7 (June 11, 1982): 13.

45. "48 Indian Water Suits in 10 Western States," *The CERT Report* 4, no 9 (July 23, 1982): 12–15.

46. "Rights-of-Way" and "Joint Venture," in *First Decade*, a CERT newsletter, 1985, p. 6.

47. "Education," in ibid., p. 12.

48. Imre Sutton, "Indian Land Tenure in the Twentieth Century," in Duane Champagne, ed., *Native North American Almanac: A Reference Work on Native North Americans in the United States and Canada* (Detroit: Gale Research, 1994), p. 219.

49. Ambler, "Three Affiliated Tribes," p. 198.

9

BATTLEGROUNDS IN THE COURTS

Since the turn of the twentieth century, American Indian tribes have learned new ways to defend the natural resources on their reservations. The days of sending warriors against the U.S. Army have faded into history, and Indian leaders have adopted new tactics as the battleground has shifted. A long history of exploitation has rudely taught today's sophisticated leaders to depend on the law, for they now understand that trust relations with the United States are their best weapons to use in defending their rights and resources in the federal courts. This approach was tried before, but success for the tribes did not occur consistently until the twentieth century. How to make the law work for them has been the objective, but an understanding of the law and its forum is a prerequisite for the tribes.

The key lies in recognizing, first, that the trust status between the United States and the Indian tribes binds the federal government to a set of responsibilities to the tribes and, second, that the courts and laws should be used to ensure that those responsibilities are met. Since the 1970s, tribes have learned to use the trust status to their maximum advantage in protecting their natural resources, preserving their lands, and reminding the federal government of its obligations as established in treaties.

The trust relationship between the United States and the tribes is legally imbedded within 389 treaties (and agreements) that were signed and ratified during the eighteenth and nineteenth centuries. The treaties are understood to be legally binding when one sovereign makes an agreement with another sovereign. But criticism and disagreement about the legality of the treaties have developed due to the age of the agreements and the fact that the tribes have become more dependent on the federal government in the intervening years.

In order to understand the U.S.-Indian trust relationship, the definition of *trust* must be considered. Trust is "a right in property held by one person, called the trustee, for the benefit of another, call the beneficiary, or *cestui que* trust."[1] This particular trust relationship is also considered to be an active trusteeship because the federal government has been considerably active in its trust responsibilities via the Bureau of Indian Affairs and the Department of the Interior. The trustee (the federal government) has continuously attempted to act in the best interests of the tribes, although the tribes have criticized the government for frequent, incompetent paternalism.

Although Chief Justice John Marshall set the legal precedent for establishing the concept of "trust" in Indian-U.S. relations, the original concept developed from early Spanish debates over Indian rights during the early sixteenth century. In 1532, Francisco de Victoria, a Spanish cleric and professor of theology at the University of Salamanca, argued on behalf of the human rights of Indians and the power of Spain to be responsible for the aborigines of America.[2] Almost 300 years later, Marshall stressed the precedent of "trusteeship" in his borrowing from Spanish dealings with Indians when he rendered a statement in *Cherokee Nation v. Georgia* (1831). In his famous decree, he described the Cherokee Nation as "in a state of pupilage," resembling that of "a ward to his guardian."[3] Such a statement established a significant legal precedent for all Indian nations in their relations with the United States.

With the concept of trust thus established, Marshall attempted to clarify the legal interpretation of U.S.-Indian relations in the famed case *Worcester v. Georgia* (1832). Again, trust was conceptually defined as Marshall explained the operation of this trusteeship. He described the Cherokee Nation as a "domestic nation" when he wrote that "a weak state, in order to provide for its safety, may place itself under the protection of one more powerful, without stripping itself of the right of government, and ceasing to be a state."[4] Marshall's opinion described the relationship of tribes today vis-à-vis the U.S. government. Although the legal definition of *trust* was accepted by both sides, however, it was not initially clear which agency in the government would assume this responsibility or what its duties would be.

An assistant secretary of the interior, who used to be known as the commissioner of Indian affairs, actually supervises the daily operations of federal-Indian relations. Under the Bureau of Indian Affairs, Indian Country has been divided into twelve separate regions, with the area directors empowered to make important daily decisions pertinent to the effectiveness of operations. Within these regions, almost eighty Indian agencies operate among the tribes. This multilevel bureaucracy sometimes leads to a paternalism that works against the tribes as they struggle to protect natural resources on their reservations.

The Bureau of Indian Affairs has been under constant criticism from the tribes and Indian people at large. Allegations of paternalism and ineffectiveness resulted in formal charges being brought in court in 1971 in *Rockbridge v. Lincoln,* which cited the bureau's failure to regulate Indian traders in Indian Country.[5] In an attempt to dissipate Indian criticism, the federal government has since placed Indians in the management of the Bureau of Indian Affairs, beginning with the appointment of Robert Bennett, an Oneida from Wisconsin, in 1966. However, one non-Indian contested this Indian preference as a policy directive in *Morton v. Mancari.* He claimed that "Indian preference" had been repealed by the Equal Employment Opportunity Act of 1972, but the U.S. Supreme Court ruled that such a preference was based not on racial discrimination but on the special legal status of Indians.[6]

The commissioner of Indian affairs became known as the assistant secretary of the interior via a department order from President Jimmy Carter on September 26, 1977.[7] Although both the assistant secretary and the interior secretary operate in the best interests of Indians, tribes and Indian persons have, on at least several occasions, taken the federal government to court in an effort to protect their interests.

The Interior Department functions as the supervisor of the trust relationship for the federal government. The secretary and assistant secretary must act in accordance with the law, whereby Congress usually defines the course of federal Indian policy. Over time, that policy has swung widely, from supporting Indian rights and sovereignty at one point to advocating termination of such rights at another.[8] Until 1961, the one consistency was that federal policy, whether favoring or opposing Indian interests, was largely formulated without Indian input. In 1961, that changed after a conference of Indians met in Chicago and articulated their own "Indian policy" of self-determination to the federal government.[9]

The fact that other units of government have assumed responsibility and provided services regarding Indian affairs should also be noted. Since the 1970s, the usual policy objective of mainstreaming Indian people has decreased the BIA and Interior Department's exclusive relations with Indian tribes and their members. Indian services have been dispersed to the Department of Health and Human

Services, the Department of Education, and the Department of Housing and Urban Development. This development has not, however, reduced Indian criticism against the BIA and Interior Department since land relations and trust status are still under the supervision of these branches of the federal government.

But with Indian affairs so widely represented in Washington, how have the mining companies gained control to excavate so much of Indian Country? The most common method has been through leasing Indian land, and since the 1970s, the tribes have fought successfully to renegotiate those leases, although much more needs to be done to protect Indian Country and the tribes' natural resources and tribal assets.

In order to effectively guard their natural resources, tribes have had to look at the issue of land in a new way, especially when bringing related matters to court. Instead of perceiving their lands in a shared, communal way, according to "tradition," tribes have learned to proclaim their properties as their own "real estate." Thinking like American capitalists, they have gone further to imitate business corporations while demanding their legal, sovereign rights within the "white" justice system. A changed attitude among Indian leaders and a different tribal mindset has become essential for developing defensive tactics and corporate strategies to save tribal natural resources. The first essential step was to understand the legal definitions of basic elements regarding tribal resource rights as they apply in U.S. courts. The tribes' realization that they would need to acquire and apply legal expertise took the struggle to a new battleground—the courts.

One of the first concerns of tribal leaders has been to understand the legal definition of *Indian Country*. In terms of criminal and civil jurisdiction, the courts provided the following definition of *Indian Country* in 1948: "(a) all land within the limits of any Indian reservation under the jurisdiction of the United States government, notwithstanding the issuance of any patent, and, including rights-of-way running through the reservation, (b) all dependent Indian communities within the borders of the United States whether within the original or subsequently acquired territory thereof, and whether within or without the limits of a state, and (c) all Indian allotments, the Indian titles to which have not been extinguished, including rights-of-way running through the same."[10]

Since 1948, other definitions have been advanced, all with a similar interpretation. But even with the legal basis of Indian Country established, problems have arisen involving state regulation of conservation programs; the interventions of federal agencies such as the U.S. Army Corps of Engineers[11] and the Bureau of Reclamation; water programs;[12] and taxation efforts.[13] Added to this is the fact that more non-Indians live on the 291 reservations than Indians. Consequently, the original concept of Indian Country has become convoluted, shaped by various federal agencies' interests, state programs, and sometimes divided tribal views. The most disruptive interest and the most dangerous threat to the tribes has come not from governmental agencies but from the private sector—the mining corporations. The competition for Indian resources has placed political pressure on the legal definition of the term Indian Country.

In defending their tribal interests, the tribes are frequently plagued by the age-old problem of internal disagreement, which weakens tribal governments and has historically worked against Indian people.[14] This unfortunate problem also has had a bearing on the effectiveness of the tribes in court. As a minority on their own reservations, the tribes are sometimes fractionalized and have to work hard to resolve political differences in order to present a unified front. In the process of unification, the tribes are not always united in support of their leadership and legal representation.

An unforeseen concern that has arisen, given the magnitude of the potential losses in natural resources, involves the definition of Indian tribe. Until 1980, the U.S. Congress had established a uniform federal definition for this term in the United States.[15] Since 1980, some tribes that were not federally recognized have sought federal recognition, which has, in turn, challenged the point that the federal government has the authority to define an Indian tribe. It is imperative for an Indian tribe to be federally recognized in order for it to be able to protect its natural resources and rights in the U.S. courts. Tribes that are recognized only by states have considerable difficulty since the federal government does not recognize them to be tribes. And tribes that are not recognized by either federal or state governments have little legal recourse. In 1993, approximate twelve tribes were recognized by state governments only, and an estimated twenty-four were petitioning or preparing cases for federal recognition.

Under the Indian Gaming Act of 1988, the U.S. Congress has defined an Indian tribe as "any Indian tribe, band, nation, or other organized group or community of Indians which — (A) is recognized as eligible by the Secretary [of the Interior] for the special programs and services provided by the United States to Indians because of their status as Indians, and (B) is recognized as possessing powers of self-government."[16]

Since natural resources are contained in the earth of Indian Country, most of the competition for oil, gas, coal, uranium, water, and other resources affects the legal rights of the tribes. Tribal leaders have understood that their legal rights are established within the 389 treaties and agreements signed and ratified between the tribes and the United States.[17] Another factor affecting the successes or failure of efforts to defend tribal resources is how a given reservation was created, that is, whether it was created by treaty, by congressional law, by executive order of the president of the United States, or by a state government.

The jurisdiction and supervision of Indian Country is a bureaucratic maze. The issue of jurisdiction remains in flux and is subject to change, according to the legal definition. Of course, revisionary laws or amendments keep jurisdiction matters in limbo for the tribes while mining issues remain important.

As early as 1902, the secretary of the interior authorized the first oil and gas leases on Indian lands in Oklahoma, although statehood for the area would not occur until five years later. On the average, leases last about twenty-five years, but some run as long as ninety-nine. The leases cover many interests in coal and uranium mining, drilling for oil and natural gas, timber cutting, housing, grazing, general agricultural, and water.

The Department of the Interior has represented the interests of both the United States and the American Indian tribes, and it sees no conflict of interest in this position. Past leases negotiated for the tribes by the interior secretary, however, have not favored the tribes. The secretary has complete power over Indian lands held in trust—almost 2.3 percent of all land in the United States.[18]

Also during 1902, Congress passed the rest of the allotment legislation that divided the lands of the Five Civilized Tribes. Four years later, the Burke Amendment removed the restrictions from the allotment acts to enable non-Indians and shrewd mixed-bloods to gain control of oil lands from the full-blood Indians of the Five Civilized Tribes. Legislation passed at the demand of non-Indian interests, as illustrated in the case of the Osage, has undermined Indian interests in the fossil fuel resources.

The first major court case of the twentieth century regarding Indian resources did not involve oil, or gas or coal but water. The dispute over the Milk River, which feeds the Fort Belknap Reservation in Montana, reached the U.S. Supreme Court in 1907. Known as the *Winter's* Doctrine, the case was decided in favor of the Gros Ventre Tribe, giving all tribes a major court victory for protection of their water rights (but not their oil rights).[19] Indian water rights remained a strength for the tribes in the following decades, until the ultimate test came in the form of the Bursum bill in 1923, which threatened Pueblo irrigated lands in the Southwest. Unusual support for the Pueblo communities and the passage of the Pueblo Lands Act in 1924 favored all Indian water interests. In succeeding years, congressional water legislation sought to undermine this strength, but anti-Indian water interests encountered a more serious setback in the early 1960s. In 1963, the *Arizona v. California* case reinforced Indian water rights. Almost ten years later, another case, *Pyramid Lake Paiute Tribe v. Morton,* resulted in a district court ruling against the water allocation made by the interior secretary, in violation of the government's trust responsibility.[20]

The status of Indian water rights will continue to be challenged as the population in the Southwest and in lower California increases and the demand for this precious commodity rises. Tribal communities and their governments understand that leasing of their lands entails the right to use the land's water, but the leasing of water rights to non-Indians for uses on other lands was not made clear in the *Winter's* decision. Nonetheless, the tribes should retain the reserve right interest of their water rights. Of all their rights related to natural resources, the Indians' water rights have been the most protected, even as their rights regarding fossil fuels and hunting and fishing have been under severe attack.

Another resource—wildlife—has played a major role in the life of Native Americans throughout their history, given the intimate connection Indians feel to animals. However, as with other natural resources on their lands, their rights in regard to wildlife have also been challenged in the twentieth century. In the Pacific Northwest, the issue exploded in the mid-1960s when traditional fishing tribes in the state of Washington protested to secure such rights—rights that non-Indian fishermen did not want them to have in regard to Washington's rivers. The resulting *Boldt* decision in 1974, which favored the tribes, set a significant precedent for Indian fishing rights that depended of earlier treaties.[21] This important decision affected Indian rights in Minnesota, Michigan, and Wisconsin.

The main concern has involved special rights for Indians (which are established through provisions written in the 1800s), but specific controversy has occurred regarding the Indians' practice of spearfishing. The *Fox* decision of the 1970s protected Indian fishing in Michigan and the *Voigt* and *Crabb* decisions of the 1980s protected such rights in Wisconsin, but Indian fishing rights continued to be challenged nonetheless. In 1984, in *United States v. Adair,*[22] Klamath tribal hunting and fishing were legally protected based on the reserved water right and the manner in which the reservation was established. Based on the provisions of a treaty, the amount of water reserved to supply the reservation was the quantity needed for the Klamaths to hunt and fish for their livelihood.

The legal controversy on fishing rights has increasingly involved the issue of state governments' supervision over Indians. Specifically, the states' concerns over conservation matters have often conflicted with Indian interests. And when the federal government began to transfer responsibility for Indian affairs to the states, the states started to usurp tribal sovereign rights. P.L. 280 (passed in 1953 and amended in the same year) gave five states—Wisconsin, Minnesota (except Red Lake Reservation), Nebraska, California, Oregon (except Warm Springs Reservation), and, five years later, Alaska—jurisdiction over criminal and civil violations of laws.[23] Since then, the conservation movement developing out of the 1960s has increased federal support of state interests and conservation programs that interfere with Indian interests and rights.

In 1986, the important case of *South Carolina v. Catawba Indian Tribe, Inc.* allowed cases involving civil and criminal violations to be heard in state courts, as opposed to federal or tribal courts.[24] This court ruling delivered a crucial blow throughout Indian Country, threatening Indian sovereignty. To meet this challenge, the tribes, bolstered by the federal policy of "self-determination" as established in legislation in 1975, have developed their own system of tribal courts. More than 100 tribal courts exist, most having developed since the 1970s, and the tribes are now seeking to protect their natural resources in their own courts of law. The problem has been a federal reversal that prevents the tribes from trying non-Indians in a tribal court.

The *Oliphant* decision in 1978 represented another critical blow to the Indians' sovereignty over their own lands. The ruling of the court overturned the Suquamish Tribe's arrest of a young non-Indian man named Mark Oliphant who lived on the reservation; the tribal court found him guilty of resisting arrest for drunk and disorderly conduct on the tribe's reservation in the state of Washington. Oliphant claimed that he was not legally subject to the Suquamish tribal authority, and the Supreme Court ruled in his favor.[25] That meant that, although tribes had jurisdiction over their own tribal members (except for the crimes listed in the Major Crimes Act), they did not have control over non-Indians.

Oliphant and similar cases have continued a trend of usurping the inherent sovereignty of Indian people and their tribes. Among such cases is the recent *Duro* decision, involving an Indian of a different tribe who murdered a fourteen-year-old Indian male on another reservation. The U.S. Supreme court ruled that the tribe had no jurisdiction over a nontribal member.[26] Although the obvious concern in that case was tribal rights, the individual rights of Indian people are equally important in other areas, such as protecting individuals from the intimidation of mining companies. So the tribes must protect both tribal and member interests against mining factions and perils posed by other external forces.

Over the years, the interior secretary's influence over Indian leases has declined as federal laws protecting other interests have interceded. Such laws as the Omnibus Indian Mineral Leasing Act,[27] the National Environmental Policy Act,[28] and segments of the Surface Mining Control and Reclamation Act of 1977 have worked against the tribes.[29] Conservationists' efforts to get rid of pollution and to oversee governmental projects have frequently interfered with the interests of tribes holding natural resources.

Since the 1980s, when the federal government began to increase its support of state interests, state governments have challenged the legal rights of tribes in court. However, the states have not always prevailed. For example, the state of Arizona was defeated in *Arizona v. San Carlos Tribe*,[30] a 1983 water rights case, when a federal court ruled that the state enabling acts that gave the states jurisdiction over Indian lands did not empower them to adjudicate Indian water rights. Federal policy also halted states from officially interceding in matters involving Indian water rights and stipulated that a federal presence was necessary in adjudicating such rights.

In the last decade of the twentieth century, tribal legal rights having been under siege from both state and federal laws. With the large potential of tribal natural resources hanging in the balance, tribal, state, and federal courts have become the battlegrounds for disputes over the interpretation of Indian treaty rights—the basis of tribal protection of natural resources. Much of the battle for tribal rights depends on the life of the current federal policy of Indian self-determination. At present, federal laws maintain the balance in preserving the tribes' natural resources while tribal governments are developing their own judicial and economic strengths to clearly articulate the importance of tribal control over natural resources.

NOTES

1. *Trust* is defined here according to the fifth edition of *Citron's Law Lexicon*, compiled by William C. Citron (Cincinnati, Ohio: Anderson Publishing, 1973), pp. 290–291.
2. Robert N. Clifton, Knell Jessup Newton, and Monroe E. Price, eds., *American Indian Law: Cases and Materials*, 3rd ed. (Charlottesville, Va.: Michie, 1991), p. 15.
3. *Cherokee Nation v. Georgia*, 30 U.S. (5 Pet.) 1 (1831).
4. *Worcester v. Georgia*, 31 U.S. (6 Pet.) 515 (1832). For a discussion of the

evolution of the trusteeship, see Clifton, Newton, and Price, *American Indian Law*, pp. 17–18.

5. *Rockbridge v. Lincoln*, 449 F.2d 567, 9th Cir. 1971.
6. *Morton v. Mancari*, June 17, 1974, 417 *U.S. Reports* 541–45, 550–555.
7. Order by President Jimmy Carter for an assistant secretary of the interior position to "administer the laws, function, responsibilities, and authorities related in Indian affairs and matters" to "assume all the authorities and responsibilities of the Commissioner of Indian Affairs"; *Federal Register* (October 3, 1977): 42:53682.
8. See the discussion of H.C.R. 108 officially introducing "termination" as federal policy in Donald L. Fixico, *Termination and Relocation: Federal Indian Policy, 1945–1960* (Albuquerque: University of New Mexico Press, 1986).
9. The conference was held at Midway near the University of Chicago campus and was organized by Professors Sol Tax of Chicago, Nancy Lurie of the Milwaukee Public Museum, and the late Robert Thomas (a Cherokee).
10. 18 U.S.C.A. § 1151 (1948).
11. See Michael L. Lawson, *Damned Indians: The Pick-Sloan Plan and the Missouri River Sioux, 1944–1980* (Norman: University of Oklahoma Press, 1982).
12. Refer to the McCarran Amendment regarding water rights for state programs.
13. In 1992, state governments and the federal government began to tax tribal bingo operations under the regulatory provisions of the Indian Gaming Act of 1988.
14. The U.S. government used the concept of divide and conquer against tribes in various instances. In treaty negotiations in 1825 at Prairie du Chien, Wisconsin, and at other sites, for example, Indians who signed land cession agreements were recognized as the new tribal leaders; see Charles J. Kappler, comp. and ed., *Indian Treaties, 1778–1883*, 3rd printing (New York: Interland Publishing, 1975), pp. 211–273.
15. L. R. Westherhead, "What Is an 'Indian Tribe'?—The Question of Tribal Existence," *American Indian Law Review* 8, no. 1 (1980): 1.
16. "Indian Gaming Regulatory Act," October 17, 1988, *U.S. Statutes at Large*, 102:2467–69, 2472, 2476.
17. See Kappler, *Indian Treaties*, for all of the ratified treaties signed by the tribes and the United States.
18. American Indians who own their land (without trust status) on an individual basis are not under the control of the federal government.
19. "Winter's Doctrine," January 6, 1908, 207 *U.S. Reports* 565, 573, 575–577.
20. "Pyramid Lake Paiute Tribe v. Morton," 354 F.Supp. 252 (D.D.C. 1972).
21. The *Boldt* decision in 1974 was based on the Treaty of Medicine Creek, signed in 1854.
22. *United States v. Adair*, 723 F.2d 1394, 1412–15 (9th Cir. 1983), cert. denied, 467 U.S. 1252 (1984).
23. P.L. 280, 67 Stat. 588 (1953), as amended, 18 U.S. C.A. SS 1161–62, 25 U.S.C.A. §§ 1321–22, 28 U.S.C.A. § 1360 (1953).

24. *South Carolina v. Catawba Indian Tribe, Inc.*, 476 U.S. 498, 506 (1986).
25. *Oliphant v. Suquamish Indian Tribe*, March 6, 1978, 435 *U.S. Reports*, 206–212. Two other cases in 1978 involved separate issues of sovereignty: The courts ruled in favor of Indian sovereignty in both *United States v. Wheeler*, affecting a Navajo being tried for the same crime in a tribal court and a federal court, and in *Santa Clara Pueblo v. Martinez*, supporting the tribe against the charges of violating the Indian Civil Rights Act of 1968; see *United States v. Wheeler*, March 22,1978, 435 *U.S. Reports*, 322–28, 332, and *Santa Clara Pueblo v. Martinez*, May 5, 1978, 436 *U.S. Reports*, 56–59, 62–64, 72.
26. *Duro v. Reiner*, 110 S. Ct. 2053 (1990).
27. *Indian Mineral Leasing Act*, 25 U.S.C.A. § 396a–g.
28. *National Environmental Policy Act*, 42 U.S.C.A. § 4321.
29. *Surface Mining Control and Reclamation Act*, 30 U.S.C.A. § 1300(c), 1977.
30. *Arizona v. San Carlos Apache Tribe*, 463 U.S. 545 (1983).

10

ENVIRONMENTAL ISSUES AND
TRIBAL LEADERSHIP

I n the history of Indian-white relations, the ownership of land has
been greatly contested, with almost 2,000 wars and hostile en-
gagements being waged. The outcome became one-sided by the
late nineteenth century, and the legacy of exploitation continues today. The essential problem is one of capitalistic greed—a quality that
the American mainstream frequently views as mandatory for success.
Indeed, this ideology is one of the driving forces of American capitalism. Such a value orientation is incongruent with the fundamental
values of Indian tribal life and tribal leadership in regard to environmental issues on reservations.

Like their predecessors of more than three generations ago,
American Indians and their tribal communities are confronted with
the demands of a nation that has an ever-growing need to support its
energy-dependent lifestyle. Fossils fuels are becoming more scarce
with each day, and increasing attention is focused on the tribal lands
and the rich resources they contain. Once thought to be useless ter-
rain, reservation lands are now known to possess a wealth of coal
veins, pools of oil, and vast supplies of water. In the end, water is the
most precious natural resources of all, and the Indians and whites will
continue to fight for, as already proven in the Southwest and other
parts of North America.

Growing demands on natural resources in the West and on Indian
lands in particular have forced tribal leaders into two arenas—
economics and law. Tribal leaders face enormous pressures while dealing with energy companies, the federal government, and their own

constituents. With the advice of business councils, lawyers, and CERT, they frequently must make decisions and act in the best interest of their people. In order to lead their tribes successfully in the modern era, the leaders must comply with the methods and practices of the mainstream society and its culture. Meanwhile, Indian critics say that their tribal leaders have forgotten the old ways and have become more like white people.

Unfortunately, the cultural meaning of Mother Earth to many tribes becomes less important as their people seek sufficient education, well-paying jobs, modern health services, updated housing, and adequate food supplies. To be sure, cultures change with time, but the observation here is that the increasing demand for natural resources is accelerating the cultural change for tribes who happen to possess coal, oil, timber, water, uranium, and other natural resources necessary for sustaining human life.

Cultural change for most of the energy tribes involves a major transformation to modern American society's norms, and many Native Americans have made this transition during the last two or three generations. Not all tribes participate directly in the mainstream society, but the energy tribes and their leaders have to compete with the mainstream if they are going to successfully defend their natural resources. Under such circumstances, the two cultures are dynamically establishing a dialogue with each other and making demands on each other, much as they bartered in trade centuries ago. But the conditions today are far more complex.

The area of increasing concern is economics. In the twentieth century, tribes and their leaders have learned to think and function like members of the mainstream society. This requires adopting the values of the free enterprise system of American capitalism. Further, tribal leaders have to be more proficient than their competitors to successfully protect their natural resources, and they do not have many chances to make mistakes. With the accumulation of wealth, tribes will have the financial resources to improve the livelihood of their people. As this emphasis increases, a desire for a more mainstream lifestyle will become a part of the daily life in Indian communities and therefore a part of the changing culture of the tribes. At risk are the traditional tribal values, which do not stress the accumulation of wealth for most tribes. Thus, given burgeoning energy demands and the urgent need for tribal natural resources, economics becomes a vital factor and usually it is a catalyst for cultural change in such a situation, even if that change is voluntary. The problem becomes acute when economic change occurs faster than cultural change or cultural adaptation, as happened with Jackson Barnett and the Osage in the 1920s.

The second area of grave concern is federal Indian law. As tribal leaders negotiate intensely at a business level, with assistance from the Council of Energy Resources Tribes, the courts will remain the battleground in the struggle between Indians and white opportunists. The competition for Indian natural resources may very well be the last era of Indian-white confrontation, for, when all is said and done, the tribes will have nothing left that white society wants (although the Indian gaming industry has constantly lured non-Indians to reservation bingos and tribal casinos throughout Indian Country since the 1980s). For most of the twentieth century, the tribes and energy companies or white interest groups have continued to compete in the market arena and in the courts. Consequently, the tribal leaders and CERT have had to educate themselves in the law in order to defend their natural resources and represent tribal interests to the best of their ability while negotiating with energy companies and the federal government. One specific instance illustrates this point: In the 1970s, working with hired attorneys, the Northern Cheyenne Tribe found thirty-six illegal sections in their coal contracts; this type of illegality convinced the Bureau of Indian Affairs to cancel the contracts.[1]

The energy tribes have also been aided by the Native American Rights Fund, an Indian legal group committed to helping Native American organizations and individuals; it is based in Boulder, Colorado. In one case, NARF represented the Crow Tribe against white ranchers trying to halt the Crow from mining coal. In *Redoing et al. v. Morton et al.*, the Crow Tribe succeeded in having the lawsuit originally filed by ranchers dismissed.[2]

In July 1975, the Crow Tribe faced misunderstandings and tough negotiations with Shell Oil Company over several leasing offers that Shell officials proposed to the tribe.[3] After the Crow and Shell made their positions known, they hammered out agreements for mining leases.

In the current situation regarding oil, coal, uranium, timber, and water on tribal lands, the legal stakes are better identified. Legislation establishes the rules or regulations for confrontations in these areas, and previous court cases have set legal precedent. However, history has proven that laws may be changed by amendments or superseded by new laws, according to the prevailing national policy. The current federal policy supporting Indian self-determination shifts the government's responsibilities to the tribes. But the limit of tribal sovereignty remains undefined since the federal government can exercise its plenary authority to intervene.

In 1982, Congress passed the Indian Mineral Development Act, which is often referred to as the "Melcher law." In support of Indian sovereignty, Senator John Melcher of Montana introduced the bill as a departure from the past, allowing the tribes to negotiate their own mineral contracts and to participate as part owners in the mining development. In the following years, however, the tribes encountered frustration. "It seems that somebody at BIA doesn't want Indians to use this new law," tribal attorney Reid "Bill" Halton criticized at an Indian mineral institute held in 1988.[4]

Coal and oil have caused more bad memories than good results for tribes in Indian Country. In fact, it seems that some tribes, such as the Osage, are the perennial victims of wrongdoing. In the early 1980s, the Osage had 9,970 oil wells pumping crude—and ongoing troubles caused by interference from the U.S. government. The problem was that water and oil do not mix. The Corps of Engineers planned to build dams and reservoirs needed for flood control in northeastern Oklahoma, but this action threatened to cover up 83,000 acres of oil-rich land belonging to the Osage. In addition, the National Park Service wanted to obtain another 97,000 acres for the Tallgrass Prairie National Park. Thus, since the mid-1950s, the corps constructed dams and reservoirs that have submerged 45,000 acres of Osage land.[5]

As a national energy crisis in the second half of the 1970s increased the demand for Osage oil, the conflict between water and oil interests provoked the Osage to file a suit in 1976. Tribal leader Sylvester J. Tinker, seventy-eight years old at the time, took aim at the federal government and led his tribe to claim rights to minerals beneath the water reservoirs on their tribal lands. The federal court ruled that the Osage still owned the oil under the reservoirs and that the United States had no authority to condemn the Osage land for construction. This court decision halted the corps's Candy Lake project and threatened the future of the Skiatook Lake project where the dam was already built at a cost of $44 million, but the issue of Osage mineral rights remained superior to the government's surface rights. If additional federal construction had continued, the Osage argued, they would have lost 436 oil and gas wells and more than $1 million a year in royalty payments. Fighting on behalf of his people, Tinker was hostile to the government efforts to flood Osage land, and he made several trips to voice his views. "We've got 9970 pumping oil wells in the county right now," he said. "Hell, we can't get enough rigs in here to drill the new ones. And still those sorry sons of bitches in Washington are telling us to cover it up."[6]

On January 12, 1981, the *Los Angeles Times* reported that theft of oil from the Wind River Reservation in Wyoming was only a small part of the problem of oil theft and fraud on federal and Indian lands, amounting to $3 billion and $5 billion, respectively, and involving oil and gas operations in as many as twelve states.[7] Stealing gas is difficult because it is hard to transport, which has only increased the stealing of oil on federal and Indian lands. In actuality, oil can be stolen two ways—by removal of waste oil (or diverted good oil) from waste oil pits and by removal of production oil from on-site storage tanks. Since production of oil is measured by the sale of crude, theft via diversion during measuring is commonly done prior to a sale, and this is difficult to detect. On-site security is the only means to monitor such fraud, but this is costly and time consuming. Arrests and convictions have occurred for oil thefts in Oklahoma, New Mexico, and California, although most legal actions have involved violations on private land.[8] Such fraud alerted other parts of Indian Country, prompting the Assiniboine and Sioux Tribes of the Fort Peck Reservation in Montana to investigate oil theft on their own properties.

As seen throughout the twentieth century, clever thieves can steal in various ways. For example, The General Accounting Office (GAO) of the federal government reported in 1979 that energy companies underpaid tribes by as much as seven to ten percent annually. In 1981, the GAO reported that hundreds of millions of dollars may have been going uncollected each year. The Linowes Commission, set up to monitor such fraudulent activities, proposed an emergency fund that would use Indian moneys to audit royalty payments for reimbursing states and tribes. These entities have responded that the federal government should pay for its own royalty management responsibility. Projected costs to the tribes indicated that those with gross royalties of $164 million could pay $1.6 million into the emergency audit fund each year.[9] If the amount of Indian oil stolen remains at current levels and the underpayment of royalties continues, the tribes will also need to learn how to protect themselves from theft and fraud—ugly manifestations of blatant greed.

In 1980, forty-five Indian nations had tribes with oil resources. The BIA estimated that these tribes earned a combined $169,011,012.96 from oil and gas production on 5.3 million acres of tribal lands. Also in the 1980s, Indian reservations in twelve states constituted the heartland of Indian oil production. The leading oil-producing tribes included the Osage of Oklahoma; the Navajo of Arizona, New Mexico, and Utah; the Shoshone and Arapaho of Wyoming; the Jicarilla Apache of New Mexico; and the Uintah and Ouray Ute of Utah. Oklahoma had more oil production on Indian lands than any other state, with production occurring on a total of twenty-one separate tribal lands and yielding a total income of $70,266,407.33 in 1980. Wyoming was a distant second, with an income of $17.3 million in 1980, and New Mexico was third, with an income of $17.1 million involving six tribes.[10]

In 1997, the Bureau of Land Management (BLM), the federal agency in charge of inspecting Indian tribal oil and gas activity on reservations, decided to hand this responsibility to the tribes. BLM Director Pat Shea said that the bureau would provide the twenty-nine affected tribes with up to 100 percent of the necessary funding to inspect oil and gas wells on their reservations.[11]

The need for additional fossil fuel reserves became apparent during the early 1980s, compelling the Reagan administration to establish a national energy policy. The administration sought to decontrol the domestic oil and gas prices and to expand coal production. Issued through the Department of Energy, the Reagan policy also called for further regulation of the usage of nuclear power, particularly the disposal of nuclear waste.[12]

Further federal involvement and the growing needs of society forced the energy tribes to respond to demands for their natural resources and related concerns. The Flathead and Coeur d'Alene Tribes negotiated agreements with the Northern Tier Pipeline Company for the Alaska pipeline crossing twenty miles of Coeur d'Alene land in Montana and the Flathead Reservation (the forty-two-inch pipe transports Alaska crude from Port Angeles, Washington, to Clearbrook, Minnesota, a distance of approximately 1,500 miles).[13]

Another Washington State tribe, the Colvilles, negotiated for two and one-half years over the Mount Tolman Project with AMAX, Inc. The agreement called for an open-pit mine for copper-molybdenum, a flotation mill plant to produce copper and molybdenum concentrates, waste disposal sites, and support facilities including a transmission line and a water pipeline. Projected to be a forty-three-year operation, the tribe chose AMAX over nine other companies and expected to obtain over $1 billion in profit.[14] On the Wind River Reservation in Wyoming, action from the Interior Department forced two oil companies, Amoco Production of Denver and Sohio Petroleum of Oklahoma City, to demonstrate why their leases with the tribe should not be canceled after attorneys for the tribe charged the two companies with (1) failing to properly account for or pay royalties on 500,000 barrels of oil produced between November 1968 and May 1981, and (2) failing to pay royalties between November 1968 and October 1970. Tribal attorneys also charged the oil companies with defaulting on royalty payments for 471,000 barrels of oil between June 1972 and March 1981.[15] Such action taken by a tribe has compelled oil companies to formulate new strategies for dealing with rigorous tribal leadership.

The energy tribes have responded by taxing mining companies for mineral development on their lands, causing a deluge of court cases. In 1982, the Jicarilla Apache taxation case led the energy companies to complain about this new tribal power, which was enforced by the U.S. Supreme Court decision recognizing Indian sovereignty in implementing taxation on tribal lands. Other tribes also considered using the power of taxation and challenged the ability of states to tax mining companies operating on Indian lands; in Montana, for example, both the Blackfeet and the Crow Tribes contested state taxation. On the flip side of the same issue, the Kerr-McGee Corporation challenged the legality of New Mexico's taxing of uranium production on the Navajo Reservation. In the Crow case, the U.S. Court of Appeals for the Ninth Circuit reversed a Montana district court dismissal of the tribe's suit on the basis that federal law preempts state taxation, intending to promote tribal autonomy over mineral development on reservation land.[16]

The issue of terminating Indian rights was nearly resurrected in 1982 when Congress considered the Ancient Indian Land Claims Settlement Act. The bill was an attempt to retroactively legalize the taking of lands originally owned by Eastern tribes but now owned by states, municipalities, and private individuals. At least seven tribal cases would have been affected had the bill not failed to pass into law.[17]

Two individuals—Pat and Opal Pourier of Pine Ridge, South Dakota— had the first Indian-owned gas company. Purchased in 1973 from Amoco, after Pat worked as a driver for the company for three years, the company was renamed the Lakota Gas Company; Pat and Opal operated it with the help of their twelve children. Although the early years proved difficult, they gained experience and struggled hard to stay in business and were ultimately successful. Pat and Opal stressed the importance of good bookkeeping, solid credit arrangements, and having enough capital for the first year of operation in advising other Indian businesspeople.[18]

Since the 1980s and actually in the last decades of the nineteenth century as well, tribes such as the Klamath and others in the Pacific Northwest, the Menominees in Wisconsin, and various Chippewa bands in the western Great Lakes region have experienced huge losses of timberlands, and they are now carefully trying to protect their remaining forests. As of January 1981, 104 tribes had a total market of 5.8 million acres of timber across the United States. This was estimated to represent an income of $89.9 million, but the risks inherent in developing this resource should be noted. In the Southeast, for example, the U.S. Forest Service reported that approximately forty-two hectares, or thirty to fifty percent of all forest land in the area, had disappeared due to excessive harvesting.[19]

Currently, an estimated one-third of the coal west of the Mississippi River lies under tribal lands. Since World War II, energy companies have intensely mined coal, particularly since the 1970s. With one-third to one-half or more of the documented reserves of uranium in the United States located in the Four Corners area alone, CERT has a huge responsibility in protecting Indian interests in the Southwest.[20] Uranium will be the new natural resource that the tribes need to know more about in order to protect it. In January 1989, the Havasupai who live in Nataract Canyon of the Grand Canyon faced the possibility of a seventeen-acre mining operation for uranium at Red Butte, near the south rim of the Grand Canyon. This area is near the original site of the Havasupai's historical territory, and it is considered to be a sacred area. "The preparation of the mine which is being [developed] now wounds the earth at a sacred and vital place. A mine will kill it," said Havasupai leaders.[21] Earlier, New Mexico had released a 216-page report, on February 4, 1982, stating that the Bureau of Indian Affairs lacked the staffing and technical skills necessary to properly advise and represent Indian people in negotiations involving energy affairs.[22]

Water is perhaps the most precious natural resource of all, and land without water is useless, as was proved in the Pueblo lands controversy of the 1920s. In the future, the tribes in the Southwest and other parts of Indian Country who have sufficient water tables will have to protect their water rights in the courts. Since the *Winter's* decision established the Indians' "reserve right" in 1908, tribal groups have been facing a growing threat as the state governments increasingly challenge Indian water supplies, as indicated in the *Arizona v. California* water case in 1963.[23] Although the court ruled that five reservations had the right to water on the lower Colorado River, the case raised the issue of "practicably irrigable acres"—a ruling that would have implications for future federal and tribal water cases. Indian Country, especially in the Southwest, felt the pressure for this resource even earlier, when Congress passed the McCarran amendment in 1953. The law vested state courts with jurisdiction to determine water rights comprehensively, if the water usage was a part of a larger usage such as a national forest, a wildlife refuge, or a certain type of national recreation area.[24] Congress intended the McCarran amendment to end piecemeal federal adjudication of water rights by granting this privilege to the states, but it did not mention Indian water rights as being subject to state court jurisdiction.

Since the late 1800s, non-Indians have depended on the Desert Lands Act of 1877 for their entitlement under the states' jurisdiction to water supplies for use in developing lands in the West.[25] Westerners convinced Congress of the need for water legislation, noting that the states varied with regard to water supplies. In response, Congress granted states plenary control over all nonnavigable streams so that they could develop their own water laws.[26] Fortunately for the tribes, most states adopted a seniority system based on prior appropriation; thus, the states recognized Indian water rights protected under *Winter's*.[27] Although the states acknowledged senior water rights, however, they stressed that the tribes should continue to use the water.[28] In this light, the states recognized the issue of competing needs for water.

Tribes must realize (1) that their water rights are senior to those of others using water, as stipulated under *Winter's*, and (2) that they will not lose those rights even if they do not use the water. It is mainly farming corporations and individuals in need of large amounts of water in the West who are attempting to pressure the federal government to pass laws giving the states greater water rights than Indians have. Furthermore, if the reserved water right for Indians does not yield an adequate supply of water for tribal uses, the United States could appropriate or purchase additional water for the tribes.[29]

On an individual basis, an Indian allotment owner may sell his or her right to reserved water to a non-Indian. In a case involving the Colville Reservation, a court decided that this right included sufficient creek water for the development and maintenance of fishing grounds and that the state of Washington could not grant water permits to a non-Indian who had purchased an Indian allotment.[30]

Furthermore, eleven states—Alaska, Arizona, Idaho, Montana, New Mexico, North Dakota, Oklahoma, South Dakota, Utah, Washington, and Wyoming—disclaimed jurisdiction over Indian water rights in their state constitutions. In fact, Congress intended for the McCarran amendment to help the states determine water rights comprehensively and to reiterate that federal and Indian water interests are determined in the federal courts. Since 1980, Western interests have continually attempted to undermine Indian water rights. In early 1982, the National Congress of American Indians met in an executive council from January 27 to 29 with Senator William Cohen of Maine and Representative John Seiberling of Ohio, both members of the Indian Affairs Committees, to reject a draft of a national Indian water rights bill prepared by the Western Regional Council. The bill sought to place all Indian water rights under state control, after a two-year commission recommended specific water quantifications for each of the tribes by 1984.[31]

The legal war for water had already begun. By 1982, there were forty-eight lawsuits on Indian water rights in ten Western states. Tribal leaders in Arizona, Utah, Washington, and California entered a new political period of protecting water rights for their peoples. In eleven states, a total of ninety-seven irrigation projects were being developed, producing crops worth more than $178 million.[32] During the early 1980s, sixty-eight percent of the groundwater in the country was used for agricultural irrigation, with approximately ninety percent of the irrigated lands existing in seventeen Western states. After eighty-five percent of the water consumed in the West went to irrigated croplands, the remaining fifteen percent was divided among domestic, municipal, and industrial uses. By 1990, more than four million hectares in the United States, an estimated fifth of the nation's irrigated areas, were watered by excessively pumping recycled water. Using such amounts during the early 1980s dropped the lower water tables in Texas, California, Kansas, and Nebraska—four primary food-producing areas. In Texas, as an example, the water tables fell about fifteen centimeters (six inches) per year beneath 1.54 million hectares, or seventy-two percent of the state's total irrigated area, amounting to a total of thirty percent of that land between 1974 and 1987.[33]

CERT has warned the tribes about future battles for retaining water rights, obtaining ownership, securing a needed supply of water, and getting funding for water programs. In 1982, CERT described the water situation as confused and stated that time and water were running out on the tribes. Intertribal cooperation was posed as one way to amass enough influential power to oppose the water interests of the federal and state governments, non-Indian agriculture, industries, and municipalities as their water needs increased.

Although all Indian tribes legally had water rights, many did not actual possess water. Consequently, both ownership *and* possession were paramount in the formation of water policy. Throughout the twentieth century and certainly well before, as in the case of the Pueblos in the Southwest, Indian water rights have been abused and Indian water has been stolen. The diversion of streams around reservations frequently was authorized by federal authorities and state officials, who sometimes allowed non-Indians to siphon off reservation groundwater. Ironically, even as dry lands on reservations lay in dire need of water, the federal government subsidized non-Indian agricultural users. CERT claimed that the tribes lacked political power to overcome this exploitation and that they needed to be better informed about their water rights and resource management.[34]

In 1989, the U.S. Supreme Court began to reexamine Indian reserve water rights when it agreed to review a 1988 Wyoming Supreme Court decision. The decision had awarded extensive federal reserved water rights to the Shoshone and Northern Arapaho Tribes on Wyoming's Wind River Reservation, establishing that the tribes had 477,000 acre feet of water for agricultural purposes but none for industrial or municipal usage. The state of Wyoming and the tribes appealed the decision. The Supreme Court rejected the state's petition to deny the tribes any reserved water rights but agreed to review the quantification of those rights based on the "irrigable" standard.[35]

Water is the source for human life—and also the source of unfortunate conflict. Because the money involved is not as substantial as that represented in energy negotiations for oil and coal; water does not arouse immediate concern. Yet the war for water is approaching and is already evident in some parts of the country. This precious natural resource is the most valued of all, for it is essential to everyone. The by-products of water, such as geothermal energy and hydroelectricity, are important as well, but they are secondary to human needs.

Using water as a means of wielding power, the Warm Springs Confederated Tribes have developed the only Indian-owned hydroelectric project in the United States. The project was planned in June 1978, and the tribe received a grant of $86,000 from the Department of Energy for a feasibility study to develop the hydropower plant at the Pelton Reregulating Dam, built in the mid-1950s. The $30 million project, completed with $10 million in tribal funds, $15 million raised by a state bond issue, and a $5 million federal loan, is expected to produce annual net revenues of approximately $4 million to the Warm Springs Tribes.[36]

One innovative project is a wind generator belonging to the Muscogee Creeks in Oklahoma. The generator was designed to provide electricity for the tribal offices at Okmulgee with wind speeds as low as eight miles per hour. The Creeks obtained a grant from the Department of Energy, and the windmill can produce a maximum of 2,100 watts of electricity, costing the tribe $10,000.[37]

In another imaginative effort, the Navajo town of Steamboat, Arizona, located forty miles west of the tribal capital of Window Rock, purchased 32 solar-cell lighting systems as part of a continuing tribal program to bring solar electricity to remote residents. (The tribe was estimated to have 10,000 to 11,000 homes without electrical service in 180 towns on the 26,000 square miles of the Navajo Reservation.) By 1982, 191 photovoltaic-powered systems had been installed on the reservation. Costing $40,000, the system at Steamboat was funded by the tribe as a part of a rural Solar Energy Project started in March 1982. By contrast, the average cost of bringing in utility service to the Navajo on the reservation (which stretches across portions of Arizona, New Mexico, and Utah) was $11,000 a mile.[38]

A serious problem affecting one tribe is the nearby location of a nuclear energy plant. The Yakima Tribe in Washington, through the Columbia River Intertribal Fish Commission (CRIFC) of Portland, Oregon, has petitioned the Nuclear Regulatory Commission (NRC) to intervene regarding two Washington State nuclear power plants. Originally, five nuclear plants of the Skagit-Hanford Project were planned, but two were halted during funding debates. The Yakima protested that the plants were too close to the reservation and that radiological, chemical, and thermal pollution of the air and water would contaminate the Columbia River Basin, affecting their fisheries. The Yakima are the first tribe in the United States to pass a tribal resolution to prohibit the transport of nuclear waste, residues, fuels, and by-products across reservations by land, rail, air, or water.[39]

In another related affair, Browning-Ferris Industries (BFI) of Houston, Texas, one of the largest waste disposal firms in the United States, started a campaign to locate toxic chemical disposal sites on tribal lands. In 1982, BFI negotiated with the Fort Mohave Reservation on the Colorado River and contacted the Chemehuevi and Hualapai in Arizona, the Duckwater Shoshone in Nevada, reservations in southern Utah, the Eastern Cherokee in North Carolina, and possibly the Winnebago of Nebraska; it also attempted to locate a site on Muscogee Creek lands in Oklahoma. The Houston business firm explained to the tribal leaders that, given the federal cutbacks to tribes that would hurt their revenues, establishing waste disposal sites on their lands could help tribal economies. The tribes reported that slick promotional materials were sent to them, and apparently, the BFI campaign was persuasive, for the company has since run operations in California, Phoenix, and Salt Lake City.[40]

In a cyclic manner, mining has come back to harm Native Americans yet again, for radiation from uranium mines has contaminated Indian miners and the drinking water where they live. Among the Lakota in the Black Hills, where more than twenty-five mining companies are active, uranium mining has exposed Lakota workers to radiation. The Pine Ridge Reservation has experienced related health hazards since the 1970s.[41] In New Mexico on the Navajo Reservation, Navajo miners have worked deep below the Colorado Plateau to extract soft, yellow uranium since the 1960s, and many of the Navajo mining veterans who worked to supply the uranium needed for America's nuclear warheads during the Cold War were affected with radiation. More than 2,700 Navajo miners and their relatives have registered with the tribe's Office of Navajo Uranium Workers, but only 242 have applied for compensation under the Radiation Exposure Compensation Act of 1990. Unfortunately, the "old-timers" among the Navajo miners did not save any checkstubs or other documents to prove that they had worked in the uranium mines.[42]

In Alaska, where the Alaska Native Settlement Act of 1971 led to the return of millions of acres of land to the Indians and where millions of dollars flowed from the discovery of oil on the Northern Slope, the Natives have been now been plagued with major problems of another sort. Although the windfalls from oil royalties helped Alaska's Native communities as a whole, they hurt many individuals who could not handle large sums of wealth, much like the Osage of Oklahoma during the 1920s. This has been a problem since the 1970s. In 1997, the Alaska Native groups found themselves fighting Exxon in a lawsuit after the Exxon ship *Valdez* ran aground in 1989 and spilled millions of gallons of crude oil in Prince William Sound. Consequently, not only the Alaska Native Americans but also the fish and the fowl of the area have been affected by contamination.[43]

The last decade of the twentieth century has witnessed the heightening of environmental concerns among Americans and other citizens of the world. Global warming is increasingly a subject of international summits, as is the rapid decline of the rain forests in South America, where agriculture players strive to create more farming land and raise more livestock. Environmentalism is certainly prominent in the United States, where the redwood forest in California has dwindled from some 2 million acres 200 years ago to only about 85,00 acres today, 65,000 acres of which lie protected in parks.[44] The timber situation is becoming worse, particularly in regard to the amount of waste that occurs in converting trees to paper. Consider the issue of junk mail. Americans receive an estimated four million tons of junk mail annually, and approximately forty-four percent of them never open any of it. Put another way, every person in the country who receives junk mail has used the equivalent of one and a half trees a year. If only 100,000 people stopped their junk mail, almost 150,000 trees could be saved annually; if a million people did this, the United States could save approximately a million and a half trees per year.

Today's generation of Indian leaders and American officials will need to resolve their differences and cooperatively formulate energy policies that do not threaten the tribes. But the exploitative federal policies of the past remind tribal leaders and their people to be skeptical of new federal ideas. Since the late 1970s, America has become dependent on other oil-producing nations who are in a position to exploit the United States for its dollars; in 1973 and 1974, for example, the price of crude oil exported from OPEC quadrupled. Moreover, the demand for mineral resources is accelerating with the uncontested growth of America's population via steady foreign immigration and with its unabated dependence on gas-guzzling vehicles. Ironically, although the United States is one of the largest oil producers in the world, it is also the largest importer of oil.

The next century will record the outcome of efforts by America's capitalistic system to utilize the natural resources that lie on tribal lands. From the twentieth-century's struggles and sad accounts, it can easily be predicted that the losses will be great, for these resources are irreplaceable. But who will benefit, and what will the repercussions for the tribal communities in Indian Country be? America is a land of wasteful people who have naively exploited the abundance of natural resources for capitalistic gain. At the end of the twentieth century, the competition will be growing for the remaining natural resources. In the years ahead, tribal leaders will wage the most significant battles since the nineteenth century for the existence of their people and the protection of their homelands. Oil and coal reserves will most likely be exhausted first, followed by natural gas. Alternative fuels, including geothermal fuels, wind, and hydroelectricity, will be used, and finally, conflicting interests will be fighting over the air and water. Ironically, it is the force that has propelled the United States during the twentieth century—the "invisible hand" of American capitalism—that the tribes must guard against if they hope to secure their people's natural resources.

NOTES

1. Marjane Ambler, "Indian Energies Devoted to Self-Sufficiency," *National Forum* 71, no. 2 (Spring 1991): 22.
2. Daniel H. Israel of NARF to U.S. Representative Morris K. Udall, May 31, 1974, Lee Metcalf Papers, Folder 227–8, Box 227, Montana Historical Society Archives, Helena, Montana.
3. Vice President K. Doig of Shell Oil Company to Tom Dailey of Crow Agency, July 23, 1975, Lee Metcalf Papers, Folder 227–7, Box 227, Montana Historical Society Archives, Helena, Montana.
4. "Mineral Law Hamstrung by BIA Delay," *Lakota Times*, March 14, 1990.
5. William J. Broad, "Osage Oil Cover-Up," *Science* 208, no. 4439 (April 14, 1980): pp. 32–33, and *Final Report and Legislative Recommendation*, A Report of the Special Committee on Investigations of the Select Committee on Indian Affairs United States Senate, Senate Report 101–216, 101st Cong., 1st sess., Senate, November 6, 1989.
6. Broad, "Osage Oil Cover-Up," p. 32.
7. "Wind River Reservation," *Los Angeles Times*, January 12, 1981.
8. Russell Davis, James E. Wilen, and Rosemarie Jergovic, "Oil and Gas Royalty Recovery Policy on Federal and Indian Lands," *Natural Resources Journal* 23, no. 2 (April 1983): 399.

9. Ibid., pp. 407–409; see also Donald T. Sant, Abraham E. Haspel, and Robert E. Boldt, "Oil and Gas Royalty Recovery Policy on Federal and Indian Lands: A Response," *Natural Resources Journal* 23, no. 2 (April 1983): 417–434.

10. John Butler and Richard La Course, "45 Indian Tribes in a Dozen States Form Heartland of Indian Oil Production," *The CERT Report* 4, no. 11 (September 13, 1982): 3–4.

11. "BLM to Let Tribes Manage Their Own Mineral Resources," *News From Indian Country* 10, no. 19 (mid-October 1997): 7A.

12. John Butler, "Edwards Unveils National Energy Policy Plan," *The CERT Report* 3, no. 10 (August 10, 1981): 7.

13. "Flathead, Couer d'Alene Tribes Sign Northern Tier Agreements," *The CERT Report* 3, no. 10 (August 10, 1981): 7.

14. "Final EIS for Proposed Cooper-Molybdenum Mine Completed," *The CERT Report* 3, no. 10 (August 10, 1981): 10.

15. Richard La Course, "The Truth of Such Allegations Warrants Cancellation of the Leases on Wind River," *The CERT Report* 4, no. 7 (June 11, 1982): 3–4.

16. Frank G. Long, "Energy Critics Jump the Gun on Tribal Mineral Taxation," *The CERT Report* 4, no. 2 (June 11, 1982): 10.

17. Gary Fife, "Ancient Land Claims Bill Would Harm Eastern Indian Tribes," *The CERT Report* 4, no. 2 (February 8, 1982): 13.

18. Sharon Illoway, "Lakota Gas Co. Only Indian-Owned Gas Firm in S. D." *The CERT Report* 4, no. 7 (June 11, 1982): 11.

19. Butler and La Course, "45 Indian Tribes."

20. Philip Reno, *Mother Earth, Father Sky, and Economic Development: Navajo Resources and Their Uses* (Albuquerque: University of New Mexico Press, 1981), p. 133.

21. "Havasupais Fighting Mine Plan," *Lakota Times*, January 10, 1989.

22. "Report Says New Mexico Energy Development Creates Problems for Tribes," *The CERT Report* 4, no. 2 (February 8, 1982): 18.

23. *Arizona v. California*, 373 U.S. 546, (1963).

24. *McCarran Amendment*, (1953) 43 U.S.C. § 666.

25. *Desert Lands Act*, (1877), 43 U.S.C.A. §§ 321–339 (1970).

26. State control over water is supported in *California Oregon Power Co. v. Beaver Portland Cement Co.*, 295 U.S. 142, 163 (1935).

27. Refer to *Coffin v. Left Hand Ditch Co.*, 6 Colo. 443 (1882).

28. Frank M. Bond, "Indian Reserved Water Rights Doctrine Expanded," *Natural Resources Journal* 23, no. 1 (January 1983): 207–208.

29. David S. Brookshire, James E. Merrill, and Gary L. Watts, "Economics and the Determination of Indian Reserved Water Rights," *Natural Resources Journal* 23, no. 4 (October 1981): 750.

30. *Colville Confederated Tribes v. Walton*, 647 F.2d (9th Cir. 1981), cert. denied, 50 U.S.L.W. 3448 (U.S. Dec. 1, 1981) (No. 81–321).

31. "NCAI Opposes WRC's Draft Water Bill Affecting Indian Tribes," *The CERT Report* 8, no. 2 (February 8, 1982): 14.

32. Richard Trudell and Joseph Myers, "How Indian Water Rights Are Resolved May Determine Future of Western United States," *The CERT*

Report 4, no. 9 (July 23, 1982): 1.

33. Lester Brown and Alan Durning, *State of the World 1990* (New York and London: W. W. Norton, 1990), pp. 45–46.
34. Trudell and Myers, "How Indian Water Rights," pp. 1–3.
35. "U.S. Supreme Court to Re-examine Water Rights," *Lakota Times*, March 22, 1989, p. 11.
36. Donna Behrend, "Oregon's Warm Springs Reservation Dedicates Hydro-power Project," *The CERT Report* 4, no. 10 (August 10, 1982): 5.
37. "Tribal Energy Front," *The CERT Report* 4, no. 11 (September 13, 1982): 16.
38. Ibid.
39. Richard La Course, "Amoco Sohio Seek 'Show Cause Hearing' on Wind River Cancellations," *The CERT Report* 4, no. 8 (July 9, 1982): 2.
40. Daniel Bomberry, "Browning-Ferris Industries Giving Indian Tribes Case of 'Toxic Shock,' " *The CERT Report* 4, no. 10 (August 10, 1982): 8.
41. Amelia W. Irvin, "Energy Development and the Effects of Mining on the Lakota Nation," *Journal of Ethnic Studies* 10, no. 1 (Spring 1982): 90–99.
42. Matt Kelley, "Miners Paid Price in Cold War Effort," *South Bend Tribune*, September 8, 1997.
43. Kevin Galvin, "Natives Fight Exxon Plan for Valdez," *South Bend Tribune*, January 16, 1997.
44. Bill Barol and Lynda Wright, "Eco-Activist Summer," *Newsweek*, June 2, 1990, p. 60.

11

AMERICAN INDIAN PHILOSOPHY
AND GLOBAL CONCERNS

L ong ago, the many Indian tribes of the Americas learned to
live with the various climates, flora, and fauna of their environments. They developed a relationship with nature, charac-
terized by harmonious respect. Few generalizations cover all of their
philosophies, but there are basic points that are relevant when con-
templating the future of this planet and its limited natural resources.
One observation is that the tribes, representing various levels of civilization, ultimately understood their relationship with their environments. In general, they accepted the premise that the environment
was something greater than the mere capabilities of humans. With
this in mind, Indian people acknowledged that the natural environment directed all life and that its natural resources should be used
wisely. Practical reasoning revealed that the supplies of resources were
finite and that life would be difficult if the balance of supply and demand was disturbed.

People depended upon each other and upon nature's environment
for food and shelter. Human survival depended on cooperation, and
social relations were important, starting with the perception of one's
self as a person and one's role within the family, community, and tribe.
The person or self established a delicate equilibrium between individual development and maintaining kinship relations. For example,
among the Wintu Indians of California, a person spoke about "self" *in*
"society" rather than "self" *and* "society."[1] People preferred to be
members of the community for practical reasons—to hunt or grow
foods, for protection, and for the feeling of security. The importance of

community was vital to the societal norms and patterns that developed. Without the underpinning of a common need and moral assumptions, however, the society would disintegrate into a disordered collection of individuals.[2]

Practical needs led to the next development of social behavior and certain morals, and afterward, tribal laws, ceremonies, and protocols for leadership developed. The latter are not among the basic elements of Indian society, but they evolved as themes for culture manifestations; they are formally expressed in ceremonies, philosophies, art, music, and worldview. Cultural genesis begins with the process of interrelating the elements of people, family, and community, which produces a balance between the themes in the community and nature.[3] In the development of traditional Indian culture, establishing the first phase of personal relationships with other kinspeople, community, and the environment allowed the second phase of thematic cultural expressions to flourish, as previously mentioned.

Finding food and preparing it consumed most of the early Indian's day, compelling the family to cooperate as a social unit.[4] Families helped each other to ease the work of hunting, food preparation, and providing living accommodations. Plentiful environmental areas permitted unrelated families to interact so that communities developed; more than one community united in a collective political effort constituted a tribe, or nation (tribal nation). All of the social-kinship elements were in sync, assuring the well-being of the tribe or nation, and the people envisioned an idyllic equilibrium with other nations and the environment. Attaining such a political-social equilibrium with other tribal nations, however, proved more difficult than working within one's own tribe in balance with nature and the entire universe. The physical reality obviously differed from the idyllic one as social relations among tribes acquired political aspects. However, the tribes consistently acknowledged a creative force that was superior to mere humans.

Many tribes acknowledged that the causality of the "unexplained" resulted from supernatural forces that governed the environment and that a supreme force gave life to the entire universe. Traditional Indians rationalized that the forces of life were interlinked, expressing both positive and negative powers, and they presumed that a balance would create a positive atmosphere for life's activities. They accepted this general explanation since a time constraints prohibited scientific investigation (a privilege of bountiful civilizations and later phases of societal development); their waking hours were devoted to obtaining and preparing food.[5] When the community stabilized its economy, even for a minimal number of days, conscious reflection turned to the history, philosophy, and artistic expression of the tribe's culture, thereby further solidifying the identity of the community; rationalization and scientific inquiry would likely follow.

From traditional times to contemporary times, Indian people have struggled to maintain a dual balance, both within themselves and with the universe. Such efforts are very personal since the strength of the Indian societies rested on kinship and social relations. However, the most important relationship is not that between humans, nor is it that between humans and animals or plants. Rather, the relationship of people with the universe is the most significant relationship, and Indians have learned that the way in which humans view themselves in this role is important for an understanding of the essence of life and "the natural order of things."[6] The enormity of the universe is acknowledged, and the smallness of humans in the universal order of life is accepted. Unlike Anglo-Americans who perceive themselves as the center of the universe, Indian people traditionally have viewed themselves as minuscule members of a vast universe. For example, the Western person typically refers to his or her "self" as the reference point and travels accordingly to turn right or left. The Wintu, by contrast, referred to left and right as the sides of their body but while traveling referred to the cardinal directions to avoid confusion and becoming lost. If traveling northward, a Wintu would say, the mountains are to the west; a non-Indian would say, the mountains are on the left. But in returning to go south, the Wintu would know the mountains were to the east, and the non-Indian would know they were on the right side.[7] When the non-Indian faced another direction and perhaps did this again, he or she became confused, then lost.

In kinship terms, the human relationship with the natural environment was more important than the human-to-human relationship. In time, Indian people understood that their lives depended on the environment, and knew that this source of energy—so intrinsic to life itself—deserved respect. Their collective attitude lacked an individual ego consciousness, allowing them to contemplate their societal relations and participation in the universe. Maintaining this relationship influenced cultural development and the values of life as defined according to each Indian tribal nation by its people. Over the generations, these values proved to be successful, and it is these traditional values that could offer a useful lesson as global natural resources and the environment are rapidly depleted by the progress of civilization.

Unfortunately, Victorian evolutionists in physical anthropology in the nineteenth century underestimated the value of nativistic thought and referred to so-called primitive societies as savage and of lesser intelligence, only to elevate their own race above others.[8] Such a racist view has endangered natural resources in the twentieth century as the Western mentality has appointed itself the most advanced society of human existence, while dismissing the conservation philosophies of Native Americans. Racial prejudice and cultural ethnocentricism has obstructed the global cooperation needed to achieve the best answers for halting the ongoing drain on natural resources and preserving what remains. Although the United States holds perhaps the most advanced scientific facilities and the greatest wealth for funding environmental conservation, it must overcome its own prejudice against scholars of different racial and cultural backgrounds in order to stop the depletion of the environment.[9]

The primary focus of the numerous tribal philosophies is on global concerns regarding the exhaustion of natural resources. From traditional Indian people, we can learn that kinship and social cooperation is important if the global community is to survive. Such relationships were deeply personal for the Indians, and they carefully treated other people and expected generous social treatment in return—so unlike the stoic, impersonal role that stereotypes have assigned them. (Naturally, Indian people would appear unfriendly to non-Indians since the latter decided early on that Native Americans were their enemies.) From the Indian point of view, Anglo-Americans are less open to other people, and their friendly overtures are suspicious since their mental preoccupation is focused more on scientific rationalization and less on social relations. If global scientists and government leaders could combine the personal thinking of American Indians with the Western mind's causal thinking, answers to questions of "Who is responsible for decreasing natural resources?" and "What is the cause?" could produce a better approach to conserving global resources.[10]

Before the arrival of non-Indians in the Western Hemisphere, American Indians learned from their struggles how to live within the limits of the environment. The environment had a direct impact on their cultural development and directed life's economies, leading to a focus on agriculture and hunting and gathering or a combination of the two. Among the Hurons, as among many Indian people, fishermen offered tobacco and invocations to the waters before taking fish from the streams and rivers. Certain spirits of the waters had to be appeased, lest they jeopardize the fishing.[11] Philosophically, this acknowledgment of animism stressed the positive nature of human involvement with the act of fishing so that positive results would occur.[12] Montagnais hunters who depended upon the beaver practiced conservation hunting since limited moose and caribou lived in their country. By studying the habits of the beaver, the Montagnais estimated how many animals already were taken and were able to roughly calculate how many were left so that there would always be enough to hunt. This type of cognition became one of the natural laws that the tribe obeyed.[13] This practice of conservation ensured a steady supply of food to support the estimated 10,000 Montagnais who are thought to have lived in a dozen villages.[14] Traditional Indians treated the natural environment on a social but elevated level (perhaps operating on a principle of retribution)[15] as they developed philosophical explanations for the causalities of life. They observed the activities of nature and incorporated the patterns expressed in the four seasons, in animal activities, and in plant growth into their social norms, laws, philosophy, and worldview. The commonality between traditional Indians and animals is the social outcome of their group emphasis on human-animal relations.[16] In the human-animal relationship, all partners are equal and mutually respected, so that people develop a respect for all life, including the life of plants. All three—humans, animals, and plants—possessed life, and their spirits lived within their bodies. Many Indian tribes developed clans represented by animal and plant totems, and they practiced group protection and unity. They courted the positive side of life, abhorred evil, and at times had to combat negative agents from the dark side.

Following traditional practices as their ancestors had enabled Native Americans to be protected from the evil that lay beyond their understanding of life. Success in maintaining their livelihood, even during hardship, brought a confidence that the ancestors were correct, that traditions should not be questioned but rather accepted; maintaining a healthy stasis between the people and the destructive forces of life depended on sustaining those traditions.[17] In this sense, traditional Indians were more metaphysical than their non-Indian counterparts, who eventually drifted from their early European religious beliefs toward a focus on economic gain. The unseen powers of nature convinced traditional Indians that the laws of nature were greater than their tribal political laws, and thus, much of their own laws were based on those of nature. Consequently, traditional Indians observed and continue to observe the seen and unseen forces of life, seemingly without regard to past, present, or future. In the development of tribal religions, nature represented universal determinism, and this religious concept became an important part of many Indian religions and unified the tribal communities.[18]

The Indian relationship with animals dates back to the mythical times when both were new members of the freshly created world. Cree myths in Canada describe a time when men married certain animals, such as the beaver, and speak about man's relationship with the animal world. These stories, legends, and parables taken together created an oral history tradition.[19] Waswanipi hunters in the Canadian boreal forest hunted the moose more easily after accumulating a large amount of knowledge about the animal's habits, so that the moose "surrendered" its life to the Waswanipi. The hunter respectfully killed the moose swiftly, without torture, (and not excessively for sport) in order to release the animal's spirit to return to its life in the afterworld. To ensure a successful harvest for hunting, hunters estimated the animal populations and rotated their hunting areas.[20]

America's Native populations had learned to distribute their populations to areas of a size and type that could sustain their people. Since their lives depended upon the environment, climate and other aspects of nature influenced their cultural development.[21] Furthermore, a second point of technological advancement was incorporated into this conservationist lifestyle, as recorded among the Iroquois people of the eastern Great Lakes.[22] Ethically, one does not ask for more than the amount that can be used; if this simple rule is obeyed, less misfortune will occur. Among the Ojibwa, hunters always shared the game that they killed to ensure that they would not be bewitched by others, and they did not hoard any materials for fear that misfortune would plague them.[23]

When contact with Europeans and then the Anglo-Americans occurred, a different value system, primarily an English one, became a part of the American experience, based on concepts of individualism and property ownership.[24] As other early non-English Europeans participated in capitalism, this resulting exploitation critically impacted world societies. This continues today and is especially evident in the last half of the twentieth century.[25] Motivated by greed, America's capitalistic attitude has set a dangerous precedent for other world powers and Third World nations alike. Since 1950, the world has lost almost one-fifth of its topsoil from croplands, a fifth of tropical rain forests, and tens of thousands of plant and animal species.[26]

The environmental relations among traditional Indians and among non-Indians differ. Traditional Indians developed a respectful relationship with nature, and early Europeans emulated them in their early settlements in America—until they adopted an attitude of individual, capitalistic gain. Even American Indians were learning to relate their lives to the natural environment, Euroamericans began to change that environment. The traditional Indian's natural environment is substantially different from the American man-made environment, with its domesticated animals and plants that alter the landscape; this latter environment is designed to support an industrial, modernized society with a burgeoning population.[27] This increasing population has placed enormous demands on the environment, depleting its forests and forcing farmers to use chemicals on the land to produce more and better crops. But the ultimate effects will be lingering and have many dire consequences. As other nations imitate America's aggressive consumption of natural resources and the world population increases, Thomas Malthus's theory about geometric population growth placing enormous demands on the planet's resources will soon be seriously tested.[28] Certainly, in the case of China, which must feed almost one-quarter of the world's population from an estimated seven percent of the planet's arable land, the precedent is already being established.[29]

It has been common knowledge for several years that deserts in some parts of the world are growing rapidly and that rain forests are being cut away due to the demand of world capitalism. The natural resources and animal life of the planet are being depleted at an alarming rate.

The repercussions of human greed at the individual and corporate levels will be devastating for the entire planet.[30] Throughout the history of human existence, technology has worked against world conservation. And currently, the greed in the United States has influenced the world's nations, for America's wealth is widely envied. With a population of less than six percent of the global total, America is both the largest producer and the largest consumer, using a full thirty percent of the world's energy.[31] A sad precedent has been set, for other countries are exploiting their natural resources for wealth just as this nation has done without the control of strict conservation laws, all in an effort to emulate the United States. This will place additional pressure on natural resources around the world, especially for industrial nations who depend on Middle East countries surrounding the Persian Gulf, which has over one-half of the world's low-cost oil. Presently, multinational oil companies—Exxon, Gulf, Mobil, Texaco, Standard Oil of California, British Petroleum (which is fifty percent government owned with private management), Royal Dutch Shell, and Compagnie Française des Petroles (which is partly owned by private interests but mostly governmental controlled)—are steadily draining the world's oil supply, and they will do so as long as there is little interest in fuel alternatives, such as advanced technological uses of coal.[32] In 1974, the largest spenders on oil imports were the United States at $24 billion, Japan at $18 billion, the United Kingdom at $8.5 billion; and Italy at $7.5 billion. The largest earners were Saudi Arabia at $20 billion, Iran at $17.4 billion, Venezuela at $10.6 billion, Libya at $6.8 billion, and the Union of Arab Emirates at $4.1 billion.[33] The tremendous current usage of oil and the combustion of coal produces carbon dioxide that traps solar energy in the earth's atmosphere, causing

a rise in temperature. This is the "greenhouse effect," and it is predicted to change the climate worldwide. Between 1950 and 1973, a 4.5
percent increase in carbon emissions occurred, and another 4.5 percent increase from 1973 to 1983. From 1983 to 1988, carbon emissions
increased to 3.7 percent, and a similar increase has continued through
the 1990s.[34]

The sun is a constant in our lives, and its abundant power, handled
properly, could be used to sustain life. As estimated in 1974, solar
radiation could provide more than 500 times the world's total energy
consumption.[35] Transforming the sun's rays into electricity with the
use of solar photovoltaic cells promises to be widely used by the 2020s
or 2030s. By 1990, India had 6,000 village systems in operation. The
U.S. Solar Energy Research Institute (SERI) estimated that
photovoltiacs have the potential to supply over half of America's electricity by 2030.[36]

Another natural force that could be used is the wind, a resource
that renews itself. In the 1980s, more than 20,000 windmills producing electricity were used in the world, with the potential to generate
1,600 megawatts. California and Denmark were the leading areas in
this regard, and wind generators began to appear in India and Germany. One estimate reported that wind power could provide more
than ten percent of the world's electricity by the year 2030.[37]

Another possibility is the stockpiling of energy via fossil fuels and
nuclear fuels. Western Europe and Japan are dependent on other nations' natural resources, and stockpiling may be a means of support
for such nations until new energy resources can be developed. It is
suspected that Third World nations will become industrialized, and
stockpiling could also serve their needs.[38]

Natural gas is yet another alternative that could be used to relieve the demands on crude oil since only a small portion of it is mar-
keted in world trade, except where large markets exist. Presently,
the United States has an estimated fifteen percent of the world's supply, yet it consumes more than fifty percent of the total available. The
next largest consumers are the countries of the former Soviet Union
at approximately twenty percent, which also have some of the largest
supplies; the other large supply exists in Asia.[39]

It is unfortunate that the future of the planet is so intimately tied
to political interests instead of a global concern for the environment.
It is imperative that we take steps to stave off the decimation of natural resources throughout the world. International stability in politics
is essential, especially given the sweeping political changes in 1989
and 1990 and the move to democracy and economic improvement.
Furthermore, sound national economies are important if nations are

to avoid exploiting their environmental resources to dangerously low levels. Unchecked industrial growth has forced made recovery difficult for many nations. As nations strive to reach international parity in terms of shared wealth and political status, pollution, forest destruction, and nuclear waste are among the major irreversible problems that we confront.

As examples, radioactive wastes stored in a salt dome at Lyons, Kansas, was found to have leaked. More chilling still is the knowledge that nuclear waste disposal practices in some countries have involved storing the waste in canisters and dropping them into the oceans.[40]

It is unfortunate that human beings have developed technology that has the potential to destroy their race and the environment. Without using wisdom while inventing new technologies, the human race will become its own executioner. At present, the motivation of greed prevails over the concern for environmental conservation, placing the globe on a destructive path. Until this focus on capitalistic gain is replaced by a focus on human-environmental survival, all life around the world is in danger.

Although conservation is practiced at some levels, long-range consequences must be considered. In the process, we must learn a great deal more about the delicate balance of nature, as American Indians knew long ago. We need not practice their traditions of environmental kinship and religious ceremonies, but we should understand their perspective on the role of humans within the environment and all of life. In changing the current exploitative attitude, a fresh perspective might result and lead us to fuller philosophies about life and the role of humans within the universe.

The prophetic words of Chief Seattle apply to the world today:

> If we accept your offer to buy our land, I will make one condition: The white man must treat the beasts of the land as his betters. . . . What is man without the beasts? If all the beasts were gone, men would die from loneliness of spirit. For whatever happens to the beasts, soon happens to man. All things are connected. Teach your children what we have taught ours, that the earth is our mother. Whatever befalls the earth soon befalls the children of the earth. This we know, the earth does not belong to man; man belongs to the earth. This we know. All things are connected like the blood which unites one family. So hold in your mind the memory of the land as it is when you take it. And with all your strength, with all your mind, with all your heart.[41]

Over the last century, the world population has grown from 1.6 billion to more than 5 billion people.[42] The fastest-growing areas are in water-short regions, such as northern Africa, the Middle East, and parts of the Indian subcontinent. Overall, it will be more difficult to feed all of the people in the future, increase the strain on the earth's resources. Every year, approximately 3,300 cubic kilometers of water (six times the annual flow of the Mississippi) are taken from the world's river, streams, and underground aquifers to irrigate crops. Lakes and inland seas are shrinking, and aquatic habitats are being lost.[43]

In their efforts to feed the world, farmers lose about 24 million tons of topsoil from their croplands each year. During the 1980s, they lost a total of 240 billion tons of topsoil.[44] In order to feed more people, parts of the world such as South America are clearing forests for agricultural purposes at a dangerous rate. However, ninety percent of the once massive and lengthy Atlantic forest along the east coast of South America has been destroyed for industrial and urban growth. Deforestation changes the local hydrological cycles by increasing runoff and possibly the inland rainfall. In 1997, the Amazon rain forest suffered its worst drought in twenty-five years, forcing the Brazilian government to create a policy requiring farmers to burn their land in an effort to prevent forest fires.[45]

The land is further destroyed by fertilization. Between 1950 and 1989, world fertilizer usage increased from 14 million tons to an estimated 143 million tons annually. At this stage, the world is so dependent upon fertilizer that we would suffer an estimated forty percent decrease in food production without it.[46]

Meanwhile, the air we breathe is becoming more polluted each day. In the United States, an estimated 150 million people breathe air considered unhealthy by the Environmental Protection Agency (EPA). In metropolitan Athens, the number of deaths is six times higher on heavily polluted days. In Hungary, every twenty-fourth disability and every seventeenth death in due to air pollution. In India, breathing the air in Bombay is equivalent to smoking ten cigarettes each day. In Mexico, the capital city's air is so polluted that some foreign governments have told their diplomats not to plan on having children while they are stationed there.[47]

To solve crucial problems, problems that are at the heart of our survival, the global population and all national governments must work cooperatively and in unison. In terms of solar potential, the earth receives enough solar energy every day to heat every home on the planet for one year. But our exploitative attitudes and wasteful habits must change. The average American throws out his or her own weight in packing material every month. On a global level, 27,000,000 acres of rain forest, containing one-half of the world's animal and plant life are destroyed every year—an area equivalent to the size of Pennsylvania. Put another way, we destroy roughly fifty-four acres per minute.[48]

In America, the land of free enterprise, poll after poll taken during the 1996 presidential election showed that Americans were concerned about the environment. Unfortunately, the same Americans gave higher priority to their individual economic goals. They agreed with environmentally sound practices—as long as someone else made the sacrifice.[49]

The world's environmentalists and conservationists predict that significant changes must be made by 2030. This intervening period is crucial, as the world is already at a critical phase with air in some cities too polluted to breathe, water so scare that people fight over it, and land chemically fertilized beyond any capacity to return to a normal state. The growing crisis in depleting world natural resources has forced a situation that demands global cooperation without regard to political, cultural, or racial differences. Considering the condition of the United States and the world, Chief Seattle's words become even more meaningful as a lesson in life that must be learned.

Ironically, the human race is destroying itself via its industrial technology and capitalistic attitude—all of which depends upon the earth's natural resources. In the competition for capitalistic gain at the regional, national, and global levels, the momentum becomes increasingly irreversible. Some day in the not-so-distant future, it will be too late. But until capitalistic attitudes are corrected and the preservation of the earth's diminishing resources become a priority, we will continue to destroy ourselves.

NOTES

1. Michael Kearney, *World View* (Novato, Calif.: Chandler & Sharp Publications in Anthropology and Related Fields, 1984), pp. 150–55.
2. See Emile Durkheim, *The Elementary Forms of the Religious Life* (New York: Free Press, 1967).
3. Morris Oppler also referred to "themes" in cultural development as "affirmations" of cultural practice; see Morris Oppler, "Themes as Dynamic Forces in Culture," *American Journal of Sociology* 51, no. 31 (November 1945): 198, 199, and 202.
4. Franz Boas professed that the conditions of daily life occupied primitive people, preventing them from thinking about abstract ideas, and relating everything to the social level of humans. Although socialization largely determines the traditional Indians' relationships to people, animals, and plants as Boas suggested, tribes have developed advanced philosophies interrelating the finite and the abstract of metaphysics. See Franz Boas, *The Mind of Primitive Man* (New York: Macmillan, 1938), p. 216.
5. Hans Kelsen argued that the principle of causality was unknown to primi-

tive peoples (and American Indians are often classified as such) and that primitives interpreted nature according to social norms and the norm of retribution; see Hans Kelsen, *Society and Nature, A Sociological Inquiry* (Chicago and London: University of Chicago Press, 1943), p. vii.

6. Durkheim, *Forms of Religious Life*, p. 41.

7. Dorothy Lee, "Notes on the Conception of Self Among the Wintu Indians," *Journal of Abnormal and Social Psychology* 45 (1950): 542.

8. Followers of Sir Edward B. Tylor and Herbert Spencer promoted the concept of the "primitive mind," asserting that people of darker color than Caucasians were intellectually inferior; see George Stocking Jr., *Race, Culture, and Evolution, Essays in the History of Anthropology* (New York: Free Press, 1968), pp. 120–132.

9. In commenting on the mental capabilities of different races, Daniel Brinton emphasized that racial "capacity" was based on racial "achievement." According to Brinton, Anglo-Americans have not dealt very well with the environment, and examining the philosophies of American Indian groups could be of assistance. See Daniel G. Brinton, *The American Race: A Linguistic Classification and Ethnographic Description of the Native Tribes of North and South America* (Philadelphia: N.D.C. Hodges, 1891), pp. 41–44.

10. The difference in the problem solving of "primitive man" and Western civilization's causality is covered in Kelsen, *Society and Nature*, pp. 42–43.

11. Bruce Cox, ed., *Cultural Ecology: Readings on Canadian Indians and Eskimos* (Toronto: McClelland and Stewart, 1973), p. 30.

12. Sir Edward B. Tylor, *The Origins of Culture* (New York: Harper & Brothers, 1958), p. 23.

13. Cox, *Cultural Ecology*, p. 30.

14. Ibid., p. 61.

15. Kelsen, *Society and Nature*, pp. 49–185.

16. Boas, *Mind of Primitive Man*, p. 162.

17. A similarity in Lucien Levy-Bruhl's analysis of primitive societies is applicable to traditional American Indians in their acceptance and belief in traditions and invisible forces; see Lucien Levy-Bruhl, *Primitives and the Supernatural* translated by Lilian A. Clare (New York: E. P. Dutton, 1935), p. 20.

18. Durkheim, *Forms of Life*, pp. 41 and 62.

19. Stanley Diamond, ed., *Primitive Views of the World: Essays From Culture in History* (New York: Columbia University Press, 1964), p. 65.

20. Cox, *Cultural Ecology*, pp. 119–122.

21. Boas, *Mind of Primitive Man*, pp. 175–196.

22. Cox, *Cultural Ecology*, pp. 35–36.

23. A. Irvin Hallowell discussed the importance and dangers of greed among traditional Ojibwas, in "Ojibwa Ontology, Behavior, and World Views," in Diamond, *Primitive Views*, 75.

24. During the settling of England in the thirteenth century, a deep individualism developed and was secured in the laws protecting individual rights, independence, and the freedom of thought and religion. Protection of these

rights led foreigners to observe the English as ethnocentric; they also viewed the nations of Europe as arrogant. Alan MacFarlane held the position that the origin of English individualism developed independently from Asia, Eastern Europe, the Celtic, and the continental countries of Western Europe. See Alan MacFarlane, *The Origins of English Individualism: The Family, Property and Social Transition* (Oxford: Basil Blackwell, 1978), pp. 165–166.

25. MacFarlane observed that English individualism is protected in English law and can be traced to the writing of Charles Montesquieu and his work on "The Spirit of the Laws." He studied Cornelius Tactius. See Tactius, "A Treatise on the Situation on the Manners and People of Germany," *The Works of Cornelius Tactius, An Essay on His Life and Genius*, vol. 7, edited by Arthur Murphy (London, 1811), pp. 194–201. Thus, the concept of English government derived from the example of the Germans. See Alan MacFarlane, *The Origins of English Individualism*, pp. 167–168.

26. Lester Brown and Alan Durning, *State of the World 1990* (New York and London: W. W. Norton, 1990), p. 1. This startling fact demonstrates the progress of the Western mind, whose twentieth-century attitude is unconsciously leading to self-destruction by exhausting natural resources. Though Darwinists referred in the 1800s to Native people as savages to indicate their own evolution of the human mind, ironically, it is the same Western mentality whose exploitative attitude is responsible for decreasing natural resources and jeopardizing all of life for the twenty-first century. In discussing mental evolution, George Stocking Jr. cited Sir Edward B. Tylor, "that the 'civilized man' is wiser and more capable than the savage," in the context of mental evolution; see Stocking, *Race, Culture, and Evolution*, pp. 99–100.

27. A. L. Kroeber expressed less respect for cultures of small population in his categorically emphasis that low-population societies do not produce rich or advanced cultures. Furthermore, in his discussion on cultural diffusion and intermarginality, he stated that Native American cultures were retarded when compared to old world cultures, due to their late start from population migrations across the Bering Strait; see A. L. Kroeber, *Anthropology: Culture Patterns & Processes* (New York and London: Harcourt, Brace & World, 1963), pp. 195–196, 231–232.

28. The relationship of "self" with "other" concerning individual rights, privacy, and private property is influenced by an attitude in the Western mind that is deep in consciousness and introspective of the ego; see Oswald Spengler, *The Decline of the West*, translated by C. F. Atkinson (New York: A. Knopf, 1926–1928).

29. Mason Willrich, *Energy and World Politics* (New York: Free Press, 1975), p. 3.

30 Ibid., p. 31.

31. Ibid., p. 130.

32. Brown and Durning, *State of the World*, p. 18.

33. Willrich, *Energy and World Politics*, p. 62.

34. Brown and Durning, *State of the World*, p. 25.

35. Ibid., p. 24.

36. Willrich, *Energy and World Politics*, p. 77.

37. Ibid., p. 40.

38. Ibid., p. 166.

39. Ibid.

40. Brown and Durning, *State of the World*, p. 39.

41. Chief Seattle made this speech to Governor Issac Stevens of the Territory of Washington when he surrendered tribal lands to the United States in 1855.

42. Brown and Durning, *State of the World*, pp. 39–43 and 60.

43. Ibid., p. 67.

44. Ibid., pp. 60–98.

45. Michael Astor, "Amazon Rain Forest Parched by Worst Drought in 25 Years," *South Bend Tribune*, October 29, 1997.

46. Ibid.

47. Ibid.

48. Ibid.

49. Hal K. Rothman, *The Greening of a Nation? Environmentalism in the United States Since 1945* (Fort Worth, Tex.: Harcourt Brace College Publishers, 1997), p. 208.

APPENDIX A

CERT Member Tribes and Natural Resources for 1990

TRIBE	STATE	NATURAL RESOURCES
Acoma Pueblo	New Mexico	Coal, Geothermal, Natural Gas
Blackfeet	Montana	Coal, Oil, Natural Gas
Chemehuevi	California	Oil, Uranium, Hydroelectric
Cheyenne-Arapaho	Oklahoma	Oil, Gas
Cheyenne River Sioux	South Dakota	Oil, Gas, Coal
Cherokee	Oklahoma	Coal, Oil, Natural Gas
Chippewa-Cree (Rocky Boys)	Montana	Coal, Oil, Natural Gas, Uranium
Coeur d'Alene	Idaho	Uranium, Hydroelectric
Crow	Montana	Coal, Oil, Natural Gas
Flathead (Salish and Kootenai)	Montana	Hydroelectric, Natural Gas
Fort Belknap	Montana	Coal, Oil, Natural Gas, Geothermal
Fort Berthold	North Dakota	Coal, Oil, Natural Gas, Geothermal
Fort Hall	Idaho	Geothermal, Natural Gas
Fort Peck	Montana	Coal, Oil, Natural Gas, Hydroelectric
Hopi	Arizona	Coal, Uranium, Oil, Natural Gas
Hualapai	Arizona	Uranium, Oil, Natural Gas, Hydro-electric
Jemez Pueblo	New Mexico	Uranium, Natural Gas, Geothermal, Oil
Jicarilla Apache	New Mexico	Oil, Natural Gas, Coal, Geothermal
Kalispel	Washington	Uranium, Hydroelectric
Laguna Pueblo	New Mexico	Coal, Uranium, Oil, Natural Gas
Muckleshoot	Washington	Coal, Natural Gas, Hydroelectric, Oil
Navajo	Arizona	Coal, Oil, Natural Gas, Uranium, Geothermal
Nez Perce	Idaho	Hydroelectric
Northern Cheyenne	Montana	Coal, Oil, Natural Gas
Oglala Sioux	South Dakota	Oil, Natural Gas, Uranium
Pawnee	Oklahoma	Oil, Gas
Penobscot	Maine	Hydroelectric
Ponca	Oklahoma	Oil, Gas
Rosebud Sioux	South Dakota	Oil, Natural Gas, Oil Shale, Geothermal
Saginaw Chippewa	Michigan	Oil, Gas

TRIBE	STATE	NATURAL RESOURCES
Santa Ana Pueblo	New Mexico	Geothermal
Seminole	Florida	Natural Gas, Uranium
Southern Ute	Colorado	Coal, Oil, Natural Gas
Spokane	Washington	Coal, Hydroelectric, Uranium
Standing Rock Sioux	North Dakota	Coal, Oil, Gas
Tule River	California	Hydroelectric
Turtle Mountain Chippewa	North Dakota	Oil, Natural Gas, Coal
Ute Tribe of the Uintah and Ouray Reservation	Utah	Oil, Natural Gas, Coal, Tar Sand, Oil Shale
Umatilla	Oregon	Geothermal, Hydroelectric
Ute Mountain Ute	Colorado	Coal, Oil, Natural Gas, Uranium
Walker River Paiute	Nevada	Uranium, Geothermal, Hydroelectric
Yakima	Washington	Oil, Natural Gas, Hydroelectric
Zia Pueblo	New Mexico	Uranium, Geothermal, Oil, Natural Gas

Source: Jim Pierce, CERT chief administrative officer, to author, and *CERT First Decade Report*, 1985.

APPENDIX B

Structure of the Council of Energy Resource Tribes

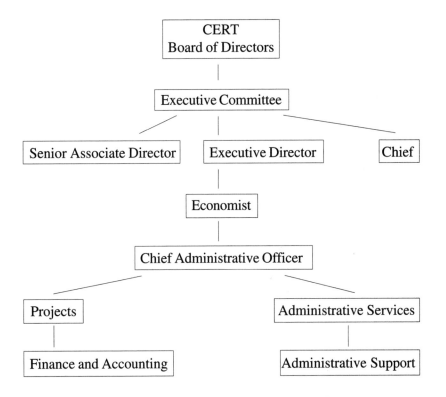

APPENDIX C
Tribal Oil and Gas Production
Subsurface Leases and Permits

TRIBE AND STATE	OIL AND GAS ACRES
ARIZONA	
Navajo Tribe (including NM, UT)	801,269.23
COLORADO	
Southern Ute Tribe	169,813.86
Ute Mountain Tribe	52,956.02
FLORIDA	
Seminole Tribe	23,040.00
KANSAS	
Kickapoo Tribe	3,886.00
MICHIGAN	
Saginaw Chippewa Tribe	18.75
MONTANA	
Assiniboine and Sioux Tribes	274,366.36
(Turtle Mountain off-reservation)	7,167.21
Blackfeet Tribe	233,017.37
Chippewa-Cree Tribe	29,881.18
Crow Tribe	102,683.14
Gros Ventre and Assiniboine Tribes	40,712.19
Turtle Mountain (off-reservation)	12,114.61
NEW MEXICO	
Isleta Pueblo	163,006.01
Jicarilla Apache Tribe	518,439.76
San Felipe Pueblo	48,516.11
Santa Ana Pueblo	27,028.85
Ute Mountain Tribe	45,481.36
Zia Pueblo	8,338.24

TRIBE AND STATE	OIL AND GAS ACRES
NORTH DAKOTA	
Chippewa Tribe	13,860.03
(Off Reservation)	39,531.78
Mandan, Hidatsa, Arikara Tribes	352,691.00
(Off Reservation)	1,920.00
OKLAHOMA	
Absentee Shawnee Tribe	6,840.73
Cheyenne-Arapaho Tribe	95,807.73
Citizen Potawatomie Tribe	1,529.15
Five Civilized Tribes Consolidated	83,033.44
Iowa Tribe	536.65
Kickapoo Tribe	1,362.86
Kiowa, Comanche, Apache Tribes	99,755.99
Osage Tribe	995,707.17
Otoe Tribe	9,994,92
Pawnee Tribe	17,938.05
Ponca Tribe	11,575.99
Sac and Fox Tribe	11,128.82
Wichita-Caddo-Delaware Tribes	64,088.37
SOUTH DAKOTA	
Cheyenne River Tribe	42,998.86
Standing Rock	160.00
UTAH	
Uintah and Ouray Tribes	385,685.36
Ute Mountain Tribe	2,080.00
WYOMING	
Shoshone and Arapaho Tribes	545,108.84

Source: Bureau of Indian Affairs, Subsurface Leases and Permits as of September 30, 1980 (printed by *The CERT Report* 4, no. 11 (September 13, 1982), p. 3. CERT estimated that these figures are the same for 1990; letter from Jim Pierce, CERT chief administrative officer, to author, February 27, 1990.)

BIBLIOGRAPHY

MANUSCRIPT COLLECTIONS

Carl Albert Congressional Center, University of Oklahoma, Norman, Oklahoma
  Elmer Thomas Papers
  William G. Stigler Papers
Dwight D. Eisenhower Presidential Library, Abilene, Kansas
  Bill File
  Fred A. Seaton Papers
  White House Central Files
Harry S. Truman Presidential Library, Independence, Missouri
  William Brophy Papers
  Official File, Harry S. Truman Papers
  Philleo Nash Papers
Montana Historical Society Archives, Helena, Montana
  Lee Metcalf Papers
National Anthropological Archives, Washington, D.C.
  Francis La Flesche File
Native American Education Services College, Chicago, Illinois
  Tribal Newspapers Collection
The Newberry Library, Chicago, Illinois
  The Indian Rights Association Papers (microfilm), original papers at Philadelphia
  John Collier Papers (microfilm), original papers at Yale University
  Tribal Newspapers Collection, D'Arcy McNickle Center for the History of the American Indian
Oklahoma Historical Society, Oklahoma City, Oklahoma
  Osage File
  Creek File
Oregon Historical Society, Portland, Oregon
  Richard Neuberger Papers
University of New Mexico, Special Collections, Albuquerque, New Mexico
  Holm O. Bursum Papers
  Albert B. Fall Papers (1916–1927)
University of Oregon, Special Collections, Eugene, Oregon
  Richard L. Neuberger Papers

University of Tulsa, Special Collections, McFarlin Library, Tulsa, Oklahoma
Alice Robertson Papers
Creek File
University of Wisconsin–Milwaukee, Golda Meir Library, Milwaukee, Wisconsin
FBI File on the Osage Indian Murders (microfilm)
Western History Collections, University of Oklahoma, Norman, Oklahoma
Creek File

RECORDS OF THE BUREAU OF INDIAN AFFAIRS

Federal Archives and Records Center, Fort Worth, Texas
Muskogee Area Office Correspondence
Records of U.S. District Courts Western District of Oklahoma, Oklahoma City
Records of the Five Civilized Tribes Agency
Records of the Osage Agency
Federal Archives and Records Center, Seattle, Washington
Klamath Agency Files
Federal Archives and Records Center, Suitland, Maryland
Bureau of Indian Affairs Correspondence

U.S. GOVERNMENT DOCUMENTS

Ray, Verne F. "The Klamath Indians and Their Forest Resources." Exhibit b–1, Docket No. 100-b–2; Indian Claims Commission.
U.S. Congress. House. Committee on Public Lands, "Emancipation of Indians." Hearings Before the Subcommittee of the House Committee on Public Lands on J.R. 2958, H.R. 2165, and H.R. 1113, 80th Cong., 1st sess., 1947.
U.S. Congress. House. Congressman Morse speaking for termination of the Klamath Indians, S. 1222, 8th Cong., 1st sess., May 2, 1947, *Congressional Record*, vol. 93.
U.S. Congress. Senate. Senator Butler speaking on removal of restrictions on certain Indian tribes, 80th Cong., 2d sess., July 21, 1947. *Congressional Record*, vol. 91.

U.S. LAWS AND COURT CASES CHRONOLOGICALLY

Cherokee Nation v. Georgia. 30 U.S. (5 Pet.) 1 (1831).
Worcester v. Georgia, 31 *U.S. Reports*, 515 (1832).
United States Trade and Intercourse Act. June 30, 1834, ch. 161, 4 Stat. 729.
United States v. Lucero. 1 N.M. 440 (1869).
United States v. Joseph. 94 *U.S. Reports*, 614 (1876).
Act of August 15, 1876. ch. 289, 19 Stat. 176, 192.
Act of February 28, 1877. ch. 71, 19 Stat. 254.
Desert Lands Act, (1877). 43 U.S.C.A. §§ 321–339 (197).
United States ex re. Standing Bear v. Crook. 25 Federal Cases 695 (Circuit Court of Nebraska) 1879.

Ex parte Crow Dog. 109 *U.S. Reports*, 556 (1883).
Elk v. Wilkins. 112 *U.S. Reports*, 94 (1884).
Dawes General Allotment Act. 1887, U.S. Statutes at Large, 22, 245, 273.
Coffin v. Left Hand Ditch Co. 6 Colo. 443 (1882).
Ward v. Race Horse. 163 U.S. Reports, 504 (1896).
Territory of New Mexico v. Delinquent Taxpayers. 12 N.M. 139, 76, Pac. 316 (194).
Act of March 3, 1905. 33, U.S. Statutes at Large, 1048.
United States v. Winans. 198 US. Reports, 371 (1905).
Winter's Doctrine. January 6, 1908. 207 U.S. Reports, 565, 573, 575–577.
Act of June 20, 1910. 36, U.S. Statutes at Large, 557.
United States v. Sandoval. 231 U.S. 28 (1913).
New York ex rel. Kennedy v. Becker. 2412 U.S. 556 (1916).
United States v. Nice. 241 U.S. Reports, 591 (1916).
"U. S. Citizenship for Indian Veterans of World War Act." November 6, 1919, U.S. Statutes at Large, 41:350.
United States v. John Ramsey and William K. Hale. No. 5660, U.S. District, Western District of Oklahoma, (1926).
Indian Reorganization Act. June 18, 1934, *U.S. Statutes at Large*, 48:984–88.
California Oregon Power Co. v. Beaver Portland Cement Co. 295 U.S. 142, 163 (1935).
United States v. Creek Nation. 25 *U. S. Reports*, 103 (1935).
Omnibus Tribal Leasing Act. May 3, 1938. 25 USCS–396a et seq., 52, *U.S. Statutes at Large*, 347.
Seminole Nation v. United States. 316 *U.S. Reports*, 286 (1942).
Tulee v. Washington. 315 U.S. 681 (1942).
Sioux Tribe v. United States. 97 Ct. Cl. 613 (1942).
Public Law 280. August 15, 1953, *U.S. Statutes at Large*, 67: 588–90.
McCarran Amendment. (1953) 43 U.S.C. § 666.
Indian Mineral Leasing Act. (1955) 25 U.S.C.A. § 396a-g.
Papago Minerals Lands Act. P.L. 47, May 27, 1955, *U S. Statutes at Large*, 69:67–68.
Kake v. Egan. 369 U.S. 60, 82 S. Ct. 562, 7 L.Ed. 2d 573 (1962).
Metlakatla Indian Community v. Egan. 369 U.S. 45 (1962).
Arizona v. California. 373 U.S. 546 (1963).
Indian Timber Act. P.L. 88–301, April 30, 1964, *U.S. Statutes at Large*, 78:186–87.
Puyallup Tribe v. Department of Game Supreme Court of the United States. 1968. 193 U.S. 392, 88 S.Ct. 1725. 20 L.Ed.2d 689.
United States v. Sioux Nation. 448 U.S. 371, 385 (1968).
Menominee Tribe of Indians v. United States. 391 *U.S. Reports*, 404 (1968).
Great Lakes Inter-Tribal Council, Incorporated v. Voigt. No. 68-C–95, U.S. District Court, W. D. Wisconsin, January 26, 1970, *Federal Supplement*, vol. 309.
Rockbridge v. Lincoln. 449 F.2d 567, 9h Cir. (1971).
Pyramid Lake Paiute Tribe v. Morton. 354 F.Supp. 252 (D.D.C. 1972).
State of Wisconsin v. Richard Gurnoe, Thomas Connors, et al. March 2, 1972, Supreme Court of Wisconsin, 192 N.W.2d 892.

Puyallup II Department of Game v. Puyallup Tribe. 414 U.S. 44, 94 S.Ct. 330, 38 L.ed.2d 254 (1973).

Morton v. Mancari. June 17, 1974. 417 *U.S. Reports,* 541–45, 550–555.

Sioux Nation v. United States. 33 Ind. C. Comm'n 151 (1974).

U.S. v. Washington. U.S. Court of Appeals, Ninth Circuit, 1975. 520 F.2d676, certiorari denied, 423 U.S. 1086, 96 S. Ct. 877, 47 L.Ed.2d 97 (1976).

Bald Eagle Protection Act. 16 U.S.C. secs. 1361–1407 (1976).

Endangered Species Act. 16 U.S.C. secs. 1531–1543 (1976).

Sohappy v. Smith. 302 F. Supp. 899 (D. Dr. 1969), affirmed and remanded, 529 F.2d 570 (9th Cir. 1976).

Migratory Bird Treaty Act. 16 U.S.C. secs. 668–668d (1976).

People of the State of Michigan v. A. B. LeBlanc. December 27, 1976, Supreme Court of Michigan, 246 N.W. 2d 199.

Puyallup III, Puyallup Tribe, Inc., v. Department of Game. 433 U.S. 165, 173–77 (1977).

State of Minnesota v. C. John Forge Jr., James Olson and Richard C. Larsen. October 14, 1977, Supreme Court of Minnesota, 262 N.W.2d 341.

Surface Mining Control and Reclamation Act. 30 U.S.C.A. § 1300 (c), (1977).

American Indian Religious Freedom Act. P.L. 95–341, May 15, 1978, *U.S. Statutes at Large,* 92:469.

Baldwin v. Fish & Game Commission. 436 U.S. 371, 391 (1978).

State of Minnesota v. Bernard Clark, Jack Fulstrom, et al. August 3, 1979, Supreme Court of Minnesota, 282 N.W.2d 902.

State of Minnesota v. Everet F. Keezer and Wallace James. June 23, 198, Supreme Court of Minnesota, Minn., 292 N.W.2d 714.

Salmon and Steelhead Conservation Act. P.L. 96–561, December 22, 1980, *U.S. Statutes at Large,* 94:3275–3302.

United States v. Sioux Nation of Indians. 448 U.S. 371 (1980).

Colville Confederated Tribes v. Walton. 647 F.2d (9th Cir. 1981), cert. denied, 50 U.S.L.W. 3448 (U.S. Dec. 1, 1981) (No. 81–321).

State of Wisconsin v. Richard Lowe and Kenneth J. Mosay. November 16, 1982, Wis. App., 327 N.W. 2d 166.

Fools Crow v. Gullet. 541 F.Supp. 785 (D.S.D. 1982).

Indian Mineral Developing Act. P.L. 97–382, December 22, 1982, 96, *U.S. Statutes at Large,* 1938.

Federal Oil and Gas Royalty Management Act. P.L. 97–451, January 12, 1983, *U.S. Statutes at Large,* 96–2457.

J. Gregory Merrion and Robert L. Bayless, et al., and Amoco Production Company and Marathon Oil Company v. Jicarilla Apache Indian Tribe. January 25, 1982, 455 U.S. 130, 71 L.Ed. 2d21, 102 S.C. 894, in *U.S. Supreme Court Reports, Lawyers' Edition,* vol. 71.

U.S. v. Bouchard, U.S. v. Ben Ruby and Sons, and Lac Courte Oreilles Band of Lake Superior Chippewa Indians v. Voigt. Nos. 76-CR–70, 72-C–366, 74-C–313, U.S. District Court, W.D. Wisconsin, *Federal Supplement,* vol. 464.

Lac Courte Oreilles Band of Lake Superior Chippewa Indians v. Voigt. 1983, Nos. 76-CR–70, 72-C–366, 74-C–313, U.S. District Court, W. D. Wisconsin.

Arizona v. San Carlos Apache Tribe. 463 *U.S. Reports,* 545 (1983).

U.S. v. State of Wisconsin. Nos. 78–2398, 78–2443 and 79–1014, U.S. Court of Appeals, Seventh Circuit, January 25, 1983, *Federal Reporter,* vol. 700 F.2d.

State of Wisconsin v. John and Peter Lemieux. February 15, 1983, Supreme Court of Wisconsin, Wis., 327 N.W. 2d 669.

United States v. Adair. 723 F.2d 1394, 1412–15 (9th Cir. 1983).

Pacific Salmon Treaty Act. P.L. 99–5. March 15, 1985, *U.S. Statutes at Large,* 99:7.

Sioux Tribe v. United States. 7 Cl. Ct. (1985).

South Carolina v. Catawba Indian Tribe, Inc. 476 *U.S. Reports,* 498, 506 (1986).

State of Wisconsin v. Thomas Newago, John H. Pero Jr., and John Lemieux. October 28, 1986, Court of Appeals of Wisconsin, 397 N.W.2d 107 (Wis. Appl. 1986).

Indian Gaming Regulatory Act. October 17, 1988, *U.S. Statutes at Large,* 102:2467–69, 2472, 2476.

Review of Tribal Constitution Act. P.L. 100–581, November 1, 1988, *U.S. Statutes at Large,* 102:2938–49.

Indian Environmental Regulatory Enhancement Act. P.L. 101–408, October 4, 1990, *U.S. Statutes at Large,* 104 pt. 6:883–84.

National Indian Forest Resources Management Act. P.L. 101–630, November 28, 1990, *U.S. Statutes at Large,* 104 pt. 6:4532-44.

Duro v. Reiner, 110 S. Ct. 2053, 1990.

U.S. GOVERNMENT REPORTS

Final Report and Legislative Recommendation, "A Report of the Special Committee on Investigations of the Select Committee on Indian Affairs United States Senate," Senate Report 101–216, 101st Cong. 1st sess. Senate, November 6, 1989.

John R. Swanton, "Social Organization and Social Usages of the Indians of the Creek Confederacy," *Forty-Second Annual Report of the Bureau of American Ethnology, 1924–1925.* Washington, U.S. Government Printing Office, 1928.

INTERNATIONAL DOCUMENTS

Treaty of Guadalupe Hidalgo. February 2, 1848, United States-Mexico, 9 Stat. 922, T.S. No. 207.

TRIBAL LAWS, RESOLUTIONS, AND MEMORIALS

Acts and Resolutions of the National Council of the Muskogee Nation of 1893 and 1899, Inclusive. Muskogee. Phoenix Printing. 1900.

Alphabetical List of Creek Indians by Blood and Creek Freedmen. 60th U.S. Congress. May 21, 1908.

Certified Roll of Members of the Osage Tribes of Indians of Oklahoma of

*Less Than One Half Indian Blood, of One Half Indian Blood or More
[and Members According to Band].* Washington, D.C. U.S. Interior De-
partment. 1921.
"Memorial of the Muskogee Nation by its National Council to the President
and Congress of the United States, October, 1889.
Constitution and Laws of the Muskogee Nation. Comp. and codified by A. P.
McKellop. F. C. Hunnard, Printer. 1893.
Constitution and Laws of the Osage Nation. Washington, D.C. R. O.
Polknshorn, Printer. 1883.
Rules of the House of Warriors. December 7, 1903. Okmulgee. Chieftain Print-
ing House. n. d.

BOOKS

Barsh, Russel L., and James Henderson. *The Road, Indian Tribes and Po-
litical Liberty.* Berkeley. University of California Press. 1980.
Boas, Franz. *The Mind of Primitive Man.* New York. Macmillan. 1938.
Brinton, Daniel G. *The American Race: A Linguistic Classification and Eth-
nographic Description of the Native Tribes of North And South America.*
Philadelphia. N.D.C. Hodges. 1891. (Reprinted New York. Johnson Re-
print. 1970.)
Brown, Joseph E., Jr., ed. *The Sacred Pipe: Black Elk's Account of the Seven
Rites of the Oglala Sioux.* Norman. University of Oklahoma Press. 1953.
Brown, Lester, and Alan Durning. *State of the World 1990.* New York and
London. W. W. Norton. 1990.
Burton, Lloyd. *American Indian Water Rights and the Limits of Law.*
Lawrence. University of Kansas Press. 1991.
Casey, Robert J. *The Black Hills and Their Incredible Characteristics.* In-
dianapolis and New York. Bobbs-Merrill Company. 1949.
Champagne, Duane, ed. *The Native North American Almanac: A Reference
Work on Native North Americans in the United States and Canada.* De-
troit. Gale Research. 1994.
Clinton, Robert N.; Nell Jessup Newton, and Monroe E. Price, eds. *Ameri-
can Indian Law, Cases and Materials.* 3rd ed. Charlottesville. Michie.
1991.
Cochran, William C., comp. *Cochran's Law Lexicon,* 5th ed. Cincinnati, Ohio:
Anderson Publishing. 1973.
Cohen, Felix S. *Handbook of Federal Indian Law,* Washington, D.C. Gov-
ernment Printing Office. 1942. (Reprinted by University of New Mexico
Press. Albuquerque. 1986; also, reprinted by Michie Bobbs-Merrill.
Charlottesville, Va. 1982.)
Cox. Bruce, ed. *Cultural Ecology: Readings on Canadian Indians and Es-
kimos.* Toronto. McClelland and Stewart. 1973.
Dale, Edward E. *The Indians of the Southwest, A Century of Development
Under the United States.* Norman. University of Oklahoma Press. 1949.
Danziger, Edmund J., Jr. *The Chippewas of Lake Superior.* Norman. Univer-
sity of Oklahoma Press. 1979.
Debo, Angie. *And Still the Waters Run: The Betrayal of the Five Civilized*

Tribes. Princeton, N.J. Princeton University Press. 1940. (Reprinted New York. Gordian Press. 1966.)

———. *A History of the Indians of the United States*. Norman. University of Oklahoma Press. 1970.

———. *The Road to Disappearance, A History of the Creek Indians*. Norman. University of Oklahoma Press. 1941.

Deloria, Vine, Jr., and Clifford M. Lytle. *American Indians, American Justice*. Austin. University of Texas Press. 1983.

Diamond, Stanley, ed. *Primitive Views of the World: Essays From Culture in History*. New York. Columbia University Press. 1964.

Doherty, Robert. *Disputed Waters: Native Americans & the Great Lakes Fishery*. Lexington. University of Kentucky Press. 1990.

Dunbar, Willis F. *Michigan: A History of the Wolverine State*. Grand Rapids, Mich. William B. Eerdmans Publishing. 1965. (4th printing, 1968.)

Durkheim, Emile. *The Elementary Forms of the Religious Life*. New York. Free Press. 1965.

Dutton, Bertha P. *American Indians in the Southwest*. Albuquerque. University of New Mexico Press. 1983.

DuMars, Charles T., Marilyn O'Leary, and Albert E. Uton. *Pueblo Indian Water Rights: Struggle for a Precious Resource*. Tucson. University of Arizona Press. 1984.

Erodes, Richard, and Alfonso Ortiz, eds. *American Indian Myths and Legends*. New York. Pantheon. 1984.

Fixico, Donald L., ed. *An Anthology of Western Great Lakes Indian History*. Milwaukee. American Indian Studies, University of Wisconsin. 1988.

———. *Termination and Relocation: Federal Indian Policy, 1945–1960*. Albuquerque. University of New Mexico Press. 1986.

Foster, James S. *Outlines of History of the Territory of Dakota*. Yankton, S.D. M'Intyre and Foster. 1870.

Franks, Kenny A. *The Osage Oil Boom*. Oklahoma City. Oklahoma Heritage Association. 1989.

Glasscock, C. B. *Then Came Oil: The Story of the Last Frontier*. Indianapolis and New York. Bobbs-Merrill. 1938.

Green, Donald, and Thomas V. Tonnesen, eds. *American Indians: Social Justice and Public Policy*, vol. 9, *Ethnicity and Public Policy Series*. Milwaukee. University of Wisconsin System Institute on Race and Ethnicity. 1991.

Hardin, Terri, ed. *Legends & Lore of the American Indians*. New York. Barnes and Nobles Books. 1993.

Hughes, J. Donald. *American Indian Ecology*. El Paso. Texas Western Press. 1983.

Hutton, John. *The Mystery of Wealth, Political Economy—Its Development and Impact on World Events*. Cheltenham, England. Stanley Thornes. 1979.

Iverson, Peter, ed. *The Plains Indians of the Twentieth Century*. Norman. University of Oklahoma Press. 1985.

Jorgensen, Joseph G., ed. *Native Americans and Energy Development*, vol. 2. Boston. Anthropology Resource Center & Seventh Generation Fund. 1984.

Kappler, Charles, ed. and comp. *Indian Treaties, 1778–1883*. New York. Interland Publishing. 1975.

Kearney, Michael. *World View*. Novato, Calif. Chandler & Sharp. 1984.

Kelsen, Hans. *Society and Nature: A Sociological Inquiry*. Chicago and London. University of Chicago Press. 1943.

Kime, Wayne R. *The Black Hills Journals of Colonel Richard Irving Dodge*. Norman. University of Oklahoma Press. c. 1996.

Kluckhohn, Clyde, and Dorothea Leighton. *The Navajo*. Cambridge, Mass. Harvard University Press. 1958.

Knaut, Andrew L. *The Pueblo Revolt of 1680: Conquest and Resistance in Seventeenth-Century New Mexico*. Norman. University of Oklahoma Press. 1995.

Kroeber, A. L. *Anthropology, Cultural Patterns & Processes*. New York and London. Harcourt, Brace & World. 1963.

Laarus, Edward. *Black Hills/White Justice: The Sioux Nation Versus the United States, 1775 to the Present*. New York. Harper Collins. 1991.

Lawson, Michael L. *Damned Indians: The Pick-Sloan Plan and the Missouri River Sioux, 1944–1980*. Norman. University of Oklahoma Press. 1982.

Levy-Bruhl, Lucien. *Primitives and the Supernatural*. New York. E. P. Dutton. 1935.

MacFarlane, Alan. *The Origins of English Individualism: The Family, Property and Social Transition*. Oxford. Basil Blackwell. 1978.

McFee, Malcom. *Modern Blackfeet: Montanas on a Reservation*. New York. Holt, Rinehart and Winston. 1972.

McGuire, Paul. *Osage County, Osage Indians, History, People*. Pawhuska. Adrin. 1969.

Malthus, Thomas. *The Principle of Population as It Affects the Future Improvement of Society*. n.p. 1798.

Meriam, Lewis., Ray A. Brown, Henry Roe Cloud, Edward Everett Dale, Emma Duke, Herbert R. Edwards, Fayette Avery McKenzie, Mary Louise Mark, W. Carson Ryan, Jr., and William Spillman, comps. *The Problem of Indian Administration*. Baltimore, Md. Johns Hopkins Press. 1928.

Milton, John R. *South Dakota, A Bicentennial History*. New York. W. W. Norton. 1977.

Morris, John W. ed., *Drill Bits, Picks, and Shovels, A History Of Mineral Resources in Oklahoma*. Oklahoma City. Oklahoma Historical Society. 1982.

Olson, James S., and Raymond Wilson. *Native Americans in the Twentieth Century*. Provo, Utah. Brigham Young University Press. 1984.

Parker, Watson. *Gold in the Black Hills*. Lincoln and London. University of Nebraska Press. 1982.

Peattie, Roderick, ed. *The Black Hills*. New York. Vanguard Press. 1952.

Perdue, Theda. *Nations Remembered, An Oral History of the Five Civilized Tribes*. Westport, Conn. Greenwood Press. 1980.

Philp, Kenneth R. *John Collier's Crusade for Reform*. Tucson. University of Arizona Press. 1977.

Price, Monroe E. *Law and the American Indian: Readings, Notes and Cases*. Indianapolis. Bobbs-Merrill. 1973.

Prucha, Francis Paul. *The Great Father: The United States Government and the American Indians*, vol. 2. Lincoln and London. University of Nebraska Press. 1984.

Raventon, Edward. *Island in the Plains: A Black Hills Natural History.* Boulder. Johnson Books. 1994.

Reno, Philip. *Mother Earth, Father Sky, and Economic Development Navajo Resources and Their Use.* Albuquerque. University of New Mexico Press. 1981.

Rollings, Willard H. *The Osage: An Ethnohistorical Study of Hegemony on the Prairie-Plains.* Columbia. University of Missouri Press. 1995.

Rosen, Peter. *Pa-Ha-Sa-Pah, Or the Black Hills of South Dakota.* St. Louis. Mo. Nixon-Jones. 1895.

Rothman, Hal K. *The Greening of a Nation? Environmentalism in the United States Since 1945.* Fort Worth. Harcourt Brace College Publishers. 1997.

Satz, Ronald. *Chippewa Treaty Rights: The Reserve Rights of Wisconsin's Chippewa Indians in Historical Perspective.* Madison. Wisconsin Academy of Sciences, Arts and Letters. 1991.

Schusky, Ernest L. *The Forgotten Sioux: An Ethnohistory of the Lower Brule Reservation.* Chicago. Nelson-Hall. 1975.

Simmons, Marc. *New Mexico, A Bicentennial History.* New York. W. W. Norton. 1977.

Smith, Theresa S. *The Island of the Anishnaabeg: Thunders and Water Monsters in the Traditional Ojibwe Life-World.* Moscow. University of Idaho Press. 1995.

Spengler, Oswald. *The Decline of the West.* Translated by C. F. Atkinson. New York. A. Knopf. 1926–1928.

Stern, Theodore. *The Klamath Tribe: A People and Their Reservation.* Seattle and London. University of Washington Press. 1965.

Stocking, George, Jr. *Race, Culture, and Evolution: Essays in the History of Anthropology.* New York. Free Press. 1968.

Sutton, Imre. *Indian Land Tenure: Bibliographical Essays and a Guide to the Literature.* New York and Paris. Clearwater Publishing. 1975.

Tanner, Helen, ed. *Atlas of Great Lakes Indian History.* Norman. University of Oklahoma. 1987.

Taylor, Theodore W. *American Indian Policy.* Mt. Airy, Md. Lomond Publications. 1983.

Trigger, Bruce, ed. *Handbook of North American Indians: Northeast*, vol. 15. Washington, D.C. Smithsonian Institution. 1978.

Tylor, Edward B. *The Origins of Culture.* New York. Harper & Brothers. 1958.

Utley, Robert M. *The Last Days of the Sioux Nation.* New Haven and London. Yale University Press. 1963.

Willrich, Mason. *Energy and World Politics.* New York. Free Press. 1975.

Wilson, Terry P. *The Underground Reservation: Osage Oil.* Lincoln and London. University of Nebraska Press. 1985.

Wright, Leitch J., Jr. *Creeks and Seminoles: Destruction and Regeneration of the Muscogulge People.* Lincoln. University of Nebraska Press. 1986.

ARTICLES

Ambler, Marjane. "Indian Energies Devoted to Self-Sufficiency." *National Forum* 71, no. 2 (Spring 1991): 21–23.

"American Indians Bargain 'Arab Style' to Cash in on Resources." *U.S. News and World Report.* June 3, 1974, p. 53.

Anderson, Owen L. "Indians—Hunting and Fishing Rights: State Law Must Yield to Federal Treaty." *North Dakota Law Review* 48, no. 4 (Summer 1972): 729–737.

Barol, Bill, and Lynda Wright. "Eco-Activist Summer." *Newsweek.* July 2, 1990, p. 60.

Bean, Jerry L. "Off Reservation Hunting and Fishing Rights: Scales Tip in Favor of States and Sportsmen?" *North Dakota Law Review* 51, no. 1 (Fall 1974): 11–30.

Beck, Melinda; Jeff B. Copeland, and Merril Sheils. "Resources: The Rich Indians." *Newsweek.* March 20, 1978, p. 61.

Boeth, Richard; Jeff B. Copeland, Mary Hager, and Phyllis Malamund. "A Paleface Uprising." *Newsweek.* April 10, 1978, p. 40.

Bond, Frank M. "Indian Reserved Water Rights Doctrine Expanded." *Natural Resources Journal* 23, no. 1 (January 1983): 205–212.

Bradimore, Kathleen. "Indian Law—Treaty Fishing Rights—the Michigan Position." *Wayne Law Review* 24, no. 3 (March 1978): 1187–1204.

Bransky, James A. "The Political Status of Indian Tribes in Michigan." *Michigan Bar Journal* 65, no. 5 (May 1986): 444–450.

Brazil, Wayne D. "Special Masters in Complex Cases: Extending the Judiciary or Reshaping Adjudication?" (Paper presented at the "Symposium on Litigation Management.") *University of Chicago Law Review* 53, no. 2 (Spring 1986): 394–423.

Broad, William J. "Osage Oil Cover-Up." *Science* 208, no. 4439 (April 4, 1980): 32–35.

Brom, Thomas. "The Southwest: America's New Appalachia." *Ramparts* 13 (November 1974): 17–20.

Brookshire, David S.; James E. Merrill; and Gary L. Watts. "Economics and the Determination of Indian Reserved Water Rights." *Natural Resources Journal* 23, no. 4 (October 1981): 749–765.

Burchardt, Bill. "Osage Oil." *Chronicles of Oklahoma* 41, no. 3 (Autumn 1963): 253–269.

Chapman, Berlin B. "Dissolution of the Osage Reservation. Part One." *Chronicles of Oklahoma* 20, no. 3 (September-December 1942): 244–254.

———. "Dissolution of the Osage Reservation. Part Two." *Chronicles of Oklahoma* 20, no. 4 (September-December 1942): 375–386.

———. "Dissolution of the Osage Reservation. Part Three." *Chronicles of Oklahoma* 21, no. 1 (March 1943): 78–88.

———. "Dissolution of the Osage Reservation. Part Four." *Chronicles of Oklahoma* 21, no. 2 (June 1943): 171–182.

"The Chippewas Want Their Rights." *Time.* November 26, 1979, p. 54.

Churchill, Ward. "The Black Hills Are Not for Sale: A Summary of the Lakota Struggle for the 1868 Treaty Territory." *Journal of Ethnic Studies* 18, no.

1 (Spring 1990): 127–142.

Claasen, Sharon E. "Taxation: State Transaction Privilege Tax: An Interference With Tribal Self-Government." *American Indian Law Review* 7, no. 2 (1979): 319–333.

Coggins, George Cameron, and William Modrcin. "Native American Indians and Federal Wildlife." *Stanford Law Review* 31, no. 3 (February 1979): 375–423.

Colby, L. W. "The Sioux Indian War of 1890–'90." *Transactions and Reports of the Nebraska State Historical Society* 3 (1892): 144–190.

Crawford, Mrs. Wade. "An Indian Talks Back." *American Forests* 63 (July 1957): 4, 48–50.

"A Crow Indian Threat to Western Mines." *Business Week.* October 13, 1975, p. 37.

Davis, Russell; James E. Wilen, and Rosemarie Jergovic. "Oil and Gas Royalty Recovery Policy on Federal and Indian Lands." *Natural Resources Journal* 23, no. 2 (April 1983): 391–416.

Dean, William. "Klamath Hearings in Oregon." *American Forests* 63 (November 1957): 12, 65–67.

Deletka, Diane H. "State Regulation of Treaty Indians' Hunting and Fishing Rights in Michigan." *Detroit College of Law Review* no. 4 (Winter 198): 1097–1122.

Fey, Harold E. "The Indian and the Law." *The Christian Century* 72, no. 10 (March 9, 1955): 297–299.

Finnigan, Richard A. "Indian Treaty Analysis and Off-Reservation Fishing Rights: A Case Study." *Washington Law Review* 51, no. 1 (November 1975): 61–95.

Fixico, Donald L. "The Alliance of the Three Fires in Trade and War, 1630–1812." *Michigan Historical Review* 20, no. 2 (Fall 1994): 1–25.

Forbes, Gerald. "History of the Osage Blanket Lease." *Chronicles of Oklahoma* 19, no. 1 (March 1941): 70–81.

Foulke, William Dudley. "Despoiling a Nation." *The Outlook* 91 (January 2, 1909): 40–44.

Goldberg, Carol. E. "A Dynamic View of Tribal Jurisdiction to Tax Non-Indians." *Law and Contemporary Problems* 40, no. 1 (1976): 166–189.

Harris, Fred, and LaDonna Harris. "Indians, Coal, and the Big Sky." *The Progressive* 38, no. 11 (November 1974): 22–26.

Hobbs, Charles A. "Indian Hunting and Fishing Rights II." *George Washington Law Review* 37, no. 5 (July 1969): 1251–1273.

Hood, Susan. "Termination of the Klamath Tribe in Oregon." *Ethnohistory* 19 (Fall 1972): 379–392.

"Indians Want a Bigger Share of Their Wealth." *Business Week.* May 3, 1976, pp. 101–102.

Irvin, Amelia W. "Energy Development and the Effects of Mining on the Lakota Nation." *Journal of Ethnic Studies* 10, no. 1 (Spring 1982): 89–101.

Israel, Daniel H. "The Reemergence of Tribal Nationalism and Its Impact on Reservation Development." *University of Colorado Law Review* 47 (Summer 1976): 617–652.

Jenkins, Myra Ellen. "The Baltazar Baca Grant: History of an Encroachment." *El Palacio* 68 (Spring-Summer 1961): 47, 51–52.

Jones, Quentin M. "Mineral Resources: Tribal Development of Reservation Oil and Gas Resources Through the Use of a Nontaxation-Based Tribal Joint Development Program." *American Indian Law Review* 9, no. 1 (1981): 161–194.

Kelley, W. F. "The Indian Troubles and the Battle of Wounded Knee." *Transaction and Reports of the Nebraska State Historical Society* 4 (1892): 30–50.

Kinney, J. P. "Will the Indian Make the Grade?" *American Forests* 60 (December 1954): 24–27, 52–53.

Lee, Dorothy. "Notes on the Conception of Self Among the Wintu Indians." *Journal of Abnormal and Social Psychology* 45 (1950): 538–543.

Littlefield, Daniel F., Jr., and Lonnie E. Underhill. "The 'Crazy Snake Uprising' of 1909: A Red, Black, or White Affair?" *Arizona and the West* 20, no. 4 (Winter 1978): 307–324.

McGee, Pattie Palmer. "Indian Lands: Coal Development Environmental/Economic Dilemma for the Modern Indian." *American Indian Law Review* 4, no. 2 (1976): 279–288.

McLoone, John J. "Indian Hunting and Fishing Rights." *Arizona Law Review* 10, no. 3 (Winter 1968): 725–739.

Merrill, James L. "Aboriginal Water Rights." *Natural Resources Journal* 20, no. 1 (January 198)): 45–70.

Moore, John H. "Racism and Fishing Rights." *The Nation* 225, no. 8 (September 17, 1977): 236–238.

Neuberger, Richard L. "Solving the Stubborn Klamath Dilemma." *American Forests* 64, (April 1958): 20–222, 40–442.

Noble, Jim, Jr. "Tribal Power to Tax Non-Indian Mineral Leases." *Natural Resources Journal* 19, no. 4 (October 1979): 969–995.

"An 'OPEC' Right in America's Own Back Yard." *U.S. News and World Report.* August 2, 1976, p. 29.

Oppler, Morris. "Themes as Dynamic Forces in Culture." *American Journal of Sociology* 51, no. 3 (November 1945): 198–206.

Palma, Jack D., II. "Considerations and Conclusions Concerning the Transferability of Indian Water Rights." *Natural Resources Journal* 20, no. 1 (January 198): 91–100.

Paulson, Michael I. "Indian Regulation of Non-Indian Hunting and Fishing." *Wisconsin Law Review*, no. 2 (1974): 499–523.

Philp, Kenneth R. "Albert B. Fall and the Protest From the Pueblos, 1921–23." *Arizona and the West* 12, no. 3 (Autumn 1970): 237–254.

Reno, Philip. "The Navajos: High, Dry and Penniless." *Nation.* March 29, 1975, p. 359.

Reynolds, Laurie. "Indian Hunting and Fishing Rights: The Role of Tribal Sovereignty and Preemption." *North Carolina Law Review, Part 2* 62, no. 4 (April 1984): 743–793.

Roderick, Janna. "Indian-White Relations in the Washington Territory: The Question of Treaties and Fishing Rights." *Journal of the West* 16, no. 3 (July 1977): 23–34.

Rollins, Willard H. "Indian Land and Water: The Pueblos of New Mexico (1848–1924)." *American Indian Culture and Research Journal* 7, no. 1 (1983): 1–21.

Sant, Donald T.; Abraham E. Haspel, and Robert E. Boldt. "Oil and Gas Royalty Recovery Policy on Federal and Indian lands: A Response." *Natural Resources Journal* 23, no. 2 (April 1983): 417–433.

Seaton, Fred A. "Seaton Outlines Klamath Indian Proposal to Congress." *American Forests* 64 (February 1958): 12–13, 38–39.

Spier, Leslie. "Klamath Ethnography." *University of California Publication in American Archaeology and Ethnology* 30 (1930): 1–338.

Stern, Theodore. "The Klamath Indians and the Treaty of 1846," *Oregon Historical Quarterly* 57 (1956): 229–273.

Talney, Mark A. "Question Validity of Klamath Plan." *The Christian Century* 73, no. 30 (July 25, 1956): 882–884.

Taylor, William B. "Land and Water Rights in the Viceroyalty of New Spain." *New Mexico Historical Review* 50, no. 3 (July 1975): 189–212.

Thurtell, John. "Troubled Waters, The Struggle on the Great Lakes for an Ancient Way of Life." *The Progressive* 44, no. 9 (September 1980): 48.

Veeder, William H. "Water Rights in the Coal Fields of the Yellowstone River Basin." *Law and Contemporary Problems* 40, no. 1 (1976): 77–96.

Viers, Becky J. Miles. "Environmental Law: Uranium Mining on the Navajo Reservation." *American Indian Law Review* 7, no. 1 (1979): 115–124.

Westernhead, L. R. "What Is an 'Indian Tribe'?—The Question of Tribal Existence." *American Indian Law Review* 8, no. 1 (1980): 1–47.

Wilkinson, Charles F., and Eric R. Briggs. "The Evolution of Termination Policy." *American Indian Law Review* 5, no. 1 (1977): 139–184.

Williams, Dennis; Gerald L. Lubenow, and William J. Cook. "Where the Coal Is Not a Problem." *Newsweek*. March 20, 1978, p. 35.

Williams, Rob. "Redefining the Tribe..." *Indian Truth*, no. 262 (April 1985): 5–11.

Wilson, Raymond. "Dr. Charles A. Eastman's Report on the Economic Conditions of the Osage Indians in Oklahoma, 1924." *Chronicles of Oklahoma* 55, no. 3 (Fall 1977): 343–345.

Young, Lise. "What Price Progress? Uranium Production on Indian Lands in the San Juan Basin." *American Indian Law Review* 9, no. 1 (1981): 1–50.

Zimmerman, David R. "Can Indians and Environmentalists Find Common Ground?" *The Progressive*. December, 1976, p. 28.

NEWSPAPERS

"Killing the Earth, Air, Water." *Akwesasne Notes* 9, no. 1 (Spring 1977).

"The Northern Cheyenne ... Defending the Last Retreat ..." 10, no. 1 (Early Spring 1978).

"The Black Hills Alliance." *Akwesasne Notes* 2, no. 2 (May 1979).

Garity, Michael. "The Pending Energy Wars, America's Final Act of Genocide." *Akwesasne Notes* 11, no. 5 (December 1979).

"Blackfeet Tribe Forms New Company." *Akwesasne Notes* 2, no. 9 (November 23, 1983).

"Unique Deception Methods Used by Federal Agents in Solving Mysterious Cases Revealed Here." *Butte Daily Post*. September 30, 1938.

"Accord With Tribe May Smooth Waters." *Chicago Tribune*. October 2, 1989.

"Burial Rites for Barnett Halted by U.S." *Daily Oklahoman*. June 1, 1934.

Farrell, John A. "Empty Promises, Misplaced Trust." New Indian Wars Series, *Denver Post*. November 20, 1983.

Fenwick, Robert W. "U.S. Efforts to Aid Indians Clumsy and Costly." *Denver Post*. January 15, 1960.

"Governor Meets Voigt Tribes." *Lac Courte Oreilles Journal, A Chronicle of the Lake Superior Ojibway*. February 1987.

"Ft. Peck Sioux Sign Agreement on Oil & Gas." *Lakota Times*. April 22, 1983.

"Indian Mineral Development Act." *Lakota Times*. January 6, 1983.

Ambler, Marjane. "Controversial Speech Draws Ire at CERT Convention." *Lakota Times*. November 9, 1983.

———. "The Forgotten People." *Lakota Times*. November 2, 1983.

———. "Victories for Tribes in Tax Cases." *Lakota Times*. September 14, 1983.

"Indians Received $161.4 Million in Minerals Royalties in 1981." *Lakota Times*. November 18, 1982.

"Rosebud Chairman Elected to CERT Executive Board." *Lakota Times*. December, 9, 1982.

"OST Wins Major Victory in Land Claims." *Lakota Times*. December 5, 1986.

"Mickleson Lists Objections to Bradley's Hills Bill Measure." *Lakota Times*. May 13, 1987.

"Oldest Land Claim May Not Be Over Yet." *Lakota Times*. August 19, 1987.

"The Hills Are Not for Sale, Says Reader." *Lakota Times*. December 30, 1987.

"Havasupais Fight Mine Plan." *Lakota Times*. January 10, 1989.

"U.S. Supreme Court to Re-Examine Water Rights." *Lakota Times*. March 21, 1989.

"Tribal Factions Agree to Disagree Over Black Hills." *Lakota Times*. March 28, 1989.

"Mineral Law Hamstrung by BIA Delay." *Lakota Times*. March 14, 1990.

"Watt Approves Coal Mining Agreement." *Lakota Times*. April 14, 1983.

"Wind River Reservation," *Los Angeles Times*. January 12, 1981.

"Chairmen Define Key Issues With Gov. Thompson." *Masinaigan, A Chronicle of the Lake Superior Ojibway*. February, 1987.

"The Voigt Decision." *Masinaigan, A Chronicle of the Lake Superior Ojibway*. March, 1987.

"Court Decision Favorable to Tribes." *Masinaigan, A Chronicle of the Lake Superior Ojibway*. September, 1987.

"Earl Aide Bridges Gaps for Indians, State," *Milwaukee Journal*. July 1, 1984.

"Indian Leader Offers Solution." *Milwaukee Journal*. May 11, 1985.

"Treaty Rights, Tourist Dollars Back on Trial." *Milwaukee Journal*. December 9, 1985.

"70 picket spearers at boat landing." *Milwaukee Journal*. April 20, 1987.

"Unruly Crowd Taunts Spearfishers." *Milwaukee Journal.* April 27, 1987.

"3 Arrested in Protest at Flowage." *Milwaukee Journal.* April 29, 1987.

"Chippewas Seek More Input With DNR to Manage Resources." *Milwaukee Journal.* March 22, 1987.

"Conservationist Urges Lease of Fishing Rights." *Milwaukee Journal.* September 21, 1986.

"Hanaway Invites Indians to Treaty Talks." *Milwaukee Journal.* April 29, 1987.

"Of Course Racism Plays Role in Treaty-Rights Battle" and "Boycott Leads Brewery to Drop Treaty Beer." *Milwaukee Journal.* August 16, 1987.

"Chippewas Are Willing to Listen." *Milwaukee Journal.* August 21, 1987.

"Long Trial Ahead for Indian Treaty Talks." *Milwaukee Journal.* August 23, 1987.

"Pro-Treaty Group Says Stickers Incite Violence." *Milwaukee Journal.* October 13, 1987.

"Doyle Says Indians Must Comply With State Fishing Regulations." *Milwaukee Sentinel.* June 2, 1984.

Editorial, *Milwaukee Sentinel.* September 10, 1984.

"Chippewas Argue for Treaty Rights." *Milwaukee Sentinel.* September 25, 1985.

"Few Indians Out on Last Days of Hunting From Vehicles." *Milwaukee Sentinel.* September 30, 1985.

"Ill Judge Withdraws From Chippewa Suit." *Milwaukee Sentinel.* March 21, 1987.

"Racism Cited in Fishing Dispute." *Milwaukee Sentinel.* April 11, 1986.

"Indians Should Return to Primitive Fishing." *Milwaukee Sentinel.* May 12, 1986.

"Are Chippewas Victims of Racism and Greed?" *Milwaukee Sentinel.* May 27, 1986.

"Earl Plans to Set Up White-Indian Panel." *Milwaukee Sentinel.* May 31, 1986.

"Old Tribal Treaties Threaten State's Future." *Milwaukee Sentinel.* June 10, 1986.

"Treaty Ruling May Restrict Sport Fishermen." *Milwaukee Sentinel.* February 21, 1987.

"Treaty Rights Ruling in Effect Now." *Milwaukee Sentinel.* February 24, 1987.

"Spearing Accord Called 'Bad News'," *Milwaukee Sentinel.* March 16, 1987.

"Final Indian Treaty Sets Up Reservations." *Milwaukee Sentinel.* March 18, 1987.

"Century of Changes Strains Treaty Terms." *Milwaukee Sentinel.* March 21, 1987.

"Cold Weather Delays Indian Spearfishing." *Milwaukee Sentinel.* April 1, 1987.

"Shooter Near Spearing Not Charged." *Milwaukee Sentinel.* April 24, 1987.

"North Woods seen as `pressure cooker' after spearfishing." *Milwaukee Sentinel,* May 2, 1987.

"Lac du Flambeau Reject Treaty Pact." *Milwaukee Sentinel.* October 26, 1989.

"Cab Driver to Tell of Elopement." *Muskogee Daily Phoenix.* July 7, 1926.

"Creek Chief Calls Upon His People." *Muskogee Daily Phoenix.* July 7, 1926.

"Deeds to Creek Lands Recorded." *Muskogee Daily Phoenix.* January 3, 1903.

"Mrs. Barnett Moves to Home of Husband." *Muskogee Daily Phoenix.* August 31, 1926.

"Seize Barnett for Contempt!" *Muskogee Daily Phoenix.* August 21, 1926.

"Confession to Slaying Accepted." *Muskogee Times-Democrat.* June 21,1926.

S. Arne, "No More Women! for Jack Barnett." *Muskogee Times-Democrat.* August 24, 1926.

"Indian Bill Will Destroy Pueblo Life, Says Indians in Memorial to Country," *(Santa Fe) New Mexican* 51, no. 235 (November 6, 1922).

"Delegation of Pueblos To Petition Congress," *New York Tribune,* January 8, 1923.

Elizabeth Shepley Sergeant, "Big Powwow of Pueblos," *New York Times Magazine,* November 26, 1922.

"BLM to Let Tribes Manage Their Own Mineral Resources," *News From Indian Country* 10, no. 19 (mid-October 1997).

Astor, Michael. "Amazon Rain Forest Parched by Worst Drought in 25 Years." *South Bend Tribune.* October 29, 1997.

Galvin, Kevin. "Natives Fight Exxon Plan for Valdez." *South Bend Tribune.* January 16, 1997.

Kelley, Matt. "Miners Paid Price in Cold War Effort." *South Bend Tribune.* September 8, 1997.

Smith, E. N. "Low-Sulfur Coal Puts Wyoming at Top of Heap," *South Bend Tribune.* August 18, 1997.

"Nefas ad Narrandum," *Taos Valley News.* March 4, 1923.

Emery, Dorothy. "Fiendish Killing in Ravine Told By Murderer." *Tulsa Tribune.* June 3, 1926.

"Find Fraud in Indian Estate," *Tulsa World.* July 30, 1926.

"Energy and Land Use Questions on Indian Lands." *Wassaja* 5, no. 6 (September 1977).

"Tribes Being Plundered." *Wassaja* 6, no. 11 (December 1978).

"2 Million for Tribes; CERT." *Wassaja* 6, nos. 9–1 (October-November 1978).

Kenyon, Richard L. "If We Give Up Our Ways, We Die." *Wisconsin: The Milwaukee Magazine.* July 23, 1989.

REPORTS

Stanford Research Institute. "Preliminary Planning for Termination of Federal Control Over the Klamath Tribe. Menlo Park, California: Stanford Research Institute, 1956.

Uncommon Controversy Fishing Rights of the Muckleshoot, Puyallup, and Nisqually Indians. A report prepared for the American Friends Service Committee. Seattle. University of Washington Press. 1970.

DISSERTATIONS AND THESES

Bland, Benay. "Jackson Barnett and the Oklahoma Probate System." M.A. thesis. University of Texas, Arlington. 1978.

Brown, Charles C. "Identification of Selected Problems of Indians Residing in Klamath County, Oregon—An Examination of Data Generated Since Termination of the Klamath Reservation." Ph.D. diss. University of Oregon, Eugene. 1973.

Clifton, James A. "Explorations in Klamath Personality." Ph.D. diss. University of Oregon, Eugene. 1960.

Moorman, Donald R. "A Political Biography of Holm O. Bursum: 1899–1924." Ph.D. diss. University of New Mexico, Albuquerque, 1962.

INDEX

Italic page numbers indicate pictures;
n after a page number indicates a note.

A

AAIA. *See* Association on American Indians
Abeyta, Pablo, 69
Acoma, 55, 57
Adams, Sherman, 90–91
Administration for Native Americans, 166, 168, 173
Age of Reform, xvii
Agriculture, 214
AIO. *See* Americans for Indian Opportunity
AISES. *See* American Indian Science and Engineering Society
Alabama Jane, 129
Alabama-Coushatta, 84
Alameda Oil Company, 31
Alaska Native Settlement Act, 201
Algonkian, 106
Allison, William B., 127
Allotment, 3, 159, 182, 186n., 197; and Klamath, 81, 86, 87; and Muscogee Creek, 6–13; and Osage, 27, 32–33, 34–35
All-Pueblo Council, 66–67
Alternative energy, 199, 211, 212
Amax, 147, 148, 194
American Baptist Home Mission Society, 12
American Civil Liberties Union, 117
American Indian Defense Association, 67
American Indian Religious Freedom Act, 131
American Indian Science and Engineering Society, 172–173
American Museum of Natural History, 86
Americans for Indian Opportunity, 161
Amoco Production Company, 152, 194, 195
ANA. *See* Administration for Native Americans
Anasazi, 55
Ancient Indian Land Claims Settlement Act, 195
Anishnabe, 105, 106–107
Anthony, Harold B., 86
Apache, 58. *See also* Jicarilla Apache
Apache Indian Industries, 152
Arapaho, 127, 152, 169, 193, 198–199
Arizona, 197–198
Arizona, University of, 172
Arizona Public Service, 169
Arizona State University, 172
Arizona v. California, 183, 196
Arizona v. San Carlos Tribe, 185
Arkansas, 28
Arkansas River, 28
Assimilation, 154–155. *See also* Klamath
Assiniboine; oil and gas, 149, 168, 169, 193

Association on American Indians,
  95
Atwood, Stella, 66, 67, 69, 70
A'ukckni, 80
Audubon Society, 92

B

Bacone College, 12, 17
Bad River Band (Chippewa), 114
Bailey, Elmer, 16, 17
Barnett, Anna Laura Lowe, 14–20,
  21, 39
Barnett, Hubert Howard, 21
Barnett, Jackson, xvi, 3–4, *4*, 5,
  190; and Anna Laura Lowe
  (wife), 14–20, 21; and Carl J.
  O'Hornett, 13, 14, 15–16, 17;
  death of, 20–21; donation to
  Baptist Church, 13–14, 15, 17;
  early life, 13; and Elmer Bailey,
  16, 17; estate, 21; heirs and
  "heirs," 21–22; houses, 15, 17,
  18; oil lease, 13; suspension
  between white and Indian ways,
  20, 22
Barnett, Maxine Lowe, 15, 16
Barnsdall Oil Company, 36
Baruch, Bernard, 70
Bear Butte, 131, 133
Bennett, Robert, 179
BerryHill, Willie, 12
BIA. *See* Bureau of Indian Affairs
Bicket, 14
Bigheart, George, 42
Bigheart, Grace, 41
Bigheart, James, 29, 30
Black Dog, 34
Black Elk, 131, 136–137
Black Hills, xvi, 123; buffalo, *124* ;
  Camp Yellow Thunder, 130–131;
  cities, 129; coal and fossil fuels,
  132–133, 136, 137, 150–151;
  conflict between Lakota and
  whites, 125–129, 131, 135; gold,
  125, 126, 127, 128, 129; Harney
  Peak, 131; legal efforts by

Lakota, 129–130, 131–136; Mato-
  Paha (Bear Butte), 131, 133;
  other minerals, 129; *Paha Sapa*,
  125, 131; railroads, 128; spiritual
  significance, 124, 131, 136–137;
  as state park, 130; tourism, 130;
  uranium, 138n., 200–201
Black Hills Alliance, 133
Black Hills Placer Mining Com-
  pany, 128
Black Hills Sioux Nation Treaty
  Council, 135
Black Hills Steering Committee,
  134, 135
Blackfeet, 127, 160–161, 171; oil and
  gas, 149, 153, 167–168, 195
Blocker Drilling Ltd., 149
Blumberg, Paul, xix
Blumenschien, Ernest L., 66
Board of Indian Commissioners, 126
Boas, Franz, 215n.
Bob, Daniel, 11
Boldt case, 104, 183
Bozeman Trail, 125
Bradley, Bill, 134–136
Brinton, Daniel, 216n.
Brophy, William, 83
Brosius, S. N., 64
Brown, Anna, 39–41
Brown, Edwin, 45
Brown, Ode, 39–40
Browning-Ferris Industries, 200
Brule, 123, 127. *See also* Lower
  Brule
Brunot, Felix, 126
Bryan, William Jennings, 70
Bureau of Indian Affairs, 70, 87, 88,
  89, 90, 93, 94–95, 96, 147, 148,
  150, 152, 153–154, 160, 162, 165,
  166, 170–171, 178, 191, 196;
  criticisms of, 179, 180; and
  Department of the Interior, 178,
  179, 186n.; regions, 178–179
Bureau of Land Management, 194
Bureau of Mines, 161
Bureau of Reclamation, 180
Burke, Charles H., 16, 20, 38, 65
Burkhart, Byron, 41

189–190; by tribe, 219–220; and
U.S., 208, 210, 211, 217n. *See
also* Black Hills; Barnett,
Jackson; Osage
Navajo, 160–161; and CETA
grants, 169; coal, 144, 145, 146,
151, 153, 169, 172; election
between Zah and MacDonald,
168–169; Energy Department
Authority, 167; oil, 193; solar
electricity project, 199; ura-
nium, 151; uranium radioactiv-
ity, 200–201. *See also*
MacDonald, Peter
Navajo Agricultural Products
Industries, 169
Navajo Indian Wood Products, 152
Nebraska, 28, 184
Neuberger, Richard, 88, 89, 90, 92,
93–94, 96
Neutral tribe, 106
New Mexico, 55, 59, 60, 62, 72, 193,
195
New Mexico Enabling Act, 62
New Republic, 67
Nixon, Richard, 162
North Dakota, 143, 171–172
Northern Cheyenne, 127, 160; coal,
143, 144, 145, 147, 172, 191; oil
and gas, 167. *See also* Cheyenne
Northern Pueblo Enterprises, 152
Northern Tier Pipeline Company,
194
Nuclear energy, 200
Nuclear Waste Policy Act, 171

O

Office of Surface Mining, 166
Oglala, 123, 127, 133–134
Oglala Sioux Tribal Council, 134,
135
O'Hornett, Carl J., 13, 14, 15–16, 17
Oil, xvi, 11–12, *30*, 193; Alaska, 201;
and Albert Fall, 64–65. *See also*
Teapot Dome; inspections, 194;
leading oil-producing tribes,

193; production by tribe, 223–
224; thefts, 166–167, 192–193;
towns, 29; U.S. dependence on
imports, 201–202; world
resources and users, 211–212.
See also Barnett, Jackson;
Osage
Ojibwa, 105, 210, 216n. *See also*
Chippewa
Oklahoma, 6, 7–8, 10, 28, 144, 151,
166–167, 182, 193
Oklahoma, University of, 172
Old Oraibi, 57
Old Person, Earl, 160–161
Oliphant, Mark, 184
Oliphant decision, 184
Omnibus Indian Mineral Leasing
Act, 185
Omnibus Tribal Leasing Act, 148
Oñate, Don Juan de, 58
Oneida, 106
Onondaga, 106
OPA. *See* Osage Protective
Association
OPEC. *See* Organization of
Petroleum Exporting Countries
Open Hills Association, 134
Oregon, 94–95, 184
Orenda, 113
Organization of Petroleum Export-
ing Countries, 150, 162, 201
Osage, xvi, 190; Allotting Commis-
sion, 34–35; and allotment, 27,
29, 32–33, 34–35; Business
Committee, 34; constitution, 33,
34; and dams and reservoirs,
192; factionalism, 32–34; and
family, 27–28, 48–49; farming,
29; gas and oil royalties, 35–36;
land cessions, 28; mineral
resources, 151; mineral rights
(headrights), 35–36; National
Council, 30, 31, 34, 37, 39; oil,
29–32, *30*, 35–38, 48, 144, 192,
193; reign of terror, 27, 28, 39–
47; reservation, 28–29, 31; and
Tallgrass Prairie National Park,
192; termination of trust status,

Western Regional Council, 164, 197
Westmoreland Resources, 151
WESTPO. *See* Western Governors'
    Policy Office
Weyerhaeuser Timber Company,
    92
White Eagle Industries, 152
White Earth Equal Rights, 113
Whitehorn, Charles, 41
Wild Horse Kate, 129
Wildlife, 86, 89, 92, 93, 118, 183. *See
    also* Chippewa
Wildlife Department, 92
Wilkinson, James, 58
Williams, Robert L., 18, 21
Wilson, Francis, 67, 68, 69–70
Wind energy, 199, 212
Wind River Reservation, 152, 153,
    166–167, 169, 192, 194, 198–199
Winnegabo, 108
Winter's Doctrine, 182, 183, 196,
    197
Wintu, 205, 207
Wisconsin, 108, 109–110, 116, 184;
    tourism, 111–112
Wisconsin Advisory Committee,
    113
Wisconsin Alliance for Rights and
    Resources, 113
Wisconsin Conservation Congress,
    111
Wisconsin Department of Natural
    Resources, 103, 112, 114, 115
Wisconsin Equal Rights Council,
    113

Wisconsin Greens, 113
Wisconsin Indian Resource
    Council, 113
Wisconsin NOW, 113
Wisconsin v. Lemieux, 110–111
Woodenlegs, John, 147
Worcester v. Georgia, 178
Work, Hubert, 70
Worten, Jesse J., 43
Wounded Knee Massacre, 129
WRC. *See* Western Regional
    Council
Wright, J. George, 49
Wyoming, 152, 153, 155, 171–172,
    193, 198–199

Y

Yahi, 136
Yahooskin Band, 83–84, 95
Yakima, 171; and nuclear power
    plants, 200
Yankton, 127
Yatay Industries, 152
Yates, Sidney, 153–154
Young, Omar, R., 21

Z

Zah, Peterson, 168–169
Zarb, Frank, 161
Zimmerman, William, 83
Zuni, 55
Zuni Enterprises, 152